About the Author

Eric Werner is professor emeritus of liturgical music at the Hebrew Union College, where he was the successor of the late A. Z. Idelsohn. He is the author of *Mendelssohn: A New Image of the Composer and His Age,* the standard biography of Felix Mendelssohn; *A Voice Still Heard . . . ,* a comprehensive study of the musical tradition of the synagogue; and *Three Ages of Musical Thought,* a volume of essays on musical and philosophical matters. In addition he has contributed to the *New Grove Dictionary of Music,* the *Encyclopaedia Britannica,* the *Interpreter's Dictionary of the Bible,* the *Encyclopedia of Religion,* and *Die Musik in Geschichte und Geggenwart,* and has published more than 200 articles and studies in American, European, and Israeli scholarly journals. He is a Guggenheim Memorial Fellow, holds several honorary degrees, and is a member of several Academies of Science.

THE
SACRED BRIDGE

The Interdependence of Liturgy and
Music in Synagogue and Church
during the First Millennium

VOLUME II

THE
SACRED BRIDGE

The Interdependence of Liturgy and

Music in Synagogue and Church

during the First Millennium

VOLUME II

ERIC WERNER

Professor Emeritus of Liturgical Music
Hebrew Union College—Jewish Institute of Religion
New York—Cincinnati

KTAV PUBLISHING HOUSE, INC.

NEW YORK

1984

Library of Congress Cataloging in Publication Data
(Revised for volume 2)

Werner, Eric.
  The sacred bridge.

  Vol. 2 has imprint: New York, Ktav Pub. House.
  Includes bibliographical references and index.
  1. Chants (Jewish)—History and criticism. 2. Chants
(Plain, Gregorian, etc.)—History and criticism.
3. Judaism—Rituals—History. 4. Catholic Church—
Liturgy—History. I. Title.
ML166.W43   783.2   59–16191
ISBN 0–88125–052–X (v. 2)
                                        Rev.

Manufactured in the United States of America

Memoriae
Professoris Curt Sachs
Professoris Jefim Schirmann,
Msgr. Dom. Higini Anglès
Professoris Egon Wellesz,
Dennis Dobson, M.A.
amicorum sapientium ac fidelium
hic liber est dedicatus

Contents

Foreign terms not explained in the text of this volume, are to be found in the Glossary at the end of Volume 1.

Preface

THIS supplementary volume was originally destined to appear in 1974; technical and personal difficulties have delayed the appearance of the book, and technical factors have also necessitated the retention of British punctuation and spelling style. It stands in place of a second, greatly enlarged and revised edition of the first volume, which appeared first in 1959. It is to serve several specific purposes:

(1) To bring the studies of the basic problem up to date;
(2) To fill certain lacunae of the first volume;
(3) To correct some, but by no means all, errors;
(4) To reexamine certain sources and questions *de novo*.

The following list will indicate where items 1–4 are dealt with *ex professo:*

(1) The Dead Sea (Qumran) Scrolls contain some material of importance for the relationship between 'traditional' and 'art'-music (Chaps. II, VII).

(2) The results of new research about the Old Synagogue's cycle of Psalm-lessons afford new evidence of a regular Psalm-pericope, possibly the origin of the early Christian *Graduale*.

(3) The title, position, and function of the old Roman *levita,* which was misunderstood in Vol. I, are clarified (Ch. VIII).

(4) The hitherto mysterious origin of the *Improperia* and their function are discovered and interpreted (Ch. VI).

(5) The genesis of the liturgical *Tersanctus* and its primeval forms, the accusation of deicide in the Early Church, and the concept of angelic choir all originate in certain little-known theological writings that mirror the unfolding rivalry between the expanding Church and the receding Synagogue of the Near East during the first centuries of Christianity (Chaps. V, VI).

(6) The deeply grounded connection between the Sanctorale, the Martyrologies in the calendar of the Church, also the relationship of the Christian beatification of martyrs, and the Jewish divergent attitude required a thoroughly new investigation (Ch. IV).

(7) The concluding chapter on the transmitters of ancient Syna-gogue traditions and their impact on the incipient Church discusses the most important theories and their champions from the patristic age until ca. 1900, when H. Riemann, G. Adler, Peter Wagner, and A. Gastoуè first paid serious attention to Jewish scholars and sources.

II

The first volume of this work was published more than twenty-five years ago. On the whole it met with a most appreciative reception by the learned world; albeit not all the expectations with which I sent it out on its way have been fulfilled. To the main postulate, an integration of theological, liturgical, historical, and musical studies in a unity of aims and methods applied, rarely attention has been paid. Still, some of the foremost Catholic scholars, while critical of the 'rationalistic, historicistic, evolutionistic' aspects of the book (*Ephemerides Liturgicae*) have most intelligently pursued the line of integration I envisaged. A number of their critical comments are discussed in this book and have been heeded where relevant. In contradistinction, however, most German Protestant theologians and liturgiologists still tend to ignore or to minimize all Jewish scholarship, as of old.

Some of my theses have been accepted. Some were rejected, usually for reasons given in the 'grand manner'. 'Outside of ritual there is little else that would be contrived for divine services beyond Scripture reading, prayer-formulae and song . . . the point of departure need not be here; it comes with the whole Christological concept' (*Catholic Historical Review,* April 1960, p. 54).

The most concrete result of my findings seems to me the decision of the Anglican-Episcopalian Churches to dispose with the *Impropе-ria* and some lessons of Good Friday. Yet, some critics emphasized that most of my findings were old and well-known truisms; if they are so obvious, why have they been ignored by almost all Catholic textbooks?

Still, the postulates of Ecumenism, hopefully ubiquitous these days, sound highly encouraging to this author. Do they not urge a scientific and 'fraternal' dialogue between representatives of Christianity and Judaism? For those of us who still believe in the possibility of pure research, free and untrammeled, the planned dialogues or colloquies between Synagogue and Church, so different from the ugly 'disputationes' of the Middle Ages, promise new insights and a new dimension of mutual comprehension. Such hopes remain vivid in spite of certain relapses into all-too-rigid habits of thought.

With this volume, I conclude my lifelong occupation with the Sacred Bridge that spans the gulf between Judaism and Christianity. I cannot but remember the assumptions under which I first set to work, in days dark and desperate. At the time I was convinced that both Church and Synagogue were bent on guarding and preserving their oldest and most cherished traditions regardless of any practical applicability, yet with due consideration for their authenticity and correct interpretation.

I could not have been more mistaken on every count: both institutions have followed courses diametrically opposed to my expectations. The Catholic Church, yielding to internal pressure, has relinquished a good deal of its liturgico-musical tradition, including part of its magnificent Latin heritage, in the hope that thereby the understanding of (translated) ritual texts by the lay-communities will be furthered and the worshippers afforded a more active part of the service. The Synagogue of the Diaspora, completely thrown off balance by the Holocaust, has been following the dictates of a 'survivalist' policy, untroubled by academic questions of authenticity or modern interpretations. It has made concessions to every movement, right or left, secular or orthodox, that promises to attract new congregants. Hence no clear trend is, at this moment, discernible to the author. In Israel, on the other hand, the dictatorship of an ultra-orthodox Rabbinate is today endangering the democratic structure of the state. Any historical and/or critical evaluation of the liturgical tradition is *ab initio* taboo. Thus the fossilization of Orthodox Judaism may soon be accomplished in Israel. This situation, however, is liable to be radically altered and perhaps altogether reversed in due course, for the majority of Israelis will not forever tolerate the 'spiritual' hectoring of a politicized rabbinate.

A certain utilitarian spirit, disguised as 'progressive thinking' has made inroads into the discussions of liturgical or musical subjects by the supposedly 'non-pragmatic' body of theologians, Jewish and Christian alike. This is regrettable, and the historical background of this book is presented with a view to counteract these trends. To an author who is not ashamed to be called an 'old-fashioned humanist', and who does not regard the *Zeitgeist* as an infallible *arbiter rerum,* it is no more than proper to declare his unwavering allegiance to the Judaeo-Christian system of values.

As in Vol. I, practical considerations have militated against the inclusion of a systematic bibliography. To be useful, such a bibliography would have to be critical, which would increase both the size and the price of the book beyond tolerable limits. However, the notes contain an entire detailed and documented list of the sources and the literature used. Together with the index they represent a non-systematic bibliography.

Quite a few Christian scholars were somewhat perplexed by the completely and consistently Masoretic-Protestant numbering of the Psalms. Apart from minor deviations, the following table will facilitate matters for the attentive reader who is accustomed to the numeration of the LXX or the Vulgate:

Masoretic	LXX and Vulgate
Ps. 1–9	1–9:21
Ps. 9–10	9:22–39
Ps. 11–113	10–112
Ps. 114–115	113
Ps. 116:1–9	114
Ps. 116:10–19	115
Ps. 117–146	116–145
Ps. 147:1–11	146
Ps. 147:12–20	147
Ps. 148–150	148–150

Once more it is my most pleasant duty to gratefully acknowledge the encouragement of a number of friends and colleagues. Outstanding among them are my revered late friends Msgr I. Anglès, Rome, and Prof. E. Wellesz, Oxford. I am equally indebted to Professors A. Stuiber, Bochum, the late Solange Corbin, Paris, Ch.

Chailley, Paris, Sh. Simonsohn, Tel Aviv, I. Adler, Jerusalem, and Martin Cohen, New York. My thanks also go to several devoted former students of mine, especially Rabbi D. Z. Levy and J. Goor. I am keeping in faithful memory my late friend, Prof. Y. Schirmann, Jerusalem, for his wise counsel and his translation of a difficult text (in Ch. IV). Last, but not least, my thanks go to Miss Elizabeth Dobson, London, who carefully edited text and notes, and to Mr. Irving Ruderman, who was the editor of this publication.

By taking an active interest in the basic problems of this book they have revived my hopes for sincere mutual recognition, frank dialogue, and perhaps even for a spiritual solidarity.

E. W.

New York City, 1982.

Acknowledgements

FOR the friendly permission to use quotations and excerpts from my articles, grateful acknowledgement is made to the *Musical Quarterly*, New York, the *Journal of the American Musicological Society*, New York-Philadelphia, *Acta Musicologica*, Paris-Kopenhagen-Kassel, the *Hebrew Union College Annual*, Cincinnati, and the *Jubilee Volume in Honour of Prof. E. Wellesz*, Oxford.

Abbreviations

BLEW F. E. Brightman, *Liturgies Eastern and Western* (Oxford, 1896, 1924)

CGES *Corpus Graecae Ecclesiae Scriptorum*

CSEL *Corpus Scriptorum Ecclesiae Latinae* (Vienna, 1866-1939)

DACH *Dictionnaire d'archéologie chrétienne,* ed. Leclercq and Cabrol

DSS Dead Sea Scrolls

ELB I. Elbogen, *Der Jüdische Gottesdienst,* 3rd ed., CF 1931.

HUCA *Hebrew Union College Annual,* 1919-1968

IDB *Interpreter's Dictionary of the Bible* (New York, 1962)

JAMS *Journal of the American Musicological Society*

JBL *Journal of Biblical Literature* (Philadelphia)

JE *Jewish Encyclopedia* (New York, 1901-1906)

JQR *Jewish Quarterly Review* (Philadelphia)

LXX *Septuagint*

MGG *Musik in Geschichte und Gegenwart,* Kassel-Basel

MGWJ *Monatsschrift für die Geschichte und Wissenschaft des Judentums* (Breslau, 1851-1938)

MQ *Musical Quarterly* (New York)

NOHM *New Oxford History of Music* (Oxford, 1954)

NT New Testament

OHM *Oxford History of Music,* ed. P. C. Buck and Sir W. H. Hadow

OT Old Testament

PG *Patrologia Graeca,* ed. Migne

PL *Patrologia Latina,* ed. Migne

WGM P. Wagner, *Einführung in die gregorianischen Melodien* (1911-1923)

M. before Hebrew syllable quotes the respective treatise of the *Mishna*

B. before Hebrew syllable quotes the respective treatise of the *Babylonian Talmud* according to the pagination of the standard Vilna folio edition

Jer. before Hebrew syllable quotes the respective passage from the
Jerusalemite Talmud
R. added to one of the names of biblical books refers to the
respective *Midrash Rabba,* e.g., Lam. R. equals Lamentations Rabba, Vilna edition. References are given according to the scriptural chapter and verse.

LIST OF TALMUDIC ABBREVIATIONS

Arach.	Arachin	Hag.	Hagiga
Ta'an.	Ta'anit	Sanh.	Sanhedrin
Bikk.	Bikkurim	Meg.	Megilla
Ber.	Berakoth	Yeb.	Yebamoth
Sabb.	Sabbath	Pes.	Pesachim
Hull.	Hullin	Sof.	Soferim

CHAPTER ONE

Liturgical Music in Hellenistic Palestine

I

IN his *Antiquities of the Jews,* Josephus Flavius, once a priest at the Temple, then general of the Jewish army, and historian of the Jewish people, explains the symbolic significance of many of the Temple's institutions. There we read: 'If any one without prejudice and with judgment looks upon these things [matters of Jewish religion], he will find that they were every one made in a way of imitation and representation of the universe.'[1] He then explained the Temple and everything in it as the earthly counterpart, a perishable 'image' of the cosmos, or of a cosmic Temple. This mystic-allegoristic concept may be found in Philo (by whose writings Josephus was certainly impressed), and also in innumerable passages of rabbinic literature, independent of either Philo or Josephus.[2] Quite generally, in every detail the Temple was viewed as a symbol of the universe; of course, the musical instruments were treated and understood in like manner, especially the *kithara* or lyre.

It seems necessary to stress this fact at a time when this symbolic comprehension of ritual music and its instruments is being subjected to a massive critique by some archaeologists and musicologists alike, who insist upon the 'pragmatic' facts to the exclusion of anything else. Whether Philo was ever initiated into the esoteric tenets of the Jerusalem Sanctuary is irrelevant, for Josephus certainly *was* an 'illuminate', being born into the family of the High Priest; proudly he names as his direct ancestor the Hasmonean priest, Jonathan, thereby stressing his priestly as well as royal descent.[3] Nor did the many generations of rabbis, who transmitted similar ideas, learn them from Josephus, whom they despised as traitor—they had their own traditions and, in general, fairly reliable sources.[4] Even the sectarian groups shared the conception of the

1

Temple as an earthly model of the heavenly Sanctuary, as we know from the most recent discoveries.[5]

There is, on the other hand, no reason why we should echo the romantic day-dreams of past biblical historians and exegetes, who projected into the Temple their own ideas of supernatural beauty and radiance, especially into its music. Today we understand better a number of facts long known, and are in possession of others only recently discovered; in many areas previous concepts have had to be revised. Many relics, that is *realia* of instrumental music in Palestine during the Hellenistic age, have been dug up and classified during recent years; they allow us to make certain definite conclusions concerning the state, character, and practice of liturgical music.[6]

While discussing first the recent findings of instruments of the Hellenistic age, we shall confine ourselves to the most important discoveries; later we shall attempt to interpret their relevance for a realistic evaluation of the Temple's music.

(a) While the pictures of lyres and harps (on coins or graffiti) show a clear similitude to the well-known and often painted Greek patterns, there appear certain characteristic dissimilitudes, especially in the Bar Kokhba coins. As a viola differs from a violin, but is closely related to it, so the *kitharai* and lyres of Palestine are close relatives of, but not identical with, the classic models from Greece during the early Hellenistic period.[7]

(b) There is no evidence for the use of the *halil* (primitive clarinet) in the Temple until very late. However, the fertility-symbolism of the instrument is evident in many instances.[8] Small wonder that the *halil* was extremely popular as a secular instrument, especially at weddings and funerals—with the same dionysiac and orgiastic character as the *aulos*.

(c) Panpipes and double pipes, among them the *abub* or *abobas,* were quite frequently depicted in the Hellenistic period. Both the *abub* and its brother, the *'ugab,* were not considered fit for the Sanctuary. The *ambubaiae,* Syrian pipe-playing prostitutes, were notorious in Asia Minor and in Rome. Horace was not the only one who warned his friend not to get involved with them.[9]

(d) Recent comparative measurements of the priestly trumpets on the Arch of Titus in Rome, and their representations in graffiti, on coins of the Bar Kokhba period and other relics warrant the conclusion that they were very high pitched with thin body and shrill sound. In *The War of the Children of Light against the Children of Darkness* these trumpets appear clearly capable of regulating their pitch pretty accurately, as they are supposed to blow rather complicated signals in unison.[10]

(e) The sound of the Temple's orchestra, which consisted of never less than twelve instruments, but rarely exceeded thirty-six, was comparatively quiet, since plucked-string instruments predominated. The trumpets were never mixed with the rest of the orchestra—being used for signals exclusively.

(f) The one pair of cymbals admitted to the Temple ritual appears to have.had the function of a signal-instrument, not unlike the gong in the modern theatre. It is possible that the expression *'Selah'* in biblical texts referred to the cymbal-stroke, called *diapsalma* in the LXX.[11]

The degree of Hellenization, especially in musical terminology, can be gauged in the Book of Daniel, which was written—or edited—during the second century B.C.E. There we encounter the following names of instruments:

Rev. Standard Version English with Hebrew terms transcribed	LXX	Vulgate
Dan. 3 : 5 . . . that when you hear the sound of the horn (*qol qarna*), pipe (*mashroqita*), lyre (*qithros*), trigon (*sab'cha*), harp (*psantrin*), bagpipe (*sumponya*), and every kind (*z'ney*) of music . . .	ὅταν ἀκούσητε τῆς φωνῆς τῆς σάλπιγγος, σύριγγος καὶ κιθάρας, σαμβύκης καὶ ψαλτηρίου συμφωνίας καὶ παντὸς γένους μουσικῶν . . .	in hora qua audieritis sonitum tubae et fistulae et citharae, sambucae et psalterii, et symphoniae, et universi generis musicorum . . .

Qol qarna is pure Aramaic; *mashroqita* (pipe) belongs to the borderland between Greek and Aramaic, as its root *sh-r-q* (to whistle) is Semitic, but its Greek counterpart is *syrinx*, where we notice the same consonants in the root. *Qithros* (lyre or perhaps cittern) corresponds to the Greek *kithara*, from which it is derived; *sab'cha* (trigon, probably a lyre) goes back to the Greek *sambykē*, but it is questionable if that word did not originate in the Aramaic orbit; the *psantrin* is simply the Greek *psaltērion* (translated as harp or psal-

3

tery), and the *sumponya* is a contamination of our *symphōnia*.[12] The word for 'kind' or genus of music *(zan)* is of pure Iranian origin. The *psaltērion* is, according to Augustine, a triangular stringed instrument, like an inverted capital Delta—∇. It had its sounding-board above the strings, in contradistinction to the *kithara,* which had it below them.[13]

Really interesting and important among all these names is only the meaning of *sumponya.* Jerome was familiar with the then conventional translation 'bagpipe', and perhaps with another idea, that of 'the whole ensemble'.[14] C. Sachs suggested that the term be understood as the simultaneous playing by all the instruments mentioned before, after they had performed as soloists. This practice of various solo-performances, followed by their ensemble—the Turkish-Arab *pashrav*—is still very much alive.[15]

It should be noted, on the other hand, that the word *symphōnia* (in Greek), meaning bagpipe, originated just at the time when the Book of Daniel was composed. According to Polybius, Antiochus Epiphanes (who lost his ambitious war against the Maccabees) seems to have shocked public opinion by a diversion which seems harmless enough to us: he 'danced to the barbarous strains of the bagpipe' *(symphōnia).*[16] What will future historians say about statesmen of our time dancing the cha-cha with teenagers?

With all the pomp and noise of these instruments the real noisemakers are conspicuously absent: the percussion instruments. The rigid protocol of the herald's announcement is well portrayed by the fourfold, almost literal repetition of the list of instruments which are to perform the ritual. Perhaps a slightly satirical intention was not absent. . . .

For the instruments discussed are supposed to represent the royal orchestra of Nebukadnezzar at a rather noisy triumph over the conquered Jews—the triumph of a secular power over Israel's divine protector. Now, when the Book of Daniel was written, there was no longer an independent Babylonia, and perhaps the author of the book felt that, musically speaking, the conquered Jews would have done a better job—as hinted at in Ps. 137, 'At the waters of Babel'.

At the time when the Book of Daniel was composed, or edited, second century B.C.E., musical life in Israel was by no means restricted to the Temple or to religious performances. The true state of music was charmingly described in the words of praise addressed to the Hellenized Ben Sira, who, like Josephus, was a member of the priestly caste:

Ecclesiasticus 32 : 3-6:

> To you, the older man, it becomes to speak
> with consummate knowledge—
> but do not impede the music!
> Where one listens (to music)
> do not pour out talk.
> Do not annoy the listeners with lectures.
> As a ring of rubies
> shines in golden setting,
> so is the musician's ensemble
> at a banquet of wine;
> As in golden frame-work
> a precious emerald,
> so adorn melodies of musicians
> a feast of wine.
> Listen in silence!
> And for your modesty
> people will thank you.[17]
>   (Trans. E. W.)

How much more pleasant is this urbane tone than the austerity, the dour hostility of the Rabbis to all instrumental, especially to all secular, music!

As long as the Sanctuary stood, the Rabbis participated gladly in its musical festivities, especially at the 'feast of drawing water'. The Talmud has left us a few colourful descriptions of this somewhat strange festival, written by the very same rabbis, who, for their own time, resented all musical gaiety. 'He who has not witnessed the feast of drawing water has never seen real joy', they exclaimed 200 years after Temple's fall. And well they might lament!

For this was the singular occasion where the talents of amateurs and of the Temple's professional musicians (Levites) were permitted to mix for the greater glory of the festival. What and how do we know about it? For the Bible (both OT and NT), tells us nothing about it, for good reasons.

For this rain-making fertility ritual contained elements of old sympathetic magic as well as certain syncretistic traits: the *sacrum connubium* (Babylonia), the mystery-cult of Syria—which offended the strict and pure ritual of the Pentateuchal feast of Tabernacles, with which the 'drawing of water' coincided. From the musical point of view, however, it was by far the most sumptuous festivity celebrated in and around the Second Temple. We shall sketch the highlights of the celebration, according to the earliest Talmudic accounts:

> When the day grew dark the great candelabras were lighted . . . the light shed by these high lamps was so great that the whole of Jerusalem was lit up by it. . . . In the meantime spirits rose higher and higher until the 'pious men' and the 'men of (good) deeds', whose great hour this was, began to dance before the people with burning torches in their hands. It is told of the venerable Rabban Shimeon ben Gamaliel himself, that he used to dance with eight golden burning torches; he threw them high up in the air and again caught them alternately, and so great was his skill that no torch ever touched another nor did any torch ever fall to earth. . . . Other sages performed similar feats and entertained the audience with enigmatic sayings. . . . In the meantime the Levites took up positions upon the fifteen steps leading from the women's court to the inner court of the Israelites. . . . In their hands were harps, lyres, cymbals, trumpets, and numerous other musical instruments, and they began to sing, accompanying themselves. They sang the so-called fifteen 'Songs of Ascent' (Pss. 120–34). . . . The fifteen steps, the Mishna expressly states, corresponded to the fifteen Songs of Ascent. . . . While the greater part of the night was thus spent in singing, playing, and dancing, two priests stood high above the humming crowd . . . at the upper gate. . . . In their hands they held trumpets and they stood listening for the first crowing of the cock. As soon as they heard the cock crow they immediately lifted their trumpets to their lips and blew a triple blast. . . . These sounds were a signal for the cessation of the merriment. The crowd arrayed itself in the wake of the priests to descend in procession to the well of Silqam. . . .[18]

All this would not be considered licentious by the redactors of the Bible. Yet what preceded these ceremonies was apparently considered unfit for general publication: 'Originally during the festivities women used to stand within the great courtyard called the Women's Court . . . while the men were without. But the two sexes used to intermingle and to commit what is euphemistically called "lightheadedness". The sages ordained that the men and women should change places, but still "lightheadedness" occurred ("sporting between men and women"). Then the sages, having had special galleries built round about three sides of the courtyard, ordered the women to sit in them, in order to prevent the people from giving way to the temptation of the "evil inclination" that overpowers man in the hour of joy. . . .'[19] It is not known if that preventive measure was successful.

With the exception of the priestly trumpet-blowing and the Levitical chant, everything else was improvised, noisy, and exuberant. No wonder that most ancient authors believed—judging from hearsay—that this was a Bacchic wine-orgy. Plutarch maintains that the Jews invoked Bacchus during the feast of water-drawing not only in enigmatic symbols, but quite openly.[20] Similar statements were made by *Apion* and *Posidonius*.[21]

As this festival contained as its ritual centre the water and wine libation upon the altar of the Temple, the celebration fell into oblivion soon after the Temple's destruction.[22]

Apparently all instrumental music of the Temple was linked, in one way or another, to the sacrifices. The rabbinic literature no less than Josephus leaves no doubt about this fundamental connection; in fact, the Talmud usually identifies the musical activities by referring to the specific sacrifices.[23]

Whether the conspicuous number-symbolism relative to musical instruments, especially to those employed in the Temple's ritual, rests upon an indigenous and ancient Jewish concept of the relation between things terrestrial and celestial, or an early recognition of the close link between number and tone, is problematic. Such or similar ideas may just as well have been imported by disciples of the Pythagorean or of the Neo-Platonic philosophy; at any rate, we cannot ascertain how old these concepts actually are. For the conception of the Temple and Jerusalem having their celestial counterparts, the allegorization of instruments as *numerical* images of the cosmos, are found in Philo and in Josephus, who certainly were much impressed with Greek philosophy; on the other hand, we encounter such ideas also in early rabbinic literature, where Platonic influences are not likely, and especially in Scripture—and there in passages that far antedate Plato and even Pythagoras: the seven *shofars* of Joshua before Jericho; the two trumpets divinely ordered in Num. 10; the fifteen steps of the Temple's court corresponding with the number of pilgrimage psalms (120–34) and with the numerical value of the ineffable name of God. Perhaps these cosmological-musical ideas came to the Jews from Babylonia, where they were at least not unknown. For the present we ought to avoid a definite conclusion.[24]

Unique in the history of music is the firm belief in the purifying and sin-atoning power of the Temple's music, ascribed to both chant and instruments. This can only be understood if the theological concept of atonement in and by the Temple is fully comprehended. Here a few brief observations must suffice to elucidate the matter, which has produced a large theological literature.

The concept of atonement has undergone a vast development in Judaism. Starting with the conviction that blood, being the life-power of the soul, forms an indispensable part of any sacrificial atonement, we encounter statements which appear to us as shockingly crude, as well as anachronistic, in both the OT and the NT.

The Talmud contains several passages, all written long after the destruction of all sacrificial rites, which state: 'there is no atonement except with blood',[25] which runs parallel with the dictum of the Epistle to the Hebrews 9 : 22: 'without the shedding of blood there is no forgiveness of sins'.

Yet long before that time prophets and psalmists had pronounced and championed a more spiritual concept of atonement: ' "What to me is the multitude of your sacrifices" says the Lord; "I have had enough of burnt offerings of rams and the fat of fed beasts; I do not delight in the blood of bulls, or of lambs, or of he-goats. . . . Bring no more vain offerings; incense is an abomination to me. . . ." ' (Isa. 1 : 11–13); or 'Thou hast no delight in sacrifice; were I to give a burnt-offering, thou wouldst not be pleased' (Ps. 51 : 16); 'Sacrifice and offering thou dost not desire . . . burnt offering and sin offering thou hast not required' (Ps. 40 : 6). In general, five major types of atonement were developed in Jewish theology: repentance and prayer; restitution for an evil act; charity; study of the Law and fasting; martyrdom. The last-mentioned idea is already fully developed in the Psalms, where we read:

Psalm 116 : 14–15:

8

I will pay my vows to the Lord
in the presence of all his people.
Precious in the sight of the Lord
is the death of his saints.
(Rev. Standard Version)[26]

The men of the synhedrion and of the Great Synagogue, those true disciples of prophets and psalmists, had made prayer and penitence an indispensable element of every true atonement. The 'pious' group, or Hasideans, took little notice of sacrifice as a way of sin-atonement; and yet the great mass of the population preferred the showy and ceremonious kind of sacrificial atonement—notwithstanding the lip service they paid to the prophets. The Levite song was considered indispensable for the remission of sins, as indispensable as the sprinkling of blood. A few Talmudic passages will illustrate this common attitude, and the nostalgic belief in an almost magic power inherent in the music of the Temple.[27]

> The omission of song invalidates sacrifice—this is the view of R. Meir. The Sages, however, held that the omission of song does not invalidate the sacrifice. . . .[28]
> How did the Levites go wrong in the daily Psalm? Here in Babylon it was explained that they did not say any psalms at all. R. Zera . . . said that they chanted the weekday psalm along with the regular sacrifice of the afternoon. . . .[29]
> R. Simeon b. Eleazar said: the absence of priests, Levites, and musical instruments is a bar to the offering of sacrifices. . . .[30]

In other words: as the sacrifice has the function of atoning sins (individual or collective), so has the music which accompanies the sacrifice. Being an integral part of the offering, it had to be free from blemish or fault. In general, the ritual of the Second Temple eschewed magic or syncretistic elements. Yet there remained some rudiments of these earlier stages of the Jewish religion, both in the practice of the Temple (feast of drawing water), and in certain precepts for the High Priest, which dated from Mosaic and early post-Mosaic times. They were retained just because of their archaic tradition. A characteristic example of such almost animistic ideas, juxtaposed to pure monotheism, in biblical music, is the description of the High Priest's garment.

9

We read in Exod. 28 : 34–35:

> . . . a golden bell and a pomegranate, a golden bell and a pomegranate, round about on the skirts of the robe. And it shall be upon Aaron when he ministers, and its sound shall be heard when he goes into the holy place before the Lord, and when he comes out, lest he die.
> (Rev. Standard Version)

The interpretation of these verses reflects clearly the dynamism within the Jewish religion, for it did not remain stationary. At first it was understood as if the chimes or bells on the hem of the High Priest's robe had chased away the evil spirits from under the threshold of the Holy-of-Holies, where they often lurked. Yet this was only the first explanation.[31] Others followed, and the trend of Jewish thinking can be gauged by the subsequent exegeses: Philo (*De Spec. Leg.*, I) and Josephus (*Antiqu.*, III, 7,7) view the bells as symbols of cosmic harmony;[32] the Talmud (B. *Z'vachim* 88b) interprets the sound of bells as a means to atone for an 'offence of sound', or of slander;[33] elsewhere the bells are subjected to an interpretation which finds their significance in their mystic numbers (B. *Arachin* 9b).[34]

Of the numerous instruments only the *shofar* has remained in the ritual to the present day, precisely because it was *not* considered a musical instrument, and also because its theological symbolism was of paramount significance. Its original character was that of a rough signal horn, and in principle it has retained this intentionally primitive character. It is made of the horn of a domesticated or wild ram, or of an antelope, or of an ibex; very little is changed in it, and an artificial or any sort of added mouthpiece makes it ritually unfit. The verb with which the *shofar* is most frequently associated stands for 'to make the noise of an alarm'.

The *shofar* (Akkadian *šapparu*—wild ibex, in the LXX *salpinx* or *keras,* in the Vulgate *buccina* or *cornu*) is by far the most frequently mentioned instrument of the Bible. In the NT it is usually called *salpinx* (e.g., in Rev. or in 1 Cor. 14 : 8). In olden times the *shofar* sounded all signals in war and peace: it announced the new moon, the beginning of the Sabbath, the death of a notable; it warned of approaching danger; it heralded excommunications; it proclaimed exorcisms and performed magic healing (more or less clandestine).

10

Today it is used only on the New Year's day and (in very orthodox communities) on the days preceding it, as a memorial of the ram which replaced Isaac as sacrificial animal (Gen. 22—which is the main lesson of New Year just before the *shofar* ritual).[35] How close to the surface lay magic or totemistic conceptions may be seen in the prohibition on using a cow's horn instead of a proper *shofar* for the Temple's signals. The Talmud indicates that a cow's horn might seriously impair the spiritual value of a sacrifice—the cow not being a permissible sacrificial beast—because a certain spiritual affinity is postulated and must exist between the signal instrument and the sacrificial animal.[36]

In its strictly ritual usage it carried the cries of the multitude to God. At special occasions He himself or His angels may sound the *shofar* (Isa. 27 : 13; Zech. 9 : 14; Rev. 8 : 2, 6, 12; 9 : 1–13); these ideas have survived the separation of Church and Synagogue, as we can see in the *Tuba mirum* of the Requiem, or its *Vorlage,* the Byzantine hymn on the *Parousia of Christ* by Romanus.[37]

Musically speaking—which is hardly possible in connection with the *shofar*—this strange instrument can produce only the first two harmonic overtones, and these merely by poor approximation. Rarely does it appear in a general ensemble of music instruments; when it does, the ensemble bears the intention of a 'numinous' demonstration[38] (e.g., II Sam. 6 : 1; I Chr. 15 : 28; II Chr. 15 : 14). As the *shofar* is incapable of sounding a melody or even a longer series of tones clearly, its tone had not the effect of music, which might draw the listener's attention by sensual beauty or by fine melodic quality: the *shofar*'s effect is purely associative and therefore not musical in the proper sense of the word. Only in Ps. 150 is the *shofar* mentioned among most of the other music instruments—but within a list which contains both secular and Temple instruments. The *shofar*'s noisemaking, be if of earthly or of eschatological significance, has intentionally remained archaic-primitive; it is to remind Israel of his years in the desert and his awesome nearness to YHWH.

In the early rabbinic literature, *shofar* and trumpet (Hebr. *haz-zotzra*) were frequently confused. This intentionally inaccurate treatment of all music instruments was an aspect of the studied indifference to all things artistic or musical by the puritanical

11

Rabbis; it also reflects their efforts to attain in the world of the Synagogue—where they held jurisdiction—equality with the institutions of the Temple—where they had held none.[39] Jerome, who equates the *shofar* with the Roman *buccina,* is likewise mistaken, for the *buccina* was a sort of trombone, made of metal.[40] His other attempt at translation, *cornu,* approaches better the nature of the *shofar.* Such confusions do not occur in the OT or in the Dead Sea Scrolls (DSS). Both state that only trumpets, never *shofars,* could or should be blown as 'with one voice' i.e., in unison (cf. II Chr. 5 : 13; DSS *Warscroll* III). Passages such as Num. 10 : 2, 8; 31 : 6 emphasize the Aaronides' privilege of sounding the trumpets, whereas the *shofar* was normally blown by Levites.

Three kinds of signals, together with their descriptions, have been transmitted to us by ancient tradition:[41]

SHOFAR-CALLS

II

The *shofar* signals were part of the ritual performance within the Temple's precincts. Much of it is still obscure, and the questions connected with it cannot be answered satisfactorily. The more or

less sketchy descriptions of the actual music of the Temple originate, with two exceptions, from the period after the Temple's
destruction, and, what is more, from the Rabbis and their literature:
yet the Rabbis were never initiated in the arcana of the priesthood.
The two exceptions—Ben Sira and Josephus—are rather vague and
brief and more or less perfunctory, not free from discrepancies to
boot. Ben Sira, who appears as a connoisseur of secular music,
which he considers an adornment of civilized life, speaks in a tone
quite different from this about the cultic chant of the Temple; he
used the most solemn phrases, when he described (Ecclus. 50) the
chant and the trumpet-blasts of the priests on the Day of Atonement, when 'in the great hall the full sound of the psalm-singing
Levites reverberated'. Josephus tells more about the instruments,
less about the music's performance; thus we learn that the lyre
(kithara) had twelve strings, just as many as a harp, that the
primitive clarinet *(halil)* symbolized life after death, that the silver
trumpets were rather short and thin, etc. In general, however, he
limits himself to short descriptions of instruments, 'so that the
gentile reader may not be wholly unacquainted with their nature. . . '.[42]

More can be learned from the text of the *Mishna* and its subsequent discussions, but much of it is not really reliable, as it was
codified 130 years after the Sanctuary's fall; also because the Rabbis,
who compiled the *Mishna,* depicted everything connected with the
Temple in the most radiant colours. Nonetheless, a good deal of
factual observations are probably accurate—always aside from
aesthetic, or rather moralizing, evaluations.

According to these sources, both singers and instrumentalists
were strictly trained professional musicians with an average training
period of five years.[43] The choir's repertoire consisted of psalms,
canticles, and other poetic passages from Scripture; it may have
contained some noncanonical texts, which, however, have not
come down to us. The rendering of longer canticles or psalms must
have been strophic or refrain-like, as without any such repetition—
in the absence of any musical notation—it would have been impossible to keep together the vocal and instrumental ensemble. The
instrumental accompaniment was probably heterophonic—i.e., it
reproduced the vocal line instrumentally with slight melismatic

deviations. Only for signalling purposes were certain instruments used independently from the choir, such as cymbal-strokes, trumpet-calls, etc.

The daily (weekday) sacrifice called for twenty-one trumpet-blasts; a minimum of two, a maximum of six harps was normally employed, with two to nine lyres. At least, two primitive clarinets (*halilim*), at most, twelve were permitted to play, but only on the appointed twelve days of the year, in order to 'sweeten' the sound of the somewhat dry-sounding orchestra of plucked string instruments and the shrill signals of the trumpets. The occasions were: the first Passover sacrifice; the second Passover sacrifice; during the first day of Passover; on Pentecost (*Shabu'ot*); during the eight days of the festival of Tabernacles (*Succot*). In particular, the *halil* accompanied the chant of *Hallel* (Pss. 113–18), prescribed for the liturgy of those days. While there was a fixed minimum of two trumpets, their number could be increased arbitrarily; but only one pair of cymbals was permitted in the Temple.

Of choristers, twelve adult Levites constituted the minimum chorus, but the number could be augmented *ad libitum* (nine for the nine lyres, two for the two harps, and one for the cymbal). Their chant was usually 'spiced' by the sopranos and altos of their sons, who stood at their feet, and are called 'their tormentors' in the *Mishna*.[44]

The weekday's liturgy unfolded in this way: after the morning's sacrifice, introduced by the mandatory trumpet-blasts, 'the priests gave the High Priest the wine for the libation . . . and two priests stood by the table . . . with two silver trumpets; . . . they sounded a plain blast, a tremulant blast, and a plain blast, then they stood . . . by Ben Arza [the cymbalist]. When the High Priest bent down to pour out the libation . . . Ben Arza struck the cymbals and the Levites broke out in the song. When the Levites reached the end of a paragraph [or a section] they[?] blew a plain blast and the people prostrated themselves. . . . This was the rite of the daily burnt-offering in the Service. . . .'[45]

One source describes the obligatory repertoire of the Levites as Ps. 24 : 1–10, for the first day (Sunday); Ps. 48 : 1–15, for the second; Ps. 82 : 1–8, for the third; Ps. 94 : 1–23 and/or Ps. 95 : 1–10 for the fourth; Ps. 81 : 1–17 for the fifth; Ps. 93 : 1–5 for the sixth day; and

Ps. 92 : 1–16 for the Sabbath. The choice of these psalms is said to have been determined by God's activities on the first seven days of creation, and the verses which allude to them. This was, however, by no means the entire repertory of the Levitical chorus. Reports of the service for the pilgrimage festivals have come down to us which sound accurate and deserve credibility. On Pentecost, for instance:

> . . . the flute-played before the psalm-singing crowd [going upward to Jerusalem] chanting Pss. 120–34, the 'Songs of the pilgrims' or 'of ascent' [the *cantus graduum* of the Vulgate] until they drew near Jerusalem. . . . The flute played before them until they arrived at the Temple mount. . . . When the court of the Temple was reached, the Levites sang [for their welcome], Ps. 30. . . .[46]

To the signal instruments, which accompanied certain sacrifices, belonged the rather enigmatic *magrepha,* which was either a small steam siren, or a massive kind of tam-tam, which could be filled with burning coals. The Talmud is rather hyperbolic in its description of that instrument, as it invents, especially for it, an acoustic miracle: it was supposed to consist of ten pipes; each pipe had ten holes, and on each hole ten various tones could be played—so that on ten pipes a thousand tones could be produced![47]

Two generations after the Sanctuary's fall, the question—previously never raised—whether the vocal or the instrumental constituent was more important for the correctness of the ritual, was eagerly discussed. As the debaters were rabbis, not priests, they could not agree on any definite answer.[48] Indeed, certain passages were replete with contradicting or simply untenable statements about Levitical music, born of ignorance or indifference. How far the opinions diverged may be gathered from one example (which could easily be multiplied):

> How did the Levites go wrong in the daily psalms? Here in Babylon it was explained that they did not say any psalms at all. R. Zera, however, said that they recited the weekday psalms along with the regular sacrifice of the afternoon. . . .[49]

Behind all such contradictions and speculations lies an idea which we encounter quite frequently in the rabbinic literature of the first three centuries after the Temple's fall: that the arrogance and

15

negligence of the Levites was a contributing factor of guilt to the final catastrophe. Even so cool and critical an observer as Josephus was not free from this sort of splinter-seeking, where he might have thought of the mote in his eye! In his *Antiquities* we marvel at the following curious passage:

Those of the Levites . . . who were singers of hymns, urged the King to convene the synhedrion and get them permission to wear linen robes *on equal terms with the priests*. . . . The King, with the consent of those who attended the synhedrion, allowed the singers of hymns to discard their former robes and to wear linen ones such as they wished. A part of the [Levitical] tribe that served in the Temple was also permitted to *learn hymns by heart* [*hymnous ekmathein*], as they had requested. All this was contrary to the ancestral laws, and such transgression was bound to make us liable to punishment.[50]

The indignation of the high aristocrat Josephus at the Levitical arrivés, who wanted to stand 'on equal terms with the priests', is not without a comical touch; and that the Levites had the impertinence to learn a new hymn 'by heart' makes us wonder how else they should have learned them. Undoubtedly they were familiar with the texts of psalms and canticles from childhood on; thus they appear to have planned an expansion of their repertory by studying *new texts and melodies*. The remark that 'this was contrary to ancestral laws' makes sense only when applied to the linen garments, which were a privilege of the priests. It does not make sense when applied to the 'new hymns', because there was no law that limited the hymns to scriptural psalms and canticles. The psalmist's exhortation 'Sing to the Lord a new song!' was still valid and considered inspired. Was it not a cheap *vaticinium ex eventu* for Josephus to blame the despised Levites—on grounds which only a priest could understand—for the subsequent total defeat of the entire nation?

Nowhere does Josephus refer to the captain of the Levites by name, although he must have known him well. While he proudly lists his own genealogy and gives a list of High Priests, he did not bother to mention the *s'gan levi'im*, the Levites' leader. Did they have a permanent conductor? What was his title, what were his functions? Is he identical with the 'choirleader' (or 'chief musician') so often referred to in the Book of Psalms? It is, in our opinion, possible to dispose of this question once and for all. The Greek (LXX) translation, which originated about 200 years before the time of Josephus, was obviously incapable of coping with the Hebrew term *lam'natzeach*—it rendered it by the enigmatic 'to the end' (*eis to telos*); while St Jerome, instructed by a Palestinian rabbi, went back to the original source of the Hebrew term and rendered it literally correct with 'to the victor', which again does not help us much. Obviously, the precise meaning of the original Hebrew term was forgotten by the time of the Maccabees. Apparently, the term referred to the 'triumph-maker' or master of ceremonies at a royal triumph, as I have pointed out elsewhere.[51]

The discovery of the Dead Sea Scrolls during the decades following 1948 raised great hopes for all students of Hellenism and Judaism; yet while the entire religious history of that period has assumed a fundamentally new aspect, the results of these discoveries for the history of liturgy and music are rather limited in scope. The chief reason for this lack of *generally* important findings lies in the very origin of the material: it was written by a sectarian group for its own use and could not claim universal authority. This group, however we choose to call it today—and the discussion is far from being concluded, as this is written—was certainly a small minority among the population of Palestine. Nonetheless, some characteristic facts of its liturgy have come to light, especially the evolution of the antiphon form out of psalmodic structures, as we know them today in finished shape from Byzantine and Gregorian traditions. As for detailed results of the Dead Sea Scrolls, we refer to our next chapter.

One concept of ritual imagery, a remnant of the Temple's glory, has become generally popular in Judaism as well as in Christianity: the angelology, and in particular the angelic liturgy surrounding the heavenly throne. These prophetic-apocalyptic fantasies and visions were to create, it must be said in all bluntness, more poems, paintings, and sculptures than real music in all the centuries to come. Could it be that musicians were afraid to compete with the heavenly host? That no human tones were trusted to represent angelic ones, however humbly, yet adequately? That, in effect, the angelic concert could be imagined and described, but not heard, exactly as the harmony of the spheres in Pythagorean philosophy?

Whatever the reasons against musical representation of the angelic concert, its origins are now fairly clear: they go back to the time of the DSS and the intertestamentary, especially the apocalyptic literature.

Thus, while the Israelites praise the Lord in song and word during the day, the angels are silent; their time is the night. They are divided into choruses which remind us of the priestly orchestra and the Levitical divisions (*mishmarot*) of the Temple; they rival with the Israelites in their 'incessant' singing and praising the greatness of God; they are called the 'sleepless' or those 'who never lie down', terms which we encounter similarly in the language of the Byzantine court.[52]

In one way, however, the angelic chorus was quite different from the image which began to conquer Christianity from the tenth century on, and which has reached a nadir in the postcards at the Christmas season: the angels of that early literature were fire-spirits, their sound was sweet, yet 'awesome', their praise incessant but monotonous, their chant like 'the roaring of a great fire', or the 'rushing of many waters'.[53] Indeed, Goethe's lofty verses were most adequate to describe such visions:

> You cannot end, that makes you great;
> And that you ne'er began, that is your fate.
> Your song is like the starry firmament
> Revolving ever, without start or end.

One of the wellsprings of Jewish mysticism was the description of the divine chariot as envisaged by Ezekiel (Chaps. 1 and 10). During the last pre-Christian and the first Christian centuries the wheels (*ofanim*) of the heavenly chariot became a synonym for 'melodies', so that the wheels' every movement produced angelic music. The sect of the Essenes was particularly attracted to these heavenly concerts, and the fragments of an 'Angelic Liturgy' written in those circles have come down to us.[54] Two or three centuries later these visions of individuals or of small sects were incorporated in the Jewish prayer-book as the so-called *Kedusha de-Yotzer* (*Sanctus* of the morning prayer). It is a colourful paraphrase of the *Sanctus* text and has made a powerful impact upon the

18

Christian counterpart of that prayer. This will be discussed at length in Ch. V.[55]

III

Reminiscences, visions, and fantasies constituted the fabric of the dreams spun about the Temple's music after its fall. For the Rabbis took pains to eradicate both its choral and instrumental traditions; their time had arrived, and their ideas on liturgy and music were radically different from those of the priests. Yet, free from the danger of realization, they now idealized everything connected with the Temple, from the killing of the sacrifices to the sound of its music. This sounds fantastic—and the essential paradox has remained alive to this day: the very same rabbis, who prohibited any and all instrumental music in their synagogues, could not sufficiently praise that of the Temple: they spun dreams and fantasies around it. They might have reinstated it—at least the music and the non-sacrificial ceremonies of the Temple—in their own synagogues without much difficulty. Why did they fail to do so?

(1) With the fall of the Temple the priests and Levites had lost their jurisdiction. The incipient vacuum was soon filled by the chief representatives of rabbinic Judaism.

(2) One of the Temple's main functions had been the atonement of sins individual and collective; bereft of sacrifices, priests, and the numinous institution, the nation felt the pangs of a spiritual void.

(3) The official synhedrion (the organization that had supervised the Temple and the legislation) was replaced by R. Johanan ben Zakkai, who created an unofficial, temporarily clandestine High Court (*Bet Din*) in order to maintain continuity of law and tradition within the limits prescribed by the political realities.

(4) What authority did the Rabbis possess, how was it founded and justified? A full answer of this most difficult question would fill an entire book; here we shall limit ourselves to the barest essentials:

(a) The Pharisaic group had always insisted upon the oral tradition's authenticity standing on equal level with the written one; the Sadducees had denied this claim. Now the Sadducees had lost their power and jurisdiction, and the Rabbis made their fundamental assumption law and tenet of Judaism. This oral law, as well as the written one, was administered by them.[56]

19

(b) Not enough therewith: the Rabbis established a kind of pedigree of their oral tradition from Mount Sinai down to their own times. This document is still extant in the first chapter of the *Mishna Abot*. The fact itself that so old a spiritual genealogy was available at the very moment when it was most needed, lets us believe that a major part of this chapter antedated the fall of the Temple by a relatively short time only, perhaps fifty or sixty years—provided that the chapter is not a later forgery, as suggested by A. Guttmann in *HUCA*, XVI (1941).

(5) Now that a powerful group of *laymen*—for the Rabbis were and are considered laymen in Jewish law—had gained political and legal power over their priestly-aristocratic opponents and predecessors, it was necessary to set up an authoritative, prestigious clan or dynasty as a visible proof of evident authority. King Agrippa II and his sister, Princess Berenice, were disgraced, nor had the Hasmonean dynasty left many adherents outside the Hellenized aristocracy; a priestly family was rarely trusted, as long as the Sadducees maintained both their claims and their hope for a restitution of their ancient privileges. Thus an ancient patrician family, not tainted by servility to Romans, but associated with the synhedrion and its Rabbis, was to provide the best solution and to maintain the highest authority. This is why the ageing R. Johanan ben Zakkai chose as his successor in the presidency of the Academy of Jamnia (Yabne) Rabban Gamaliel II of the noble house of Hillel, the grandson of Gamaliel I, teacher of Paul.

This first rabbinic group that had attained legal power was aware of the necessity of establishing undisputed sources and reasons for its authority and made every effort to strengthen them. Jesus' constant deprecation of the 'tradition of the elders' was apparently well justified.[57] We read in one of the early rabbinic documents: 'The matter [of authority] is more serious concerning words of the Scribes than words of the [written] Law.' It was only natural that the Rabbis harped upon a rather far-fetched comparison of Deut. 13 : 2 with Deut. 17 : 11. The former passage implies that a prophet must authenticate himself by a sign or miracle, whereas the teachings and commandments of the elders are to be obeyed as a matter of course.

Equipped with newly-won prestige, unhindered by the Sadducces, the Rabbis went to work zealously and radically. One of their earliest decrees stated the theological equality of sacrifice and prayer, an originally prophetic idea, which was most useful now that no sacrifices were permitted. It was perfectly logical, then, that the Rabbis prohibited all instrumental music in the Synagogue where no sacrifices were possible; as a matter of fact, they were inclined to forbid it generally, not only for worship. Some of the *real* reasons that had motivated the Rabbis were adduced in Vol. 1, Part II, Ch. I. We shall here examine the reasons *given* by the Rabbis, which concealed the true motives.

The prohibition of instrumental music in the Synagogue was coupled with that of singing in taverns, and with the denial of antiphonal liturgical chant between men and women. It was, legally speaking, a severe and complicated measure. For these three types of musical performance demanded three different types of treatment, if their prohibition was to stand on safe legal ground. The motivation had to be provided by Scripture, but by different and disparate passages from it. Inasmuch as the Rabbis, by themselves, possessed only that much authority as they could derive from legal interpretation and interpolation of Scripture, they had to search for scriptural passages which might be twisted and interpreted, until they would suit their purposes. Since no such prohibition as the Rabbis had in mind can be found in Scripture, the rabbinic laws concerning music are inconsistent, full of loop-holes, and their derivation from the scriptural text is totally unconvincing.[58]

What was to be prohibited? (1) Instrumental music in the Synagogue and outside; (2) Loud singing or playing at banquets or in taverns; (3) Common or antiphonal singing of men and women; (4) Loud singing in public.

(1) The pertinent, but rather vague passage reads:

When the synhedrion ceased to function, song ceased from the places of feasting; as it is said 'they shall not drink wine with a song' (Isa. 24 : 9).

The text alludes to an event, which, critically looked upon, has nothing at all to do with the prohibition of music; indeed, it is a kind of camouflage. For, actually, the synhedrion lost its authority

21

before the fall of the Temple. If we are to believe Josephus, the political power of this council was abolished by the Roman general, Gabinius.[59]

Nothing is clearly said against instruments, but only against singing; this may be understood in this way: the Rabbis believed that purely instrumental music *per se* (without words) made no sense. Not so the public at large.[60] The place of music in worship is left in doubt, for at the time when this was written, it was still controversial, as we shall see presently. For the subsequent *Gemara* (Talmudic discussion) questions immediately the date of the synhedrion's loss of authority, and maintains the point of the matter—the prohibition of music—only by way of a far-fetched scriptural quotation, not by a historical or legal argument.[61] The controversialists are almost all rabbis of the third century. In order to eliminate all traces of instrumental music, R. Johanan said: 'Whoever drinks to the accompaniment of the four musical instruments, brings five punishments to the world', and recites thereafter the verse Isa. 5 : 11, totally torn out of its context.[62]

(2) His contemporary, the exilarch Mar Ukba, replied to the question: Where does Scripture tell us that it is forbidden (in our days) to sing (at carousals or banquets)? in these terms: 'Rejoice not, O Israel, unto exultation, like the nations, for thou hast gone astray from thy God' (Hos. 9 : 1),[63] 'They shall not drink wine with music, strong drink shall be bitter to them that drink it' (Isa. 24 : 9). 'From this verse it might be concluded,' says the Talmud, 'that only musical instruments are forbidden, but not song; this I learn [from the former verse].'[64] Still, there is no statement which would prohibit instrumental music at divine services. Indeed, such a prohibition is nowhere clearly pronounced, but elsewhere cunningly camouflaged. For, while the playing of instruments *ad majorem Dei gloriam* could never be forbidden in so many words, still no instruments could be played on Sabbath in the synagogue (or anywhere else), because this might violate a certain sabbatical law; and it is obviously impossible to honour the weekday-service with instrumental music when the Sabbath cannot be so adorned! Thus it came about that for the prohibition of music and song there is no systematic legislation, but one which much later had to be assembled piecemeal (from principal objections, from sabbatical

laws, from anti-assimilationist reasons, etc.), like a mosaic or a riddle, out of many different and disparate sources.[65]

(3) In order to vindicate this austere attitude, we are treated to a chain of anti-musical, *ad hoc* fabricated 'proverbs' which the Rabbis quoted with much gusto.[66] And, of course, the sinful role of female voices is not overlooked, exactly as in the contemporary Christian literature: R. Joseph said: 'When men sing and women join in, it is licentiousness; when women sing and men join in it is like fire in tow.' And: 'For what practical purpose is this mentioned at all? To abolish the latter before the former.'[67] It was the firm conviction of the Rabbis that 'the voice of woman is a *pudendum*'.[68] In the first volume ('The Conflict between Hellenism and Judaism in the Music of the Early Christian Church') the consequences of this anti-musical attitude, of this strange puritanism of the Rabbis were sketched and compared with the strikingly similar attitudes of the Church Fathers before the fourth century. As was pointed out there, the hostility of the Rabbis against all music long antedated the fall of the central Sanctuary, as we can recognize most clearly in the case of St Paul's words against musical instruments.[69]

(4) Thus, by the end of the first century C.E. we enter, in Judaism and to a certain extent also in Christianity, an age of anti-musical puritanism which lasted much longer in Judaism: not even the blooming of the so-called 'Golden Age' in Spain under the aegis of Islam could thaw the frozen music of the Jewish people. For the Rabbis stuck to the old legal formula which forbade any sort of artistic musical performance and tolerated only the 'science of music'.[70] This ruthless and senseless rabbinic suppression is responsible before history for the absence of an autonomous, organic, and independent liturgical music of the Synagogue. No choral tradition was permitted to grow in the nation which once had begotten a Levitical chorus and orchestra; and any kind of theatrical or secular musical activity by Jews was frowned upon by the Rabbis for many centuries. They did, in fact, everything in their power to put obstacles in the way of the Synagogue's liturgical music—so that first the old orthodoxy had to be overcome before any artistic standard could be aspired to. Yet just as the Rabbis paid lip-service to the Temple's musical splendour *after its downfall,* so did they emphasize and praise a musical Jewish 'tradition' for the Synagogue

in unctuous words. They stopped their ears to the tasteless offerings of their cantors, but tried everything to prevent the restitution of the ancient purity of Israel's music.[71] This very situation still prevails in the synagogues of the State of Israel, where the Rabbis hold all jurisdiction on matters of religious art.

With Paul, certain rabbinic ideas entered Christianity. His world-open line won the day and the millennium for the Church. Contemporary with him was another group in Judaism, of which we have learned relatively lately, a small, well-knit minority, resentful and isolationist vis-à-vis the world at large. These antagonistic attitudes found expression in their musical ideas and practices: the world-open line of Paul and his disciples; and the isolationist, world-weary outlook of the pious community of Qumran.

CHAPTER TWO

Away from the World—Towards the World

TWO SECTS AND THEIR MUSIC

THE states of voluntary seclusion and of worldliness, sometimes camouflaged by various catch-phrases such as 'isolationism *v.* secularism' or 'asceticism *v.* eudaemonism', have been known theological positions for thousands of years. The antinomy of evil within a world imbued by God's immanence leads to several types of ethic, all mutually exclusive. Some of the most fundamental ones are: to realize God's rule by complete submission to His actions, which by definition are just; to stabilize His rule by the enactment of His laws in the world; or to turn away from this world altogether, and strive for inner purity. The final outcome of this extreme stand is a Christian or pagan dualism which identifies all that is good with God, all that is bad with the world. The consideration that the world is also God's creation and may be an instrument of His eternal justice has often engendered agnostic or heretical ideas.

Between the extremes lie many possible views and theologies. When the Enlightenment engaged the thinkers of the eighteenth century, many naïve souls were fobbed off with empty anti-religious phraseology, and were often fed with the answers of some 'simplificateurs terribles'. The turbulent conflicts of religious history seemed finally to have come to rest. Yet our generation has seen the ancient dilemmas of Man emerging afresh, often in new and terrifying guise. After the First World War, mankind went to hell and craved redemption; one of the results was Auschwitz. . . .

The outgoing nineteenth century was inclined to regard the history of religion in general, and that of monotheism in particular, as a static, slowly unfolding discipline wherein sensations or surprises were neither expected nor desired. Yet this conservative assumption has proved to be quite mistaken. In fact all aspects of religion and the disciplines connected with it have undergone a period of almost boundless expansion under the triple impact of new findings in archaeology-history, psychology-anthropology, and natural science. The vast amount of papyri, ancient documents and epigraphic testimonies has radically altered the settled opinions held by most historians of religion at the beginning of the century. Everything seems to be in flux again, and hardly a year passes without major discoveries of significant sources hitherto unknown.

These discoveries in turn have affected the status and interpretation of ancient, indeed of canonical literature. It is being studied anew and critically, yet with greater empathy than ever before.

Below we examine two complementary aspects of music during the Hellenistic period of Judaism. One derives from a study of the Dead Sea Scrolls (DSS); the other from a critical consideration of some famous passages in St Paul's Epistles touching upon music. The first aspect reflects the position of withdrawal from the world; the second, concern with the world.

The following pages contain a number of observations on musical expressions or references to music contained in the DSS. The selection made was determined by the various musical topics, and the inferences as to actual musical performance.

MUSICAL ELEMENTS OF THE DEAD SEA SCROLLS

Whatever the final verdict on the at present still controversial Dead Sea Scrolls may be, it should clarify many points in the interplay of Judaism and Hellenism that are now obscure. The actual discoveries in the fields of theology, archaeology, and history have yielded a large crop of hypotheses. A number of important facts, however, are already agreed upon. Far from troubled Jerusalem and its cauldron of power politics there lived in a remote part of the Holy Land, some time between 150 B.C.E. and 135 C.E.—the actual dates are heatedly debated—a group of pious collectivists, provisionally identified with the Essenes. They produced a most interesting sort of literature. By thought and word they opposed the synthesizing and fermenting spirit of Hellenism. In their disci-

26

pline they anticipated Christian monasticism. In accordance with an established rule they lived in freely chosen poverty and obedience to their superior brethren, the majority in a self-imposed chastity. Before entering the order definitely the novices had to bind themselves with a tentative vow, a sort of *votum mobile*. The scrolls of this mysterious order, discovered in Khirbet Qumran near the Dead Sea, reveal a school of thought of which very little was previously known.

It is not even certain whether the group's recently excavated 'motherhouse' belonged to the 'classic' Essene sect or to one of its many offshoots; but its inhabitants must have been closely akin to that ascetic-collectivist fraternity of which Philo, Josephus, and the Gospels speak so sympathetically.

The scrolls themselves are of unalloyed Hebrew nature and show few, if any, traces of Hellenist infiltration. A similar isolationist trend appears later in the early Judaeo-Christian Church. Both groups, the Essenes and the Judaeo-Christians, were eventually crushed between the major forces of rabbinic Judaism and gentile Christianity.

Of the published scrolls at least four contain musical references. These bear on the history of musical notation, the use of instruments, and the evolution of the antiphon.[1]

I

The so-called *St Mark's Scroll* of the Book of Isaiah contains a number of marginal signs, five of which occur repeatedly. They seem to have no direct reference to the text, but perhaps to its rendition. That the signs had an ecphonetic-punctuating function may have occurred to some scholars. Yet owing to the lack of internal (or external) evidence the hypothesis has never been clearly voiced. Characteristic of the caution and restraint of the scholars is such a passage as: 'Scattered through the Isaiah scroll are interesting marginal markings, probably inserted at a later time, perhaps to mark off sections used for reading by the sect which owned the manuscripts'.[2] Five years later the same author permits himself a more extensive description:

Most striking, however, are several very elaborate and mysterious signs in the margins of these two manuscripts [Isaiah and the Habakkuk Commentary].

The meaning of all these signs has not yet been satisfactorily explained. Some of them may mark passages selected for public reading or regarded as especially significant for doctrine. Some may possibly call attention to errors in copying that require correction. Some are so elaborate as to tempt one to regard them as mere idle 'doodling' by an absent-minded scribe or student, but of course such an explanation can be entertained only as a last resort. For a convincing solution of the problem we may have to wait until comparable examples of the same kind of marking have been found in other manuscripts.[3]

It is true that there has been some speculation as to whether these markings were not primitive forerunners of the later Masoretic accentuation, the ecphonetic notation of Hebrew Scripture. Such a hypothesis would attribute a punctuating and possibly a musical function to them. In the absence of any similar or at least comparable signs in other DSS manuscripts, however, this conjecture could not be upheld.

The ten marginal signs are given here:[4]

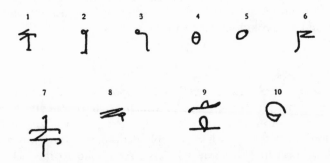

At first blush the idea of comparing these marks with Masoretic accents looks promising. Yet the signs themselves differ from Masoretic accents. The writer sought for similar signs among Roman, Syrian, and Armenian neumes, but with negative results.

Then I came across a relatively recent book on the neumes of the Old Slavonic and Bulgarian Church, which revealed some astonishing parallels. I refer to Mme Paralikova Verdeil's fine study, *La*

Musique byzantine chez les Bulgares et les Russes.[5] The following comparisons are based upon her book.

Of the many Slavonic neumes, five are either identical in shape with, or very similar to, signs found in the Dead Sea Scrolls. The Byzantine-Slavonic neumes are:

These palaeo-Byzantine neumes are found in *Cod. Laura 67,* 1753-4 of Chartres,[6] in an anonymous manuscript of the Mt Athos monastery, and in Ancient Slavonic codices. The system to which these signs belong is the so-called *notation Kontakarienne,* which bears that name because of its application to Byzantine *Kontakia,* a hymn type of the fifth to the seventh centuries. Elsewhere I have drawn attention to the strong influence of Syriac and Hebrew poetry upon the Byzantine *Kontakion.*[7] The most famous poet-composer of *Kontakia* was the great Romanus, a converted Syrian Jew. According to Mme Verdeil this type of *Kontakia* notation was used in Byzantium during the ninth and tenth centuries. It has, at least in the oldest Slavonic manuscripts, preserved its original forms.[8] A comparison of some of these neumes with signs from the Dead Sea Scrolls yields the following tabulation:

Dead Sea Scrolls	Byzantine Kontakia

29

If we permit ourselves to proceed beyond this bare statement of palaeographic evidence, we must constantly be mindful of two possible and mutually exclusive alternatives: (1) the similarity is the result of sheer coincidence; or (2) the similarity has a historical foundation. The latter assumption would imply some direct or indirect relationship between the Dead Sea Scrolls and Byzantine or palaeo-Slavonic manuscripts. *Tertium non datur.*

At the present stage of scrutiny, however, and with only part of the manuscripts published, it is futile to pursue this investigation further. At least two more hurdles must be cleared before we can reach even tentative conclusions. Palaeographic evidence will have to show whether the marginal signs were written by a later hand than the text itself, and scholars will have to search for similar markings in all the scrolls and fragments, which seem, after all, to display a common authority and doctrine.

If we could assume, with Drs Zeitlin and Kahle, that the medieval Jewish sect of the Karaites had, at one time or another, known and even handled some of the scrolls, our path would be easier.[9] The problems of a common historical origin of palaeo-Byzantine neumes and Dead Sea Scrolls signs would not seem insurmountable, for the Karaites settled in Byzantium and later in the Crimea and south-east Russia. One of their tenth-century authorities, Al Qirqisani, knew of Hebrew scrolls in south-east Palestine; moreover, they were already referred back to the 'cave-dwellers' (*Al Maghariyah*), the Arabic sobriquet for the Essenes.[10] There seems to be little doubt that some at present obscure connection existed between the Qumran sect and the Karaites; but what the Karaites had to do with the manuscripts, if they really had access to them, is still uncertain.[11]

For the moment there remains only the question whether the signs in the scrolls could have had any notational or, more specifically, ecphonetic function. While there is nothing to contradict such an assumption *a priori,* our answer must necessarily depend upon our stand towards the two principal alternatives stated above. Although five of the signs are found in both source-groups, it would be rash to base any ecphonetic significance on that evidence alone. Should newer discoveries from Khirbet Qumran or its environment contain identical or even similar signs, we might have to consider seriously the hypothesis that all such markings constitute primitive attempts at lectionary notation. A conjecture of that kind would indeed revolutionize our views on the origin of neumes. (Since these lines were first written [in 1964], many more fragments have been discovered which contain some of the signs mentioned, but no new ones. Lacking any further evidence, it is premature to form definite conclusions.)

II

Musical instruments and their use are mentioned repeatedly in the scrolls called *The War of the Children of Light against the Children of Darkness* and the *Manual of Discipline*. The names of the instruments are the same as those that so often appear in the Psalter. Even the usage appears, at first blush, to be patterned according to the standard phrases familiar to every student of the Old Testament. But this similarity is only superficial. Among these backward-harking phrases there sounds an unexpected new note, a type of thought and speech that is known to us from New Testament literature.

One of the characteristic passages of the hymn that concludes the *Manual of Discipline*, reads (*Man.*, X : 9):

Dupont-Sommer's translation	*E. W.'s translation*
I will sing with knowledge	I shall sing with knowledge
And all my lyre will vibrate of the Glory of God	And all my song will be for the glory of God
And my lute and my harp for the holy order of which He is the author	The lyre and my harp (are) in accord with His holy order[13]
And I will raise the flute of my lips on account Of his righteous cord.[12]	And I will raise the flute of my lips Following the precept of His law

The 'lute' of Dupont-Sommer's translation and also his 'vibrating lyre' are perhaps a little periphrastic. The 'holy order' refers to the succession of weeks, months, and holy days, indeed to the Essene luni-solar calendar, in which they took great pride.[14] Of greater interest than these terminological differences are expressions like, 'I will sing with knowledge'; for the very same phrase occurs in Paul's First Epistle to the Corinthians,[15] while it is absent in the Old

31

Testament. And Clement of Rome, the third Bishop, stressed, like the sect of the scrolls, the holy order, according to which all worship should be regulated.[16]

It is at this point that the question arises: Does the hymnodist refer to real instruments or are they imaginary ornaments of his poetry? Did he refer to a veritable *symphonia sacra*? For his outburst has a certain flavour which reminds us of similar allegorical passages in Paul, Philo, and the post-apostolic literature.

The trouble with all these references to musical instruments is that they were usually meant as well as understood metaphorically. A few examples will illustrate this point.

Philo of Alexandria was an older contemporary of Jesus and a sympathizer with the Therapeutes, the Egyptian branch of the Essenes. He likens the soul to a well-attuned lyre,[17] and even speaks of 'the lyre of the soul'.[18] In general he thinks that no instrument can attain the expressive dignity of the human voice.[19] And St Paul, in a famous diatribe, while not directly speaking against instruments, compares them unfavourably with song, song of the spirit and of understanding:

> Though I speak with the tongues of men and
> of angels, and have not charity, I am become
> as sounding brass, or a tinkling cymbal.[20]
>
> And even things without life giving sound,
> whether pipe or harp . . . how shall it be known
> what is piped or harped?[21]
>
> What is it then? I will pray with the spirit,
> and I will pray with the understanding also:
> I will sing with the spirit, and I will sing
> with the understanding also.[22]
>
> (Authorized Version)

In the same way the idea of 'singing with understanding' or 'knowledge' is stressed in the *Manual of Discipline*.

It is expressed more radically in the *Hymns of Thanksgiving,* the breviary of the unknown sect of Qumran:

Hymns of Thanksgiving (Hodayot), XI : 23:

I shall play upon the lyre of salvation
and upon the harp of joy . . .
Upon the flute of praise
without end . . .

CF. *Hodayot,* I : 28-29:

Thou hast created the breath of the tongue
and knowest its words.
And hast determined the fruit of the lips
even before they came into being.
Thou settest words in their due measure
and the utterance of the breath of lips in proportion.
And bringest forth measurements[23] in accord
with their secrets.
And utterances of breath in accord with
their numerical order,
to make known Thy glory and Thy wonders . . .

(Trans. E. W.)

The last four lines are open to various interpretations. Prof.
Barthélémy (*Freiburger Zeitschrift für Philosophie und Theologie,* 1959,
p. 257) speaks of 'a multitude of voices united in harmony'; while I
cannot follow him to such extremes, the passage implies, without
any doubt, a connection of words, tones and numbers. It is,
however, not clear if this link refers to music or to words.

St Paul's indifference to, and Philo's lukewarm allegorization of,
musical instruments[24] speak the same language as the passages from
the Dead Sea Scrolls. Indeed, how is it possible to interpret the
following verse from the *Hymns* in any but an allegorical way?

My adversaries roared forth their complaint
(against me)
With a lyre, accompanied by mocking songs.[25]

It seems that the poet is alluding to a verse of Lamentations (3 : 14):
'I was a derision to all my people; and their mocking song all the
day'.

Such expressions would lead us to understand the passages
dealing with musical instruments in a purely allegorical way. This
interpretation would certainly suit the puritanic-ascetic type of

33

worship described in most of the scrolls, for the sect of Qumran strongly opposed every kind of sacrifice. Instrumental music, on the other hand, as practised by the Temple's orchestra, was invariably understood as an organic accessory of the sacrificial cult. Without sacrifice the instruments had no cultic value. Hence we might dismiss the passages with reference to instruments as mere allegories.

This rule has, however, an important exception: the scroll of *The War of the Children of Light against the Children of Darkness*. This strange document purports to set down the battle order in the apocalyptic war between the forces of Good and Evil. Tactical positions, banners, lines of attack and defence, even the trumpets and signal-horns are described in minute detail. Various types of metal trumpets are referred to, all named according to their military functions, whereas the ram's horns (*shofars*) are less diversified.

The translation of the musical or semi-musical terms is by no means definite and no more than an approximation, for many Hebrew terms are unfamiliar to scholars. The words themselves are known, of course, but their technical significance is still a matter of conjecture.

Equally controversial is the question whether the entire scroll was more than an eschatalogical fantasy; but fantasy or war-ritual, the group that is glorified therein—or that glorified itself—seems to have been active in matters musical. A passage such as this:
War-Scroll, III : 17-18:

> . . . the name of the commander of the fifty
> and names of the commanders of its tens;
> on the standard of the ten they shall
> write 'Songs of God with a Harp of Ten
> Strings' and the name of the commander
> of the ten . . .

demonstrates the deep reverence in which the musical terms of the Scripture were held. For when this was written, the 'harp of ten strings', the biblical *asor*, was most probably obsolete.[26]

In this case, however, the *asor* was mentioned as a symbol of the squad of ten, not as a real musical instrument. This writer is convinced that the old number symbolism, whereby each musical instrument had its numerical and cosmological significance, was revived in Jewish sects under neo-Pythagorean influence. Such an assumption appears the more plausible in that the *Manual of Discipline,* too, stresses calendaric-cosmological ideas and principles. The Essenes leaned strongly to such speculations. Later, we encounter those speculations again in the gnosticism of the first three Christian centuries.[27]

The trumpets, on the other hand, are viewed and treated as real instruments whose signals and manner of performance are described in detail. At the moment we can only speculate on the full significance of those apocalyptic trumpet-blasts, in which the *War-Scroll* abounds. Certainly, they cannot be simply dismissed as allegorical or symbolical, since technical terms were employed that have direct application to real instruments. We quote one of many such passages:

> Then the priests shall blow the recall for them, and they shall return to the first line . . . Thereupon the priests shall sound a blast on the trumpets of assembly, (a quiet sustained note) . . . the priests shall then sound upon the trumpets a quavering blast (?) for the drawing up of the line of battle . . . And when they have taken up position in three lines, the priests shall sound a second blast—a low, subdued note for advance . . . Then the priests are to sound blasts on the six trumpets used for rousing to the slaughter—a sharp, insistent note for directing the battle. And the Levites . . . are to sound a single blast—a great warlike trump to melt the heart of the enemy . . .[28]

The *War-Scroll* contains many such passages and is full of interesting details. Each trumpet (or set of trumpets) has a function of its own, such as 'trumpets used for rousing to the slaughter' (?), 'trumpets of assembly', etc., which may be understood with reference to their signals at the varying phases of the actual battle. All these tactical regulations are couched in a strangely archaic language. They remind the reader—no doubt intentionally so—of certain military accounts as they occur in the historical books of the Old Testament.[29] Yet these books were at least three or four centuries old when the *War-Scroll* was being composed. The functions of these war-trumpets correspond roughly with the ordinances as set down in Lev. 23 : 24; Lev. 25 : 9; Num. 2-10; and especially Jos. 6 : 4-6, 8-9, 13, 16, 20. The *loci classici* are:

35

Num. 10 : 8	And the sons of Aaron, the priests, shall blow with the trumpets; and they shall be to you for an ordinance for ever throughout your generations.
II Chron. 5 : 12	Also the Levites which were the singers . . . having cymbals and psalteries and harps, stood at the east end of the altar, and with them an hundred and twenty priests sounding with trumpets.
II Chron. 7 : 6	And the priests waited on their offices: the Levites also with instruments of music of the Lord . . . ; and the priests sounded trumpets before them. . . .
II Chron. 13 : 12	And, behold, God Himself is with us for our captain, and His priests with sounding trumpets to cry alarm against you.
II Chron. 13 : 14	And when Judah looked back, behold, the battle was before and behind: and they cried unto the Lord, and the priests sounded with the trumpets.

(Authorized Version)

The biblical rule ascribes the singing and 'musick-making' to the Levites, the blowing of trumpets to the priests (Aaronides). In fact the trumpet *(hatzotzra)* was the priestly instrument. The *shofar* was usually blown by the Levites and only occasionally also by priests.

The *War-Scroll* distinguished equally sharply between priests and Levites:

One priest shall go before the men of the rank to strengthen their hands in the battle; and in the hands of the other six shall be the trumpets of assembly, the memorial trumpets, the trumpets of the war-blast, the trumpets of pursuit, and the trumpets of reassembly. And when the priests go forth to the space between the ranks there shall go with them seven Levites holding in their hands the seven rams' horns of jubilee, and three officers of the Levites before the priests and the Levites. Then the priests shall sound the two trumpets of assembly.[30]

The various numbers, six, seven, three, two, appear to have a theocratic-cosmological significance. But exactly what this significance was, we do not know. The Book of Revelation, which offers many points for comparison, also contains a vision of seven trumpets, yet here they are sounded by angels in the eschatological war between Christ and Antichrist.

Within a brief essay it is not possible to enter into a prolonged discussion of the various technical terms. Most recently Yigael

Yadin, formerly chief of operations of the Israeli army, now an outstanding archaeologist, has published an extensive monograph on the *War-Scroll*. In three chapters dedicated to the trumpets and their signals, he offers a profound analysis of the various problems raised by the terminology of the manuscript.[31] Many of his explanations are cogent and conclusive, others no more than hypothetical. In some cases he seems to have passed by important clues.

What are these clues? In our opinion, they are all concerned with the technique of trumpet-blowing as presumed by the author of the scroll. A few quotations in my own translation and with my interpretation of musical terms (printed in italic type) may indicate the problems of the manner of performance alluded to in the manuscript.

(1) And they [the priests] shall sound a steady *sostenuto legato* signal.
(2) . . . they shall sound a sharp *staccato* repeated signal [the Hebrew term suggests here a constant breaking or interrupting of tone, which might be understood as double or triple tonguing].
(3) . . . they [the priests] shall blow [on six trumpets], *as if with one voice*, a great war-blast. . . .

These battle regulations all reckon with unison blowing of the trumpets. This is even emphasized.

> Then the priests shall sound a *long-held tone*. . . .
> And the priests shall sound a second blast, a
> tone *sostenuto legato*. . . .
> And the Levites and the whole people . . .
> shall sound in *unison* a great war-blast. . . .[32]

Some of these descriptions read like paraphrases of biblical verses, such as:

And it came even to pass, as the trumpets and singers were as one, to make one sound [as in unison] to be heard in praising and thanking the Lord. . . .[33]

The term for unison (*qol chad*) is used both in this Old Testament passage and the *War-Scroll*.

What do such specifications teach us? When technical terms

37

convey ideas such as legato, staccato, sostenuto, tonguing, etc., we must assume a considerable skill in blowing. But even more important is the evidence for clearly defined pitches. For it is not possible for two or more trumpets to produce a unison sound 'as with one voice' unless the trumpeters are able to regulate the pitch with considerable accuracy. This, at least, proves decisively that the Temple trumpets had a number of definable tones and phrases. The sound of the signals themselves must have been rather shrill, since the Temple trumpets belonged to the family of the short, two-foot instruments.[34]

Another aspect of the problem with which these priestly war-trumpets confront us concerns their names: they are called trumpets of assembly, of the war-blast, used for rousing to the slaughter, of ambush, of pursuit, and of reassembly. Are we to understand that different kinds of trumpets were envisaged for these respective functions? This seems a rather fantastic assumption. And yet, the alternative interpretation that each of these designations stands for one kind of signal or another is contradicted by passages like these: 'After that, the priests shall sound for them on the trumpets of assembly a steady sostenuto legato tone.' 'The priests shall sound on the six trumpets used for rousing to the slaughter a sharp staccato signal.'

If the designations 'trumpets of assembly' or 'trumpets used for rousing to the slaughter' refer to fixed sets of signals, why was it necessary to describe the calls as a 'steady sostenuto legato' or 'sharp staccato'? These designations seem to refer to the place on the battlefield of the various sets of trumpets. Perhaps each set was envisaged at a different place as well as a different phase of the battle, and it would be irrelevant whether the battle actually took place or was just a fantasy of the author of the scroll. To him a corps of skilled trumpeters was simply essential to the battle.

III

Philo of Alexandria has left us in his famous *De vita contemplativa* a detailed description of the life and mores of the Therapeutae. It is generally held that the sect of Qumran was closely akin to that Egyptian branch of the Essenes which were called Therapeutae.

Philo's account, partly quoted by Eusebius three centuries later, mentions in a famous passage the practice of antiphony of men and women. Unfortunately, he does not quote any of their prayers or hymns, although he stresses that they 'were of many metres and tunes'. The Song of the Red Sea, Exodus 15, is the only biblical canticle mentioned in Philo's description; it was not only chanted, but it was danced in a sacred pantomime.

Actually, this often-quoted passage constitutes only a part of the general report concerning the musical liturgy of the Therapeutae. The less familiar antecedent section of the description gives details of the hymns sung at the sect's worship.

This portion reads as follows:

> . . . the President [of the sacred banquet] rises and sings a hymn composed as an address to God, either a new one of his own composition or an old one by poets of the past, who have left behind them hymns in many metres and melodies, hexameters and iambics, lyrics suitable for processions (*prosodiōn*) or libations (*paraspondeiōn*) and before the altars or for the chorus whilst standing (*stasimōn*) or dancing, set in most flexible stanzas well proportioned (*strophais polystrophois eu diamemetrēmenōn*) for the various turns. After him all the others follow in turn . . . as they are obliged to sing the refrains they have to chant closing verses (*akroteleutia kai ephymnia*): then they sound forth, all men and women together.[35]

This description would indicate an intonation of a (new or old) canticle by the senior, in metrical style or otherwise, while various groups follow in turn until the entire congregation joins them in the refrain or the closing line.

The sacred banquet celebrated every seven weeks (in intervals of a pentecontade) was concluded by a vigil-nocturne (*pannychis*).[36]

If we now compare the rules, statutes and poems pertaining to the sect of the Dead Sea Scrolls with the ritual of the Therapeutae, certain conspicuous resemblances strike the reader. Among the regulations, identical in both sources, which concern the sacred banquet, we find such items as: 'The presiding priest shall stretch out his hand first of all to bless (or to thank) God with the first fruits of bread or of wine. . . .' 'The novice shall not come into touch with the banquet of the Many before he has completed his second year in the midst of the members of the Community. . . .'[37] It is

39

superfluous to point out the similarity with the Mass, divided into the *missa fidelium* and *missa catechumenorum*. The latter part corresponds here to the role of the novices in the service.

The *Manual of Discipline* states the rules of the nightly study of the Law and the habitual prayers. Dupont-Sommer comments on these rules: 'In these sacred vigils they read the Law, commented on it, and praised God. This was no doubt a heavy obligation for men who passed their whole days in manual toil; for, we know, they laboured from morning to evening. . . . One can easily understand why from time to time one of them would be tempted to stretch out and go to sleep. But woe betide him!'[38]

The rule prescribed thirty days' punishment for such an offence. Here we are reminded of an early monastic controversy dealing with the admissibility of *troparia* and *octoechos*. The monk of this fifth-century anecdote was severely reprimanded by his abbot for always drowsing during the vigils.[39] This no doubt typical case happened in an Egyptian monastery; the sleepy but musical monk could keep awake only by frequent singing during the night service.

There has been occasion to mention the collection of poems called *Hymns of Thanksgiving* after their incipit (and presumable refrain): 'I thank Thee, O Lord', or 'I bless Thee, O Lord'. In addition, some poetic sections are contained in other scrolls, as in the *Manual of Discipline, The War of the Children of Light,* and others. It will be interesting and instructive to examine these poems against those mentioned in Philo's accounts. It might be well to point out that the poems do not constitute hymns in the accepted sense but are free compositions, like the biblical canticles.

None of these poems shows—as of now—any evidence of metrical composition. Unless the metres were exceedingly complex, which is unlikely, we must assume that no metrical style was used. Refrains and occasional strophic structure, however, are noticeable and not uncommon. If Philo's terminology is applied, *akroteleutia* and *ephymnia* (refrains and emphatic closing verses) seem to play a part in the structure of these pieces. Since we do not know anything about the way in which these texts were chanted, we cannot, of course, determine whether they were of stationary (*stasima*) or processional (*prosodia*) character. We do know, however, that these hymns were regularly chanted and that they constituted a kind of breviary. Says the poet in the *Manual of Discipline:*

> When I begin to put forth my hands and
>   my feet,
> I will bless His name;
> When I begin to go out or come in,
> When I sit down or stand up,
> And as I lie on my couch, I will sing
>   aloud to Him;
> I will bless Him with an offering of the
>   utterance of my lips
> More than the oblation spread out by men:
> Before I raise my hand to satisfy myself
> With the delights of what the world produces . . .
> In the dominion of fear and terror,
> The place of distress with desolation,
> I will bless Him, giving special thanks . . .
> When distress is let loose I will praise Him
> And when I am delivered I will sing
>   praise also . . .
> With thanksgivings I will open my mouth . . .
> Blessed art thou, O my God
> Who openest to knowledge the heart of thy
>   servant . . .[40]

The last line is an almost literal quotation from an ancient prayer. Furthermore, the often repeated 'I will bless Him' is to be understood as a kind of refrain, which opens every new stanza.

IV

To the musicologist, the *Hymns of Thanksgiving* are even more interesting. For he should regard them as the missing links in the gradual evolution from plain psalmodic-responsorial style to the full rounded form of the antiphon.

The formal structure of the classic antiphon can be described roughly as a ternary form ABA', in which A is a prefatory verse of Scripture and B is usually an inserted verse from the Psalter or the canticles. Often the last A' is replaced by the Lesser Doxology (*Gloria Patri*) or an Alleluia. The most characteristic feature is the combination of scriptural quotation with choral refrain.[41]

A number of the *Hymns of Thanksgiving* represent an intermediate

41

stage in the evolution towards the antiphon form. One cannot yet discern a clear structure, nor are the 'hymns' conceived in ternary form. Yet the elements of refrain and quotation are already combined in these poems. For example:

> I thank thee, O Lord
> For thou holdest my soul in the bundle
>   of life (I Sam. 25 : 29)
>   and thou shelterest me from all the snares
>   of the pit . . .
> And from the wreckers who seek my life,
>   because
> I adhere to thy covenant.
> And they are but a vain brood and a
>   tribe of Belial . . .
> Thou wilt ensnare the feet of those who
>   spread a net against me (Ps. 9 : 16)
> They will fall into the entanglements
>   they have hidden for my soul, but my
>   foot standeth in an even place (Ps. 7 : 16)
> In the congregations will I bless thy
>   name. . . . (Ps. 26 : 12)[42]

I have omitted some of the free poetic outbursts of the hymnodist between these quotations. Almost every one of these *Hymns of Thanksgiving* is couched in this mixture of refrains, free poetry, and scriptural quotation. This juxtaposition of quotation and original poetry presages the split in early Christian hymnody: the conservative policy of the Roman Church, which for the first five or six centuries championed a strict imitation of biblical chant and form against the free, didactic-homilectic hymns of the Eastern Churches, culminating in the edicts of the Council of Laodicea.[43]

We may well imagine the performance of such a hymn. The presiding senior of the sacred banquet intoned the hymn, and, whenever a familiar quotation occurred, the congregation joined him in traditional chant; eventually they sang the refrain or closing verse. Philo-Eusebius even speaks of antiphonal chant between men and women, but in the Dead Sea Scrolls there is no evidence of this practice. Such hymns and psalms were the patterns upon which the monastic offices of later centuries elaborated in their extensive services.

The foregoing remarks should be viewed only as a first report on a search for musical references in the scrolls. A number of scrolls or fragments of scrolls have not yet been published; and it is quite possible that the unpublished manuscripts will enrich our knowledge with new findings. The new facts cited and interpreted above seem to add unexpected data to our meagre corpus of information about music in the Hellenistic era. Yet it is only fair to admit that every new discovery raises more questions than it answers.

The position displayed by the Dead Sea Scrolls towards the world at large, and Hellenism in particular, was decidedly one of isolationism. The authors of these documents were not only puritans in the moral sense, but were also purists in linguistic and cultural respects. They shied away from using Greek words, instruments, and *as they thought,* from Greek concepts of music. In general, they shied away from the world.

It would be an error to believe that their Pharisee contemporaries were in all instances opposed to them. Yet they were interested in, concerned with, and quite open to, the world. They did not flee from it. This is perhaps the criterion which distinguishes them most clearly from the Essenes and their friends. Aside from later Talmudic sources, which to a certain extent reflect nothing but hindsight (after the destruction of the Temple), we encounter the true Pharisee's attitude to music more articulately in some sayings of St Paul than anywhere else.

'IF I SPEAK IN THE TONGUES OF MEN . . .'

St Paul's Attitude to Music

This celebrated passage (I Cor. 13:1) has often been quoted, many tracts have been written about it, and even more sermons preached. Yet in all the commentaries, ancient, medieval, or modern, I have been unable to find an explanation of this musical metaphor, which so contemptuously speaks of instrumental music; even vocal sounds uttered 'without love' (*agapēn de mē echō*) are decried. At first sight our passage reads quite easily, almost like a commonplace. For the postulate of love was nothing extraordinary or novel at a time when many a rabbinical treatise culminated in this demand for transcendent love.[44] But the descending gradation:

43

tongues of men
tongues of angels
sounding brass
tinkling cymbal

was, when it was pronounced, a revolutionary conception. For the metaphor was couched when the Temple still stood in Jerusalem with all its ceremonial music, instrumental and vocal. Did Paul not set aside at one stroke the age-old and venerated glory of the Temple, exactly as he had set aside the Law? Voices of men, even angelic choirs seemed worthless to him when bereft of love—not to speak of instrumental strains! In the above gradation, Paul cites what seemed to him the lowest instruments of the Jewish or pagan orchestra, viz. 'the tinkling cymbal'. Yet the cymbal was a highly respected instrument in the Temple of his time, for it served almost as a kind of conductor's baton. According to the *Mishna* (*Tamid* 7 : 3) the signals of the cymbal served as cues for the vocal and instrumental performance of the Levites. The *Mishna* even mentions one of the cymbal-players of the Second Temple, Ben Arza, by name. What, then, were Paul's reasons for so drastic a transvaluation of all values?

In order to fully understand any one passage, we must read it in its full context. The Corinthians, whom Paul addressed, were somewhat one-sided, not to say biased, in their scale of 'spiritual gifts'. In I Cor. 12, Paul lists these gifts (verses 4–11), and it seems to this writer that the apostle's gradation is again a descending one: from 'the utterance of wisdom' (*logos sophias*) down to the 'interpretation of tongues' (*hermeneia glossōn*). Then, as often today, ecstatic utterances such as glossolaly (speaking in tongues), or miracle-working stood in higher esteem among the gentile Christians of Corinth than sober instruction and teaching of ethics. Hence the apostle had to deal most cautiously with a group of neophytes, who were full of eager expectations (I Cor. 14 : 1–23). Those early Christians believed that with good will everybody could become his own prophet, healer, or miracle-worker. Paul recognized the danger and faced it squarely. He taught the Corinthians that their scale of spiritual gifts was far too narrow (I Cor. 12 : 14–26). Thereafter he challenged them:

Are all apostles? Are all prophets? Are all teachers? Do all work miracles? Do all possess gifts of healing? Do all speak in tongues? Do all interpret? But they all earnestly desire the higher gifts.

The apostle has not yet climaxed his harangue; but instead of a prophetic or doctrinal message he shows the Corinthians, who were losing their sense of measure, 'a more excellent way'—and he commences his sublime hymn on the power of love (I Cor. 13). The special significance of Paul's term for love (agapē) is still being debated by theologians, but as this is no theological book, we shall (with Lietzmann, Bultmann, Klausner and others) understand it as love in the widest sense of the word.

The love which Paul glorifies should not only bind man to God, but also man to fellow-man, and even to fellow-creature. This was, of course, nothing new, either in thought or in formulation. For Jesus had stressed the 'laws of love' most emphatically (cf. Matt. 22 : 37–40). Yet even then, the two commandments mentioned by Christ were nothing but literal quotations from the Old Testament, and among the most celebrated ones (Deut. 6 : 5, and Lev. 19 : 18).

The apostle goes further: he exalts love as the most timeless spiritual gift. The gifts of tongues, of prophecy, and of knowledge will pass away, but love never ends. Paul, however, makes it plain that he neither will nor can grant the good Corinthians those spiritual gifts which they crave, be they miracle-working, healing or prophesying. Love is higher than any of these gifts and of timeless value. The preamble to this hymnic manifesto is our musical metaphor. What makes it so bold is the transition from the spiritual gifts to 'the tongues of men and of angels'. It strikes us as unexpected and almost incoherent.

The transition is, as it were, subterranean. In order to appreciate it we must take into consideration the attitude of the Jewish and Greek groups of Paul's time towards music in general, and to its different types in particular.

Paul was brought up as a Pharisee. He says of himself: 'I am a Pharisee, a son of Pharisees' (Acts 23 : 6).[45] This statement implies that he and his ancestors were adherents of the Pharisaic sect. Indeed, he prides himself on having been a disciple of the great Rabban Gamaliel (Acts 22 : 3). How did the Pharisees regard music?

45

A few references will answer this question. (a) The apostasy of R. Elisha ben Abuya was attributed (by his colleagues) to the Greek instruments which were always in his home, and to Greek tunes always in his mouth. (b) The Rabbis held a particularly low opinion of certain instruments: the *halil* (a primitive clarinet, or a kind of *aulos*), the *toph* (a tambourine or hand-drum, usually played by women) and the *tziltzelim* (cymbals). A bronze gong, called *ayrus* (Roman *aes*, Aramaic *ris*, Hellenist *aes-ris*) was used in the Temple on festive occasions and at solemn weddings. It was probably the instrument most contemptible to the Rabbis. (c) The strong antagonism of Philo and the Sibyls to all cymbals and similar noise-making instruments is evident (*De vita Moysis*, II, 239; *Oracula Sibyllina*, ed. Geffcken, 8, 113).

Many reasons for the Pharisees' anti-musical attitude may be presented: Their inclination to puritanism, their original opposition to the Sadducean hierarchy in the Temple, and others. I am inclined to believe, however, that the real cause of this antagonism is to be found in the Pharisaic abhorrence of each and every kind of syncretism. These three instruments in particular (clarinet, cymbal, gong or drum) were inseparably bound up with the mystery cults of Asia Minor. Whether the divinity worshipped in these cults was the ancient Kybele, the Syrian-Babylonian Ishtar, or the Roman Magna Mater did not interest the Rabbis: they knew that all these female deities protected as well as symbolized the principle of fertility; also, that their cults were by nature orgiastic. That was enough for them.

The Corinthian group that the apostle addressed was composed of adherents of these fertility-cults; indeed, we find strong allusions to their licentiousness in Paul's Epistle (I Cor. 5; 6:9–11; 7:1–6; 10:7–9). In the latter passage idolatry is coupled with whoredom!

The apostle, however, is not content with disparaging solely the instruments used for the mystery cults; he adds another musical metaphor which indiscriminately attacks all instruments:

I Cor. 14:6–9:

Now, brethren, If I come to you speaking in tongues, how shall I benefit you unless I bring you some revelation or knowledge or prophecy or

46

teaching? If even lifeless [*apsycha*, properly 'soulless'] instruments, such as the flute or the harp, do not give distinct notes, how will anyone know what is played?
(Rev. Standard Version)

Spoken again like a true Pharisee! For this sect was actually opposed to all and every instrumental music well before the Temple's destruction. They had no power to abolish it, for the jurisdiction of the Temple rested safely in the hands of the Sadducees, a hereditary hierarchy. Pharisaic dicta such as, 'Music in the house, ruin at the threshold', or 'The ear that listens to [instrumental] music should be torn out', are significant in themselves. More important are the reasons—both real reasons and the given ones—for this hostility.

Contemporary with Paul's activities were the syncretistic Jewish sects in Asia Minor, especially in Phrygia. There the worship of Zeus Sabazios was ministered by Jewish priestesses. Even the Roman names of some have come down to us—Julia Severa and Servenia Cornuta. Indispensable to this heretic ritual was the use of musical instruments, especially of *kymbalon, tympanon* and gong. Yet the priestly authorities in Jerusalem could not excommunicate those sectarians: they identified themselves as Jews and paid the Temple-Tax faithfully. In contrast to the authorities of the Temple (the Sadducees), the Pharisees turned away from these perversions of Jewish monotheism with horror and contempt. Such abusive practices made all instrumental music suspect, even that of the Temple. As soon as the Temple fell under the incendiary missiles of Roman catapults, and all sacrificial ritual had to be abolished, the Pharisees came to power. They did not hesitate to prohibit all instrumental music, liturgical or secular. The way in which they could legally justify this negation of a millenary tradition is interesting enough, but does not concern us here (see Ch. 1).

How differently a poet of the aristocracy had felt about this very issue 200 years before! The aristocrat ben Sira advises young men of his time in the niceties of urbane behaviour as was pointed out in Ch. 1. Can we wonder at the austere Pharisees' banishment of his mundanely wise book from the Canon of the Bible? And yet, the views of the early Christian leaders, certainly those of Paul and his

47

disciples, ran parallel with those of the Puritans.[46] A surprising confirmation of this thesis (which the author suggested some years ago) has come from the Dead Sea Scrolls, which were written during the period of flourishing Hellenism (180 B.C.E.–200 C.E.).

The Dead Sea Scrolls, however, are anything but Hellenistic in spirit. They represent the thinking of neither Pharisees nor Sadducees, but are closest to the sentiments of the dissident sect of Essenism, a movement ascetic in character. The Essenes and their many splinter-groups were certainly puritans both in their morality, which viewed the life of normal men as 'wicked' and in their emphasis upon strict discipline among themselves. Indeed, we must consider Essenism in general, and the sect of Khirbet Qumran (where the Dead Sea Scrolls and the cloister of the group were discovered) in particular, as the prototype of organized monasticism.

It is curious and noteworthy that in the Dead Sea Scrolls passages occur which we can find in Paul's writing. Some of them deal with music. Exactly as the apostle uses names of instruments for metaphors and similes, so do the Dead Sea Scrolls.

Manual of Discipline, X : 9:

> I shall sing with knowledge
> and all my song will be for the glory of God.
> The lyre and my harp (are) in accord
> with His holy order.
> And I will raise the flute of my lips
> following the precept of His law.
>
> (Trans. E. W.)

The incipit of this passage is identical with I Cor. 14 : 15; the Hebrew term 'understanding' encompasses both the 'spirit' *(pneuma)* and 'mind' *(nous)*, the word chosen by Paul.

Thus far, the ideas of isolationists and Pauline Christians run parallel. But then the ways part: Paul turns to the Corinthians and teaches them the laws of love; he instructs, educates, argues and elevates. The Qumran community, however, does not proselytise; the initiants vow:

48

Not to dispute and to argue
  with the men of corruption.
To hide the counsel of law
  amongst men of wrongdoing. . .

They evade the evil world; Paul confronts it. He, too, prays and praises—it is the chanted prayer, the 'psalms and hymns and spiritual songs' of which he speaks (Eph. 5:19; Col. 3:16). The Essenes, however, could dispense with spoken or chanted worship. As we know from Philo, they also practised silent prayer—prayer in thought—a custom unacceptable to the missionary Paul. Not only are the instruments 'soundless' and 'indistinct' to him, but also silent prayer. He recognizes only prayer through words, as in I Cor. 14:9, 'If you in a tongue utter speech that is not intelligible, how will anyone know what is said?' and again (I Cor. 14:15-16): 'I will pray with the spirit and I will pray with the mind also; I will sing with the spirit and I will sing with the mind also. Otherwise if you give thanks with the spirit alone, how can anyone in the position of an outsider [i.e., pagan or unlearned] say the Amen to your thanksgiving, when he does not know what you are saying?' (A veiled attack upon the Philonic concept of silent prayer.)

It is clear that wordless prayer, hence all 'soulless' sounds, including instrumental music, is meaningless to him—even prayer 'in tongues' does not fulfil its proper purpose. There remains only the chanted prayer, inseparably linked to scriptural 'psalms, hymns, and spiritual songs'. It is possible to infer from this attitude that even the wordless *Jubili* or ecstatic songs without words did not meet with his approval. All this again reflects the rabbinic doctrine of prayer.

Viewed from the more detached angle of the history of religion, Paul's hostility towards each and every kind of instrumental music appears as a paradox. Unfolded on that higher level, it deserves a further explanation and solution.

Paul, a Jew of the Diaspora, was linked to the world of Hellenism by Greek customs, ideas, even by language; it was his natural and congenital home. The then dominant Hellenistic philosophy was the school of Stoicism, which attracted Paul by many of its conceptions. Yet both Pharisaic Judaism and incipient Christianity

49

opposed this philosophy. During his formative years, especially during his years of study under Rabban Gamaliel, Paul seems to have forgotten his leanings toward the Stoa. Then, on the road to Damascus, there befell the dramatic conversion that transformed his whole life. As apostle to the Gentiles, Paul sought and recovered his erstwhile rapport with Hellenistic thought. With one exception, however. In the eternal conflict of values between the Greek admiration of beauty, perfection, elegant moderation in life and art, and the Pharisaic transcendent awe and ethical postulate, he chose the latter. He disparaged the Jewish Law, mainstay of the Pharisees, and replaced it with his own doctrine of sin and redemption. But still he insisted upon a number of Jewish conventions, retaining, so to speak, the empty shell of rabbinic Judaism: women shall not speak or sing in the churches; they shall cover their heads lest they exhibit their hair and attract the lust of men; after the thanksgiving prayer even the uninitiated must add their Amen; psalmody and prophecy remain important constituents of Christian life and worship for him; and finally instrumental music, soulless and even unclean through syncretistic misuse, must not be heard in the service. The Torah had lost its validity for him and his adherents; Love and Grace had superseded it. Yet many of the old mores remained intact. These were the mores of the Pharisees. Hellenistic thought had been blended with Jewish practice. However, the guiding idea of this seemingly contradictory system emerges pure: no mystery cults, nothing save the sole mysterium of Jesus.

CHAPTER THREE

The Origin of Psalmody

I

THE close kinship between ritual and play has been demonstrated, with no little ingenuity, by the late Professor Huizīnga.[1] He writes:

Ritual is seriousness at its highest and holiest. Can it nevertheless be play? We began by saying that all play, both of children and of grown-ups, can be performed in the most perfect seriousness. Does this go so far as to imply that play is still bound up with the sacred emotion of the sacramental act? . . . The play character, therefore, may attach to the sublimest forms of action. Can we now extend the line to ritual and say that the priest performing the rites of sacrifice is only playing? At first sight it seems preposterous, for if you grant it for one religion you must grant it for all. Hence our ideas of ritual, magic, liturgy, sacrament and mystery would all fall into the play-concept.

Yet, if one reads the first Christian author on the subject of psalmody, the Apostle Paul, the idea of psalmody as a 'sacred game' would seem to be absurd.

During the subsequent two centuries, however, many Christian authorities praised the refreshing and wholesome power inherent in psalms and psalmody.[2] It was held in high esteem by writers and musicians.

According to historical records, the entrance of psalmody into the ancient Greek and Roman world came as something revolutionary. Persons unfamiliar with it found it astonishing. No uncertainty is left on that score by the *Ecclesiastical History* of Socrates or by the writings of Diodorus of Tarsus, Clement of Alexandria, Pliny the Younger, even Jerome—those writers who were either pagans or Christians of gentile extraction. No such amazement marks the writings of the Apostles or of others familiar with Jewish or with Syrian ways. Paul treats psalmody as nothing out of the ordinary.

51

Those to whom psalmody was a wonder contrast it with the music of the theatre and of the circus. John Chrysostom pronounced the function of psalmody to be that of producing *compunctio cordis,* contriteness of heart.[3] And: 'It is the power as well as the mystery of the Davidic Psalms that they are capable of keeping our mind free from all happenings of daily life'.[4] Eusebius speaks of psalmody as a harmony of the soul which generates goodness of conduct even if the singing is unattended by contemplation.[5] Augustine held psalmody to be a new kind of music which David invented as a mystic device for serving God. Jerome testifies repeatedly to the exquisiteness of hearing vast congregations sing psalms in such unison that 'it all but lifted the roof'.[6] The responsorial rendering of psalms at the Church service—men, women, and children participating—is likened by Ambrose to the power of the ocean.[7] The same Church Father eulogizes psalmody as 'the blessing of the people, the praise of God, the exultation of the community, the voice of the Church, the applause of everybody, the enjoyment of freedom'.[8] Chrysostom declared that the purpose of psalmody is not art but instruction—such instruction as advances and tranquillizes the soul.[9] The Rabbis also extol the Psalter, but without any amazement at its potencies, except in cabbalistic literature where it is considered a powerful mystic tool.

To prevent those misunderstandings which so often becloud the full understanding of our subject, we shall essay a clear definition of musical psalmody.

What are the musical elements that constitute the chant of psalmody? The systematization offered by the Gregorian scholars will, notwithstanding its rigidity, render us appreciable assistance. In *La Paléographie musicale,* near the beginning of the third volume, the editors express themselves as follows:

La structure psalmodique se compose de trois parties: une intonation, *initium;* une récitation, *tenor* (sur une ou plusieurs cordes); et des cadences, *clansulae,* médiantes ou finales, ponctuant, d'après des types mélodiques fixes, les membres de phrase et les phrases.

L'accent est l'expression de ce qu'il y a de plus musical dans le langage; considéré à ce point de vue, il est une mélodie. Voilà un premier caractère que nous devons retrouver dans les cantilènes liturgiques.[10]

These sentences set forth explicitly the nature of psalmody. At the same time they imply something not expressly stated, namely, the *parallelismus membrorum,* inseparable from all psalmodic structure.[11] This characteristic has to be grasped before we can understand the other characteristics, especially that of musical punctuation.

The explanation of the French scholars is mainly concerned with the *musical* phenomenon and its structure. It is not difficult to appreciate the force of its novelty in the ancient world. For the closest link of poetry and music that could be found in antiquity—in Greek music—was founded upon *metrical* properties of the text set to music. Psalmody, however, takes no cognizance of metre in the strict sense of the word. Moreover it lends itself to all kinds of performance—soloistic, choral, antiphonal, responsorial, plain, ornate, etc. Another reason for the popularity, not to say veneration, which psalmody enjoyed from the beginnings of liturgical history (including the Phoenician and Babylonian rituals), is the continuity of the form-type: Babylonian, Jewish, Syrian, Byzantine, Coptic, Armenian, and all Western Christian services cultivated it.[12]

Any study of the historical development of psalmody must concern itself with the various divisions of the Psalter, as they were and are used in the different liturgies. These divisions are sometimes the cause, sometimes the result of ritual performances, and it is by no means easy to trace them and the purposes they once served.

PARTITION OF THE PSALTER

In Judaism the 150 Psalms are divided into five books (1-41; 42-72; 73-89; 90-106; 107-50). This arrangement antedates the Masoretic revision of their (Hebrew) text made in the fifth to ninth century of Christianity.[13] It seems that this division into five parts had the purpose of establishing a cultic parallel to the Pentateuchal Law. Other divisions stress certain groups of psalms, such as the *Hallel* (Psalms 113-18), or the psalms of pilgrimage (or ascent) (Psalms 120-34), or the Hallelujah psalms (Psalms 146-50), all of which long antedate Christianity.[14] Under the name *p'suke de-zimra* (verses of song) goes a collection of psalms which in their arrangement are found in all Jewish rites with only small deviations. This collection is chanted every weekday and Sabbath morning and the choice of the constituent psalm is quite similar to that of the matutinal psalm of Catholic Christianity.[15] Apart from these ancient Jewish divisions, which are still used in Christian liturgies, other groupings of psalms are known, which have, or had, liturgical significance. Most of these aggregates of psalms were usually coordinated with the ecclesiastical year and held a considerable liturgical importance. We shall dwell on some of these forgotten collections later on.

In Eastern Christianity we encounter psalm-divisions which often, by their differences, mark the boundary between one liturgy and another.

Syrian Liturgies. (A) Jacobites

The Psalter is divided into 15 *Marm'yathe;* each of them (of 10 psalms each) into 4 *Shubbohe.* Thus there are 15 major divisions and 60 subdivisions.[16] To the Hebrew *p'suke de-zimra* correspond the Syrian *Shuraya,* a collection of matutinal lauds.[17] Another designation of this psalm-group is *Qali d'Shahra*—songs of the early morning, called *Shaharit* in Hebrew. It seems that the number 10 was arrived at as the most convenient, the easiest countable one; another possible explanation would parallel this division to that of the Compline into 3 Hallelujah psalms, plus 3 *Ba'uthas,* plus 1 *Kyrie,* plus the closing doxology: 'Blessed is the honour (*doxa*) of the Lord from His dwelling-place forever' (thrice); this verse from Ezek. 20 is followed by 'Holy and glorious Trinity, have mercy on us' (thrice), and 'Holy and glorious Trinity, be propitious and have mercy on us' (christological paraphrase of Ps. 118 : 25, 26), 'Holy art Thou and blessed is Thy name forever', a verse of Mishnaic origin and part of the prayer of 18 benedictions (*'Amida*) of Judaism. The doxology is closed by the threefold acclamations: 'Glory be to Thee, O our Lord' and 'Glory to Thee, O our hope forever'.[18]

This cento of OT, NT, and rabbinic verses appears like a theologian's concoction, inasmuch as the *Kyrie eleison* is replaced by an invocation of the Trinity and a Jewish prayer-formula ('Holy art Thou . . . ') only slightly altered.

54

THE ORIGIN OF PSALMODY

(B) Nestorians

Although the liturgical terminology resembles that of the Jacobites and seems to hark back to a common source, the categorization of the Psalter differs from the Jacobite custom: the 150 Psalms are divided either into 21 *Hullali* (praises) or into 60 *Marm'yathe*. The number 21 is interpreted as the product of the number 7, holy in the OT, with the number 3, symbol of the Trinity.[19] Every *Hullala* has normally 7-10 psalms. The entire Psalter reflects, in the manner of one great midrash, the entire *Heilsgeschichte* of both OT and NT. Thus, e.g., the first *Hullala*, which consists of the first ten psalms, reflects the first ten generations from Adam until the Flood, and is subdivided into two *Marm'yathe*: I—Psalms 1-4; II—Psalms 5-10.[20]

The end of each *Marmitha* is characterized by a device known as *Kurrahe* ('modulationes et cantiones' according to Connolly). The learned editor sensed here a musical connotation, but did not venture to give a more specific explanation. The related Heb. *Kerah* indicates 'to roll around', 'circling', but also 'turn', in musical parlance perhaps *'pneuma'*, or a melisma.[21] Of each 10 *Marm'yathe*, 7 are chanted in 'the regular Psalm Tones' and 3 in the modus of the *Qali d'Shahra*, which do not contain simple recitations.[22] In general there is—at least in early texts—reference only to 7, not to 8, Psalm Tones. All divisions and groups of psalms and other chanted prayers (*qinatha*) are, wherever possible, explained in the manner of a midrash pertaining to the liturgy. Such homiletical interpretations of the divine service are quite numerous in the Hebrew literature as well, e.g., the *midrashic* explanation of the *Kaddish* of the orphans, or the interpretation of the *Sh'ma'*.[23] Such midrashim are often arranged according to the Sabbaths and festivals of the ecclesiastical year, or to their scriptural pericopes, and we shall meet exactly the same practice in the homilies of the Syrian Churches.

Distribution of Psalms through the Ecclesiastical Year

With the recognition of the calendar's importance for the utilization and structurization of the Psalter (cf. *The Sacred Bridge*, Vol. 1, Chaps. III–V) many phenomena, hitherto inexplicable, emerged as natural consequences of the annual or monthly or pentecontadic cycles. A few examples culled from Jewish and Syrian liturgies may verify this claim.

The season-bound usage of certain psalms in the liturgy goes back to Judaism: the *Hallel*-psalms are intrinsically linked with certain feasts, especially with the so-called 'pilgrimage festivals'. The 'songs of ascent' (Psalms 120-34) owe their superscription to the annual pilgrimage of Israel's crowds, which approached Jerusalem before and during Passover, Pentecost, and Tabernacles, while singing psalms. The nightly study of the Bible can now be traced back to the DSS, where the following rule, binding for all members of the Qumran sect, is found:

The brothers of the community shall watch together a third part of all the nights of the year reading from The Book, expounding the Law and praying together.[24]

The rule is interpreted by modern scholars to mean that the members of the sect were divided into three watches that took their turns during the three spans into which the night was divided.[25] Hence the division of the psalmody into evening, midnight, and early morning groups as we encountered them.

The division of the year into pentecontades (seven weeks plus one day) which we traced in both Jewish and Christian liturgies, goes hand in hand with the grouping of the Psalms, and constituted the institution of the *octoechos*.[26] During each week of the pentecontade the Psalter had to be chanted in its entirety. In a commentary on Nestorian liturgy a midrashic interpretation of each of the pentecontades is given, e.g.:

1st pentecontade: 'First comes the pentecontade *(shabu'e)* of Moses, which metaphorically represents the time of the beginning from Abraham until Moses'.

2nd pentecontade: 'It is called pent. *(shabu'e)* of the Advent or of the Nativity: the hope of the children of Israel, when they departed from Egypt. . . . '

3rd pentecontade: 'It is the *shabu'e* of Theophany: our renewal and rebirth through Christ, and our redemption. . . . '[27]

56

The connection between the ecclesiastical year and the midrashic-homiletic assignments of certain psalms to special Sabbaths or Sundays reached a pinnacle in the liturgy of the Synagogue between the second and fifth centuries of which important documents still extant were only recently and partly published. The practice itself, however, has long ago fallen into oblivion. It is different in the Roman Church, where this link between pericopes and psalmody was strengthened more and more through the centuries and is sometimes recognizable even in the present liturgy. The details of this connection between the order of lessons and the Proper of the Mass, reaching its culmination in the distribution of Graduals throughout the year will be discussed in Ch. IV, together with a quite similar but no longer enacted synagogal order.

II

Bearing in mind the antiquity of psalm-singing and the paucity of reliable sources, we would do best to trace the development of each of these constituents separately. As psalmody is a synthesis of the three constituent elements stated above, it is not something elemental, but rather a product of reflection and organization.

A *sine qua non* of psalmody is parallelism. Parallelism, though familiar to us from the Bible and its imitations, began long before the Bible. It shows itself in the ancient literatures of Egypt, Akkad, Babylonia, and Ugarit. It is common to all Semitic and Hamitic languages. The differences among them are differences of degree and quantity, not any differences as regards the presence or the absence of parallelism.

Scholars have not always appreciated the full import of parallelism for musical forms. Investigators may have recognized the responsorial or antiphonal refrain as well as other features of psalmody, but they have neglected to trace these back to the parallelistic hemistichs which constitute fully two-thirds of the Bible. Throughout the centuries, the Bible translators have jealously preserved this trait; most of all, Jerome with his three attempts to produce an adequate translation of the Psalms. A glimpse into the learned prefaces with which Jerome introduces these several ventures will demonstrate how earnestly he grappled with the problem of retaining the Hebrew idiomatic structure in a fundamentally different language, and of doing so without introducing into that language too much that was alien. Jerome fully grasped the significance of parallelism.

Parallelism can be trace to primitive beginnings. Professor Lach had endeavoured to connect it with repetitions such as those in the speech of small children—da-da, be-be, ma-ma and the like. Lach's ideas seem to rest on certain hypotheses of the Semitic scholar, the late D. H. Müller, though Lach does not mention Müller.[28] Lach's excellent study indicates the lines to follow. There is no denying that every parallelism is a repetition. Yet, between a child's babble and such verses as:

> The sea saw it and fled;
> The Jordan turned backward,

or

> I will lift up mine eyes unto the moutains;
> From whence shall my help come?[29]

there stretch what thousands of years!

It is in Hamitic and in Semitic literatures that the earliest recorded instances of parallelism appear. Not a trace of parallelism can be found in Sanskrit or in Old Persian. We might even question whether parallelism was the origin of the dichotomic form characterizing so many kinds of metrical melody. The basic requisite of metrical music would exist where each hemistich contained the same number of words or accents. But such was not originally the case. Relatively few verses of the biblical Psalms show, in both halves, the same number of words or beats. Whatever may have been the design of ancient Hebrew prosody, if there was any design, it did not entail an equal number of words in the two halves of any verse.

While literary parallelism can be traced back to the third millennium before the Christian era, not a vestige of it appears in the literature of the Indo-European languages. Parallelism may nonetheless have prevailed in languages which have not yet been deciphered. Once adopted in the poetry of the Bible, parallelism, by way of translation, entered practically all of the world's literatures. It continues in the modern occidental literatures, though from these literatures other poetic devices such as alliteration and isosyllabism have all but vanished. In Graeco-Christian and Latin Christian literature, as we perceive from the Oxyrhynchos Hymn,[30] and from the *Te Deum* and other Christian poems of the first five Christian centuries, parallelism was deliberately imitated.

W. F. Albright aptly admonishes: 'Even today few biblical scholars have an adequate appreciation of the importance of the strictly formal element in ancient literary composition'.[31] Even musicologists and philologists, when they do not ignore it, fail to understand the importance of parallelism and its ramifications for the musical forms to which these gave birth. Winfred Douglas, in an excellent description of musical forms, pronounces of high significance 'the principle of inflected monotone, corresponding accurately to the various rhetorical pauses of prose; such as we have in the ancient tones of Lessons, Epistles. . . .'[32] Yet that author, while he discusses the regular pauses, nowhere treats them as corollaries of the parallelistic structure.

All concomitants of parallelism have been shown to exist in the less ancient Semitic tongues. These concomitants include, in particular, the punctuating melismata, that basic element of psalmody. They likewise include altered vocalization and accent or inflection at the half stops and at the full stops. Since we do not know the precise vocalization of the texts in Akkadian or Ugaritic, it is impossible to determine whether those ancient Semitic languages did or did not provide some grammatical indications of the places at which the hemistichs ended. Professor Albright appears of the opinion that some of the later Babylonian texts shift the accents to indicate the crucial points. Hebrew, Biblical Aramaic, Arabic, and Early Syriac do exhibit those characteristics.

The device of *syllabic singing* cannot, however, be pinpointed to a special family of languages or a particular geographic region. C. Sachs considered all syllabic chant a special category which he, in happy terminology, named *logogenic*.[33] Somewhat later, in his last [posthumous] book, *The Wellsprings of Music*, he was inclined to 'drop' the concept of logogenic and pathogenic music and to replace it by strictly musical considerations, the 'horizontal' and the 'tumbling' melodies respectively.[34] I may add here that I persuaded this profound thinker on music not to abandon the original antithesis altogether, and he promised me to follow my advice, but death took the pen out of his hand.

Quite informative, with respect to the forms of language-born (logogenic) chant, are the Syriac and Hebrew terminologies referring to *lectio*, cantillation and psalmody. The first two are regarded as two degrees of elevated speech (root >*qr'* and its derivatives), the last-named as musical chant (>*z mr* and its derivatives).[35]

On the other hand, it is cantillation and psalmody which belong together, for both make use of definite and definable pitch; the *lectio* structurized speech; cantillation and psalmody structurize both speech and chant, using two different approaches, about which more later on.

Lectio and pitched recitation of a text follow its grammatico-syntactic partition, which may or may not be indicated by diacritical marks or signs of punctuation.

Psalmody is the highest stage of musical recitation (the chant on one tone), whereby the one tone becomes the tenor or *tuba*, and certain ornamental deviations from it constitute the punctuating melismata. The entire text is dominated by grammatical and musical parallelism. In viewing the various practices of tonal reproduction of a text used in the ancient high cultures, we meet recitation, cantillation, psalmody, the hymnic chant, the melismatic chant, and the lyric or dramatic odes (strophes, etc.) of the Greeks. It must by no means be assumed that the historical development of these forms and practices went 'in orderly fashion' from a non-syllabic, unorganized chant to syllabism and thence to musically syllabic psalmody, or that any such 'evolutionary' or 'progressive' principle or law is discernible. The old dictum *natura non facit saltus* has become untenable in these days of quantum theory. Hence it is hardly possible to trace the beginnings of a system which assigns just one tone to one syllable. Surely, its origin must lie in language rather than in music, for it is language which operates with syllables. Moreover the practice of strict syllabism can only date back to a time when syllables constituting words were both recognized and counted. This may lead us back to the cuneiform languages and literatures. Plain psalmody and musically pitched recitation, being of syllabizing character, are artificial products of high civilizations and intellectual discipline; the practice of a fixed tenor especially is found nowhere but in developed cultures. C. Sachs classifies all such tunes as 'centric melodies', regardless of their parallelistic or non-parallelistic structure, regardless even of their close connection with artistic prose.[36]

As all such forms are word-bound, they have occasionally been confused; they stand as the group of *logogenic* melody-types against the *pathogenic*, musically autonomous melismatic tunes. This distinction was well known to the Rabbis and Church Fathers; in rabbinic literature the logogenic forms are discussed apropos of the Song of the Red Sea (Exod. 15).[37] About one hundred years later, St Ambrose, St Augustine, and other Fathers of the Church showed their familiarity with this problem, as seen in the patristic passages quoted in Vol. 1, Ch. V. The borderland between *lectio*, i.e. the articulate declamation, and recitation, the rendition of a text upon one single tone, drew the attention of St Augustine and of St Cassian, who, speaking about angelic psalmody, used the peculiar description 'Contiguis versibus parili pronuntiatione cantare' which praises the same kind of *parlando*-recitation which pleased St Augustine so well.[38]A. Baumstark was certainly right in sensing behind Cassian's clumsy Latin phrase the original Greek thought with its operative word *stichologein*. This expression stands for 'speaking in verse' or 'speaking in strict order', and, if it has a musical connotation at all, would indicate a well-articulated *Sprechgesang*, exactly that practice which Augustine praised and which the Rabbis recommend for the teaching of scriptural verses to a minor.

Psalmody and Cantillation

Although these twain practices of the chant of sacred texts frequently sound alike, it is misleading to represent *both* of them as 'phenomena of oratorical chant, the stylized imitation of the rise and fall of voice in speech'.[39] Nowhere does psalmody *imitate* speech—quite to the contrary: the exact repetition of the same pattern verse after verse, quite regardless of its logical contents, is typical of psalmody, but contrary to oratorical practice. Cantillation, on the other hand, may be considered a musically elevated imitation of oratorical cadences.[40]

Much more attention was paid in Judaism to cantillation than to psalmody, due to the central position of the scriptural (i.e., Pentateuchal) lesson and to its ecphonetic accents, systematized by the Masoretes and their successors. Of the many accents which mark punctuation and cantillation of Scripture, only three have the same function in the chant of the Psalter as in the prose books of the OT: the *p'ticha* (*initium*), *'atnah* (*flexa*, mediant), and *sof pasuq* (*punctus*).[41] Thus psalms were, as a rule, not cantillated. Obviously it is much easier to intone a psalmody than to follow all intricate details of the Masoretic accents in cantillation, which requires a considerable amount of grammatical knowledge. Almost everybody can learn to sing psalmodically, but only a few were able to retain in memory— long before there was any printing!—the minutiae of Masoretic accentuation. This fact explains the victory of the *choral* practice of psalmody in early Christianity, also the soloistic character of the scriptural lector in Judaism.

Musically speaking, the structure of cantillation does not necessarily centre around a fixed tone or tenor, nor is it strictly syllabic, nor is the initial pattern repeated verse after verse.[42] Yet both psalmody and cantillation are natural heirlooms of Semitic language and lore. The distinction between these two word-bound form-types has been most clearly established by the late Solange Corbin, that outstanding authority on the logogenic forms of chant. She writes: 'Cantillation on the one hand, applies itself to prose-texts recited by a celebrant, while psalmody is originally of *poetic* character and can be recited by the entire community. The musical *nature* of both genres is about the same, but the musical *organization* (just as the verbal) is more advanced in psalmody. . . . The musical status of psalmody is more advanced than that of cantillation, which obeys every caprice of a phrase. . . .'[43]

To these conclusive remarks we add only one observation: the farther eastward we go among the Jews of Asia, the greater becomes the resemblance between psalmody and cantillation in their traditions. This strange fact is due to two reasons: (1) the Asiatic Jews, especially those of Kurdistan and Persia, are inclined to neglect the less important accents of punctuation, so that a more or less central tone often emerges in their cantillation; (2) they use only three or four different musical motifs for their verse-endings and cadences, so that, even in prose texts, the rapidly repeated tone of recitation, together with the few stereotyped phrases and cadences, creates the impression of psalmodic chant. The only major difference lies in the greatly varying length of the prose verses, whereas the psalm verses tend to a more or less uniform, at least somehow standardized, length.[44]

Some modern scholars have introduced the concept of 'varied repetition' in their analyses of folkloristic forms. Wherever this principle is discernible in a text, its accompanying chant is never far from psalmody. Nonetheless, it would be erroneous to consider all psalmody as nothing but a stylized sequence of a fixed response to an antecedent statement.[45] Such an interpretation would neglect the parallelistic structure of the text, the chanting upon a tenor, and the phenomenon of the punctuating ornaments, that is, all three distinguishing characteristics of psalmody.

From a purely *musical* aspect B. Bartók's interpretation of the two archetypes (psalmody and cantillation), is much more satisfactory. He categorizes two styles, which he terms *parlando-rubato* (dependent upon logical-syntactic accents), and *tempo-giusto*, determined by a fixed rhythm or metre. The sole criterion is here the rhythm. In the artistically conceived prose of the OT and NT the 'totally free' rhythm leads to cantillation, whose flow is structured only by 'pausal' motifs. Yet this categorization is not stringent, as Bartók observed himself, because parallelistic texts may be kept in free rhythm or in more measured structures, as in plain psalmody—and the transition is gradual.[46] At the extremes of the two axes suggested by Bartók, we encounter plain pitched recitation on the one hand and metrical, dance-like tunes on the other. Long before Bartók, these two extremes were recognized and set against each other by the greatest Hebrew poet of the Middle Ages, R. Yehuda Halevi. In his philosophical apology of Judaism, called *Kuzari*, he states (II, No. 69-70):[47]

Kuzari: . . .'Other languages might be more advantageous by their adaptability of metrically composed poems to corresponding tunes.'
Master: 'It is well known that some melodies do not require a metrical structure; and one can sing a short or long melody to *Hodu Ladonai ki tob*

63

just as for *L'ose Niflaot G'dolot'*. . . .With respect to the metrical songs, called *Anshadiya*, let me say that they were disregarded because of more important principles.'

The poet-philosopher refers here to dance-like, usually closed form-types, such as the Arabic *Anshadiya* and other structures, often ternary or rondo-like. These new closed forms, often generated by motoric impulses, often featuring recurring melodies, bear no longer the characteristic element of small motifs or of constantly repeated variations of such elements. If the then 'conventional' tunes may be compared with mosaics made out of small stones which differ one from another but little and have a distinctly geometrical character, the new forms were much more complex: they do not abide by little variations and frequent, monotonous repetitions; they state developed themes, have them reappear with little or no variation after some contrasting part, whereby the element of *repetition* is replaced by *contrast*. Even farther goes the later Western ideal of musical form: it strives for synthesis, contrast and symmetry.[48]

In retrospect we must admit that the origin of syllabism, ténor-recitation, and punctuating melismata, all of which are indispensable in psalmody, have remained obscure. We shall try to trace them as far back as possible.

(A) Syllabism

Starting from the fact that both spoken and pitched recitation *must* be syllabic, we cautiously venture the conjecture that soloistic chant or stylized cries in early historical times were probably syllabic. The non-metrical poetry of the high cultures of the ancient Near East was chanted, and its chant, often proclaiming a law, had to be syllabic in order to be understood.[49]

Even the highly developed art songs of the Greeks were certainly syllabic.

Extant notations of Greek melodies indicate that song among the Greeks demanded an all but rigidly syllabic performance. Of melismatic passages with more than two tones per syllable, there is little trace. For one thing, Greek singing shows nowhere any bent toward an identifiable ténor. It is entirely unacquainted with parallelism and with that concomitant of parallelism, the punctuating melisma. Still, syllabizing psalmody, in some form, was well-known in the Semitic pre-Christian world.

What now are the inferences to be drawn with regard to syllabic rendition and its origin? It goes without saying that solo psalmody is older than choral psalmody. We must allow that centuries had to elapse before solo performance could become regulated. After the inception of choral psalmody and of its teaching, other centuries had to elapse before a method of group singing could attain fixity. Group singing would naturally tend toward syllabic rendition or toward an identifiable ténor; in solo performance a type of psalmody more melodious than that of dry recitation, is suggested. Confirmation of this can be found among the Fathers of the Church who either exult in the 'melodious tunes' of early psalmody or brusquely oppose all musical appreciation.[50] Basilius writes: 'Only for this one reason have the sweet melodies of the psalms been fashioned: that they who are young and immature, either in years or in spirit, may build and educate their souls while engaged in making music.'[51] Methodius observes: 'I have no desire to listen to sirens who sing one's epitaph . . . but I do wish to enjoy heavenly voices . . . not as one addicted to licentious songs, but as one steeped in the mysteries divine.'[52] Augustine reports that Athanasius had instructed his psalmodist to chant with such simplicity 'ut pronuntianti vicinior esset quam canenti' (*PL,* 32 : 800). A similar trend, according to the Talmud, prevailed among their Jewish contemporaries.

(B) *The ténor (or tonus currens)*

We observe that soloistic psalmody tends to vocal ornaments, while choral chant inclines to slur and smooth ornaments; it 'polishes' the melodic contour, as it were. The strict ténor of plain psalmody appears to be a consequence of choral performance. This might go back to Babylonian or Phoenician practice, long before the Levitical chorus followed this practice—if it did; for nothing definitive can be said about this question.[53]

If we examine liturgies such as the Syrian, the Nestorian, or the

Jewish, in which choral psalmody has been accorded a minor role, we find that psalmody has remained more melismatic and more flexible and not, like the Latin and Byzantine, rigidly insistent upon one invariable ténor, in the Byzantine theory recognizable as the neume *Ison*. Soloistic traditions abound in psalmodies with two ténors. Even the Gregorian chant incorporated two ténors in its *Tonus Peregrinus*. The plain psalmody of the Gregorian chant and the Byzantine chant must be considered the result of a regressive anti-melismatic movement which itself originated with the advent of choral intonation. Since an entire group cannot, in exact unison, chant melismatic tunes every day in the week, the more florid texture of solo psalmody that once existed became gradually polished down to the bare framework of *initium, tenor, flexa,* and *punctus* of group-singing.

(C) *Punctuating melismata*

The third and perhaps the most distinctive element of psalmody resides in the punctuating melismata. What do we mean by punctuating melismata? And what can we say about their origin and their history? There is ample reason for surmising that the melismatic type originated in the Near East, but the first attempts at ecphonetic notation stem from the circles of the Hellenistic grammarians in Alexandria. Though there were earlier efforts at punctuation in Sanskrit, it was the Greek system that came to prevail both in the East and in the West.[54] The musical expression of punctuation by a melisma became the outstanding characteristic of psalmody. But it would be erroneous to assume that what occurred was only a simple grafting of the Greek system onto Semitic practice. Forms and ideas do not follow such mechanical ways. In pre-Christian Judaism, as we have seen, the proper reading of scriptural texts, with the correct separation of words and phrases, was well established. Whether there existed any theory of punctuating melismata we do not know. In our survey of ancient psalmody, the visible punctuation will therefore serve as our *terminus a quo*.

We can readily perceive the importance of punctuation for the parallelism favoured by the old Semitic tongues. The free distich falls into hemistichs by means of the middle caesura (*mediatio, flexa, 'atnah*). All of this has been frequently observed. What has not been observed is that Semitic languages alone employ the elongated, the so-called pausal forms at the caesura and at the full stop. Elongations frequently appear also at the emphasized beginnings of verses in poems. They are called, in Hebrew, *Pe'ur;* in Arabic, *Tafchim.*[55] Falling, as they do, at the major breaks in the sentences, these embellished or lengthened forms may be considered the linguistic origin of psalmodic melismata. Some scholars such as Bauer-Leander, T. H. Robinson, and others, believe that the elongations were specially created for the solemn recital of sacred texts.[56] It is of interest to note that the ancient Indo-European languages, such as Sanskrit and Iranian, do not possess anything comparable to pausal forms or their equivalents, though Sanskrit does possess a kind of ecphonetic punctuation which certainly antedates that of the Masoretes, of the Christians, and even of the Alexandrian Greeks.[57]

The lengthened forms were of far-reaching significance for the musical rendering of the text. The full stop and the half stop now demand cadences less abrupt and a more gradual falling of the voice. This is the precise function served by the punctuating melismata. As long as strict parallelism is maintained, even a translation can, with the music of psalmody, present a fair simulation of the Semitic style.

All translations of the Bible, from the Septuagint down, took pains to preserve the parallelism even though it could not be done literally or grammatically. It was a contrivance out of accord with the spirit of the new language even when syntactically correct. From the inherently differing grammars of the respective languages, discrepancies were bound to arise.[58] The Hebrew verse, whatever its length, rarely falls into more than two parts. Such is by no means true of the Latin or the Greek or, for that matter, the English. Those other languages often require two or three verses where, for the Hebrew, one verse suffices. To illustrate, Ps. 68:5 divides as follows according to the oldest Latin and Hebrew punctuation:

Latin	*English*	*Hebrew*
cantate Deo.	Sing unto God.	Shiru lelohim
canite nomini ejus:	Sing praises to His name:	Zamru shmō,
preparate viam	Make plain . . . a highway for him	solu . . . larokheb
ascendenti per deserta:	that rideth in the desert:	ba'aravot
in Domino nomen ejus	Whose name is the Lord.	b'Yah shmō
et exsultate coram eo.	and exult ye before Him.	v'ilzu l'fanav.

67

The Latin comes from Jerome's *Psalterium Juxta Hebraeos*. J. M. Harden, who edited a recent edition of this work, points out that the subdivisions in the Codex Hubertinus 'agree, on the whole, with the Masoretic divisions of the verses'.[59] In the translations, however, melismata are attached to each *pausa*. Thus we find, for purposes of punctuation, three and even more embellishments in one verse, especially in the psalmody of the Office; while each verse in the Hebrew has not more than one *'atnah* and one *sof pasuk* (*punctus*). This could account for the many flourishes which seem to represent the abundant punctuation in the ancient solo-psalmody of the *tractus*. It was Peter Wagner's contention that, in these melismata, there are vestiges of ornamental patterns going back to ancient Hebrew lore.[60]

(D) Melismatic structures (outside the psalmody)

It is not without admiration that I find in Robert Lach's evolutionary history of melismatic chant the recognition of the very same logogenic, indeed grammatical impulses, which I traced in the last paragraph. This is the more astounding, as Lach was in no way familiar with Hebrew or Arabic linguistics. And yet he wrote:

> If we recall that the starting-point of the *tenor* . . . was the organically inserted, longer or shorter rest for breathing at the end of a . . . phrase, the following chain results: at the transition from speaking cadence to tonal fixation . . . the rest of the phonetic punctuation . . . is expressed in retarding movement at the pausal points. . . . It is here, where the development of Gregorian ornaments begins . . .[61]

and:

> We have showed before that the first impulses of melodic ideas emerged as ornamental reflections of oratorical cadences, or . . . that these cadences emerged through the *elongation of final syllables*. . . .[62]

Such an intuitive insight into the essence of logogenic music is not singular in Lach's monumental work. Indeed, he derives all melismatic chant from this very phylogenetic principle of the musical consequences of the elongation of syllables.[63]

Considerably later than this profound intuition, a similar—though much more perfunctory—hypothesis was expressed by a specialist in Gregorian studies: 'What else are these vocalises in principle but a consequence of the tendency toward elongation of certain Latin syllables, as indicated above . . . especially of the final syllables of a sentence or a phrase . . .'[64]

These opinions, which extend the principles of logogenic chant also to autonomous melismatic structures, stand in clear opposition to the concept of polarization in musical expression, which sets the logogenic (or *accentus*) chant against the pathogenic or somatogenic (or *concentus*) music without words. While Gajard, Lach, and, in his later books, Sachs championed the evolutionary point of view, others, such as B. Stäblein and W. Wiora seem to retain the idea of the polar antithesis between logogenic psalmody and autonomous melismatic chant. It seems that the decisive word on the genesis of melismatic chant will be spoken only after exhaustive study of the two complementary practices of (a) breaking up a melismatic chant into syllabic songs with texts made *ad hoc* (Sequence, Prose, etc.); and (b) the opposite idea of chanting as a melismatic vocalise an originally texted chant (*Verbeta*). The extremely interesting examples quoted by H. Anglès about this second practice should be paralleled in the traditions of other musical cultures.[65] The co-existence of melismatic and psalmodic chant in primitive civilizations will not, by itself, admit of any theory of either polarity or evolution; but the full study of the two antithetic practices, the Sequence leading from melisma to the syllable, the other from the syllable to the melisma in its totality, might afford us the answer to the question of polarity *v.* evolution with regard to these basic forms. As Anglès states, fully conscious of the importance of his evidence:

> This melisma . . . known under the name *pneuma* in the Libri Consuetudinum of medieval Catalonia, is nothing else but the exact, melismatically contracted, repetition—without text—of the notes of the foregoing textual pieces, accumulated on the last vowel of the last word of each stanza.[66]

Melismatic chant and psalmody are organically united in the Alleluia-verses of the Roman, Byzantine, and the various *Hullali-*

texts of the Near Eastern catholic rituals. In general, scholars have paid much more attention to the Sequence and Prose than to the Alleluia-verse proper. This preference may be due to the fact that it is probably easier to trace the origin of a text than that of a melody. Still, the problem of the so-called 'free' Alleluia remains unsolved. The acclamation 'Alleluia' was separated from the text of those psalms which contain it, before the time of Jerome.[67] This holds true for all of Christianity, but not for Judaism. St Jerome was quite aware of the Jewish disinclination to separate the Alleluia from its original scriptural context.[68] Notwithstanding this and numerous similar testimonies, E. Gerson-Kiwi has endeavoured to demonstrate that among present-day Yemenite Jews, 'The wish to let women and children participate in the saying of the solemn psalms fostered their performance with inserted Hallelujah-calls. These additional calls, not indicated in the biblical text, are clearly a means of popularizing biblical poetry toward a strophic and even hymnodic form.'[69] Indeed, the practice of the freely interspersed Hallelujah is twice testified to in the *Mishna*. The passages, M. *P'sahim* 10 : 5 and M. *Succa* 3 : 10, leave no doubt about the old age of the practice of using the Hallelujah as a response of the 'unlearned' at any suitable occasion.[70] The question will be elucidated more extensively in the following chapter; the two opposing attitudes in Judaism remain problematic.

Another aspect of psalm-singing in early Christianity deserves more attention: the Byzantine *proasmata* may indeed have their counterparts in the *p'tichot* (openings) of midrashic psalm-paraphrases used in the early medieval Synagogue. Of these Gerson-Kiwi gives a few impressive examples. One or two of them show resemblance with Western gradual melodies. No individual tunes are here compared, but melodic patterns and archetypes.

A few observations on these examples may be useful: the first Jewish example (a) is an ornate and extended version of the Magnificat of the First Tone (b); another parallel is the passage from the Litany of All Saints (c). In (d) we encounter a *Jubilus before* the psalm verse in an Aleppo traditional chant. Gerson-Kiwi's utilization of my findings of the etymology of the term *jubilus* is sensible; her silence about her sources is less understandable.[71]

(a) Phon. E. K. 2881

SOLO Ha - (al)- le - lu - ja _____ CHOR Hal - le - lu - ja _____

SOLO Hal - le - lu 'av - dē A - do - - nay, CHOR Hal - le - lu - ja _____

SOLO Hal - le - lu _____ et schem A - do - - nay,

CHOR Hal - le - lu - ja _____

(b)

I. Ton

Ma - gni - - fi - cat

Be - ne - - di - ctus Do - mi - nus   De - us Is - ra - hel:

(c)

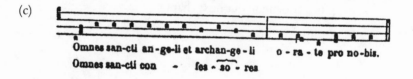

Omnes san - cti an - ge - li et archan - ge - li   o - ra - te pro no - bis.

Omnes san - cti con - - fes - so - res

(d) Ps. 92, 13: Psalmody from Aleppo (Syria), with initial Jubilus.

Phon. 2220

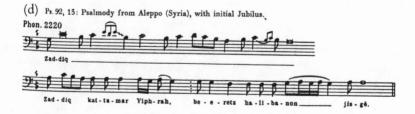

Zad - diq _____

Zad - diq   kat - ta - mar Yiph - rah,   be - e - retz ha - li - ba - non _____ jis - gě.

These opening *Jubili* are not unknown in the Gregorian repertory: B. Stäblein observes:[72]

71

The Alleluia-Jubili *before* the verse, as the *melodiae primae* . . . fit well into the typically 'mediterranean' style (exactly as do the old-Roman melismas), whereby the terms 'mediterranean' and 'oriental' were used only to indicate the small melodic steps and the constant flow of variations of a given *gestalt* of movement. . . .

As a thorough examination of melismatic chant will always lead to the Alleluia and its origin, so the Alleluia leads to the Gradual. This again, being part of the Proper of the Mass, is intrinsically linked to the ecclesiastical year and its calendar—which in turn was one of the fundaments upon which rests the *octoechos,* the system of the eight Psalm Tones. This chain of associations may also be run in the opposite direction by examining the link between psalmody and the ecclesiastical year. This is but natural, for the practice of psalmodic chant is directly and indirectly interlaced with all the rich associations of the ecclesiastical calendar. Yet the problem has an even wider scope; it comprises the *distribution* of psalmodic chant in the liturgy throughout the year. This is one of the most important criteria for the age, the provenance, the underlying concepts of every type of public worship, be it Jewish or Christian. We shall investigate the problem in our next chapter.

CHAPTER FOUR

The Connection of Psalmody with the Lesson and with the Ecclesiastical Year

LANGUAGE and poetry are clearly among psalmody's indispensable foundations; for literary parallelism is one of its basic structures. The close connection of the Psalm Tones, especially of the *octoechos,* with concepts of the calendar has been demonstrated in Vol. I of this work. Now a further dimension of psalmody's reach will be explored: it concerns the association of psalm verses to be sung between the lessons with the text of the lessons themselves. The great Catholic liturgists of the last generation, such as Duchesne, Batiffol, Eisenhofer, Baumstark and many others, accepted, albeit not without careful scrutiny, the claim of some old and heterogeneous sources which postulate a synagogal origin for the chants between the scriptural lessons. Yet this theory has never been convincingly proved.[1]

During the last decades many sources have come to light which touch upon this question, especially from the Jewish side. It seems that it may be possible to reconstruct the psalm-lectionary of the ancient Synagogue. The problem of the connection of the Gradual with its pericope, with the lectionary cycle and therefore with the entire complex of the ecclesiastical year, has not been solved as yet. If anything it has become more complex than ever.

In examining the problem in the first volume of this book, I overlooked some important evidence. Only after the book went to press did I discover new source-material concerning the ancient Synagogue. The only remark I could insert in Vol. I is found on p. 519, note 118. The (then unproved) hypothesis of the late Professor Jacob Mann about the regular psalm lesson in the ancient Synagogue served as a starting point for many new investigations, and is now becoming more and more probable. Yet the origin of the

73

double calendar of Old Christianity that seems to have taken over the Jewish psalm-lectionary has remained enigmatic, in spite of the ingenious and systematic investigations that began with Abbot Ildefons Herwegen, A. Baumstark, P. A. Dold, F. J. Dölger, Th. Klauser, O. Gatzweiler, Th. Michels, J. van Smits-Wäsberghe, O. Heiming, B. Stäblein, H. A. Schmidt, S.J., and many others. The as yet incomplete collation of ancient sources and lectionaries has evidenced a wide range of variations *between* the high Christian feasts; yet in their vicinity a certain well-established stability of lectionary texts is undeniable, thus justifying the old principle of the 'festive tides'. A good bibliography is to be found in *Hebdomada Sancta*, 'Fontes Historici', ed. H. A. P. Schmidt, S.J., Rome-Freiburg-Barcelona, 1957.

Two principal questions confront us at the outset of our examination: (a) Is there a discernible link between the text of the Gradual and the pericope for the day? (b) Does the pericope (OT, Epistle, Gospel) always depend upon the ecclesiastical calendar, or does it sometimes follow an autonomous course?

LECTIONARY AND GRADUAL

At the outset of our inquiry we shall do well to recall G. Morin's words:

. . . ce contraste si fréquent dans les productions des érudits de notre temps: les faits constatés sont exacts, pour la plupart; les conclusions que l'on prétend en déduire sont prématurées, ou dépassent, plus qu'il ne faudrait, les prémisses.[2]

In the Western orbit, to which we limit ourselves, the oldest extant documents confirming an organic link between psalmody and the lectionary come from Gallican and Aquitanian authors. It should be understood that they are not lectionaries nor books of Graduals for the various Sundays and feasts, but simply remarks that such lectionaries have been undertaken. Both sources originate in the literature of the fifth century. The first was written by Gennadius, presbyter at Marseilles, during the second half of the century. In his book *De viris illustribus*,[3] he highly praises a presbyter Musaeus, also of Marseilles, and reports:

74

Musaeus, a presbyter of the church of Marseilles, an erudite student of Sacred Scripture, excellently refined in its meaning and interpretation through most subtle experience, also a good linguist, has upon Bishop Venerius' adhortation, excerpted from Sacred Scripture the lessons suitable for the feasts of the whole year; also [compiled] those chapters of the Psalter which correspond to the seasons and the lessons. This so necessary work is now being tested by lectors in the church, so that it may remove the doubt and uncertainty. . . .

The work has not come down to us. The loss is all the more regrettable as the combination lectionary-gradual was rare before the tenth century.

Another reference to a similar compilation stems from the letters of Apollinaris Sidonius (431-89), a contemporary of Gennadius. The former, *a bel esprit* among the otherwise austere Fathers, was politically an opportunist, following the only line that promised survival, at least during a very turbulent period of history, shortly before the total collapse of the Roman Empire. He was by inclination a poet, and would not renounce poetry when he became Bishop of Clermont-Ferrand. He was a younger contemporary of the brothers Mamertus and Claudianus Mamertus, archbishop and presbyter respectively. Bishop Apollinaris sent a letter of condolence to their nephew Petreius at the death of the presbyter Claudianus Mamertus. In it he praised the close collaboration of the brothers and added a poetic necrologue.[4]

Psalmorum hic modulator et phonascus ante altaria, fratre gratulante instructas docuit sonare classes. Hic solemnibus annuis paravit, quae quo tempore lecta convenirent.

(Trans: Musician and choir-director of psalm-singing was he, standing before the altars when his brother gave thanks, and he taught the ordered classes [of the choristers] to sing. He prepared for the annual feasts whatever lesson should properly be read at its time.)

Again we encounter the personal union of a compiler of lessons and Graduals. Obviously, this was no novel office or institution. We must search further for a theological or pragmatic link between the order of the lessons and that of the chants of psalms usually coordinated with them.[5]

Stepping backwards, we come across a (rather dubious) remark in the *Liber Pontificalis,* whereby Pope Celestine I appears as the sponsor of the antiphonal chant of the Introit. As Celestine died in 432, we should assume the early fifth century as the *terminus post quem* for the chants of the Proper. Yet this is hardly convincing, inasmuch as our source was compiled considerably later. We may deduce only that the antiphonal chant was used in the Roman Mass of the fifth century.[6]

Retracing our steps again we hear from Aetherea Silvia, the woman pilgrim who reported the practice of Jerusalem;[7] and not long before her we encounter the monumental *Apostolic Constitutions,* compiled at the close of the fourth century.[8] And here we find ourselves in the (chronological) neighbourhood of St Augustine, who certainly contributed to the fixation of lessons and the chants between them. In a fine and most instructive monograph, G. G. Willis has compared, compiled, and collated the writings of St Augustine and of St Ambrose, with special reference to their attempts to establish a meaningful lectionary. In some cases the psalms corresponding to the lessons are cited, and always the homilies in which these Fathers alluded to the preceding scriptural lessons.[9]

The link between the psalm quoted and the scriptural lesson is by no means always close or convincing at first blush, although, when it is cited in the subsequent homily, it frequently appears to be convincing indeed.

The question whether the topic of a lesson motivated the psalm, or vice versa, or even whether the intended theme of the sermon helped in the choice of either, is by no means easy to determine. Only when the homilist approaches one of the great feasts, e.g., Christmas-Epiphany, Holy Week-Easter, or Pentecost, is the motif evident and the choice convincing. A few examples will illustrate the matter.[10]

Skeleton of St Ambrose's lectionary:

Wednesday before Easter	OT: Job 1 and 2
	Ps. 79
St Sebastian	NT: John 5 : 30
	Ps. 104
At Funerals	OT: Gen. 50 : 2.3
	Epistle: I Thess. 4 : 12, 13
	Ps. 86, or 24

From the skeleton of St Augustine's lectionary:[11]

Nativity	OT: Isa. 53:8 ff
	Epistle: Rom. 5 : 1, 2
	Ps. 85
	Gospel: Luke 2 : 1–39
St Stephen	Epistle: Acts 6 and 7
	Gospel: John 12 : 26
Wednesday after the	
fourth Sunday in Lent	Ps. 50
	John 1 : 19–33
Friday after the fourth	
Sunday in Lent	OT: Isa. 2 : 3
	Ps. 2
Good Friday	Ps. 22
	Matt. 26 and 27
Easter Vigil	OT: Gen. 1 : 1–5; Exod. 15 : 1–21
	Rom. 6 : 4–11
	Ps. 118 : 13:18
	Matt. 28
Easter Day	OT: Isa. 53 : 5–7
	Acts I
	Ps. 146
	Mark 16 : 1–20
First Sunday after Easter	Acts 5 : 1-11
	Ps. 116
	John 20
Ascension Day	Acts 1: Rev. 5 : 5
	Ps. 97
	Matt. 28 : 16–20; Luke 24 : 36 to end
	John 14 : 23–28; John 20 : 11–18

The links between the lessons and the chosen psalms are by no means always obvious or convincing, although the lessons of the New Testament invariably refer to events related to Christ. The Old Testament lessons are sometimes based upon the old Judaeo-Christian tradition, as e.g., Gen. 1 at the Easter Vigil,[12] or upon topics alluding to the occasion, as e.g., Gen. 50 for funerals, or Job during Holy Week.

Equally uneven is the relation between the chants of the Proper and the lessons in the medieval or recent missals. Sometimes we are hard put to it to establish any link between them (especially in the Sundays after Pentecost); sometimes the connection is obvious and even based upon cue-words. We quote a few instances of the latter type.

Missale Medicaeum sive Tridentinum:[13]

Day	Lessons	Chants of the Proper
Thursday after the fourth	OT: Ezek. 36 : 1 ff	Grad.: Ps. 34
Sunday in Lent	Isa. 1	Grad.: Ps. 33
	Gospel: John 9	Off.: Ps. 66
		Comm.: John 9
		Tract: Ps. 103 : 10
		Ps. 79 : 8–9

We find here an emphasis on purification in both OT lessons; the connection between Isa. 1 : 16–19 and John 9 : 1–39 is established by the discussion of sins inherited from parents and the question of atonement. The Offertory (Ps. 66) concludes: 'Benedictus Dominus, qui non amovit deprecationem meam et misericordiam suam a me'. The Introit anticipates Ezek. 36 : 25. The Graduals may be understood as affirmations of the OT lessons; the Tract prepares the ground for the Gospel lesson.

On this day there is no discrepancy between the Tridentine Missal and the much older Missale Sarum, except that the latter has as its Tract Ps. 25 : 17–18, and 1–4, which is perhaps not so well attuned to the subsequent Gospel pericope.[14]

Missale Tridentinum:

Day	Lessons	Chants of the Proper
Friday after the fourth	OT: II Kings 4 : 25–38	Introit: Ps. 105 : 3–4, 1
Sunday in Lent	NT: Luke 7 : 11–16	Gradual: Ps. 74 : 20, 19, 22
		Offertory: Ps. 70 : 2, 3, 4[15]
		Communion: Ps. 71 : 16–18

The analogy between the OT and NT lessons is obvious; the text of the Introit shows no connection with the lessons, but the Gradual verses refer to the poor and miserable. The Offertory would appear as an allusion to the Gradual if the *entire* psalm were read (Ps. 70 : 5 = Vulg. 69 : 6, 'Ego vero egenus et pauper sum'), but the prescribed verses do not contain a manifest link. The Sarum Missal in this instance does not diverge at all, except in the NT lesson.

If we break off our comparisons here for the present, it is only because certain links or allusions were discernible in the cases listed above. Yet this is not a generally valid principle.[16] Apart from the lessons during or just before the high feasts it may be said that for other days (aside from the Proper of Saints) the following rule holds: The older the lectionary, the less obvious are common literary or theological motifs between the texts of the Proper and the lectionary.

While this general statement cannot be maintained for the great feasts, it can be generally maintained for the Sundays after Pentecost and we must, after careful examination, subscribe to Professor Jungmann's judgement: 'While no real connection [between the texts of the chants and those of the lessons] is intended for normal Sundays, and indeed can hardly be achieved, on festive days usually a fine harmony between chant and lesson is noticeable. So e.g., if at the Feast of St Stephen, after the lesson dealing with his trial before the synhedrion, the Gradual continues with Ps. 119:23 ff "sederunt principes et adversum me loquebantur, etc." ' [17] In other words: the decisive factor in the choice of texts for the chants is not an antecedent lesson but usually a festive season or a significant part of the calendar which normally affects the structure of the lectionary.[18]

EXCURSUS: HAGIOLATRY IN JUDAISM AND CHRISTIANITY

I

The twofold nature of the Roman ecclesiastical calendar is evident and well known: the movable part, which depends mainly upon the date of Easter, and the fixed part, which follows the secular calendar. The Proper of the Saints (also the Proper of Christmas and its cycle) is fixed according to the contemporary civil calendar. As some of its chants reach back into high antiquity we might well ask if, as in the movable part, the Church followed a pattern established by Judaism. We shall see that the question is not as absurd as it seems at first blush.[19] The incredible complexity of the relation between the Proper of the Season and the Proper of the

Saints may be seen in a brief but truly substantial study: K. Gamber and P. A. Dold, *Il'ege zum Urgregorianum,* Beuron, 1956. To penetrate this liturgico-historico-calendaric jungle is anything but easy.

The main question is: How should the two calendars be evaluated as to their effect on the lectionary? Were not the saints' and martyrs' days the producers of martyrologies and their pertinent lectionaries? Did not these slowly developing orders of pericopes, fixed according to the civil calendar, counterbalance the lectionaries of the older ecclesiastical calendar? In order to decide this important question we must investigate the origins of the martyrs' and saints' days and their celebration.

It is generally assumed that the veneration of martyrs and saints is a specifically Christian institution. Indeed, its theological basis as well as the earliest documents testifying to the memorials of martyrs and saints are almost all of Christian origin.[20] The remembrance of martyrs and its cult date back to the third century; martyrdom and its veneration occur, of course, already in the canon of the New Testament.

The first authentic statement of a martyr's memorialization dates from 155 C.E., when the Church of Smyrna agreed 'to celebrate in exultation the day of his [St Polycarp's] martyrdom.'[21] Thus, the dogmatically regulated celebration of martyrdom, of which more later, as well as the historical priority of hagiolatry within the Church, stands almost free of any doubt.[22] Almost! For it will be the task of this excursus to demonstrate that the earliest traces of hagiolatry reach deep into the Second Jewish Commonwealth.

The question of what constitutes the oldest sources concerning the veneration of martyrs in the tradition of Judaism cannot, at this stage, be unequivocally answered, for none of the four *loci classici,* (a) the 'Scroll of Fasting' (*Megillat Ta'anit*), (b) the *Mishna Ta'anit,* (c) the tractates *Semachot* and *Pesachim,* also *Baba Batra* of the Babylonian Talmud, and (d) certain passages of the *Midrash Rabba* on Lamentations (*Ekha Rabba*), can be fully relied on as historically accurate, nor is their interpretation free of serious controversies. Nonetheless, certain passages, names, places and dates demand careful investigation and will be considered in the context of this essay.

The name of the 'Scroll of Fasting' is misleading: like the proverbial *lucus a non lucendo* it lists those days on which observant Jews are not permitted to fast, and cites the reasons for the rejoicing on these days. In its appended *scholion,* however, some dates are mentioned which, because of some tragic event, might be considered fast days.[23]

In the *Mishna Ta'anit* we encounter at the end a kind of litany, where various deceased pious persons and martyrs are named as possible intercessors: Abraham, the ancestors at the Red Sea, Moses, Joshua, Noah, Samuel, Elijah, Jonah, David, Solomon et al. Its counterpart in the Roman Breviary is the prayer known as *ordo commendationis animae,* consisting of fifteen stanzas, calling for intercession by Noah, Abraham, Job, Isaac, Lot, Moses, Daniel, the Three Children, Susanna, David, Peter and Paul, and Thecla.[24]

We know of similar litanies in some ancient Eastern liturgies, as e.g., in the Syrian liturgy of St James,[25] in the Egyptian liturgy of St Mark,[26] the liturgy of the Coptic Jacobites,[27] and several others. It is perhaps not too surprising that certain names appear in all such litanies, as if they were the 'stock-in-trade' of sainted martyrs. The oldest of such name-lists seems to be *Midrash Ecclesiastes Rabba* III, 15 (parallel to Leviticus *Rabba* XXVII and *Pesikta* 76a): 'In like manner [as the priests of the Temple chose their animals for sacrifice] God chose for His own the persecuted ones: Abel . . . , Noah . . . , Abraham . . . , Isaac, Jacob, and Joseph. . . .'[28]

The names of the intercessors, however, differ from rite to rite according to local customs, and even the liturgical form and function of the prayer that involved them vary. Its function may be that of a litany or of an *epiclesis,* or just an invocation of the defunct.

The practice of *celebrating* joyfully the anniversary of the martyr's death (or of his birthday) is today a purely Christian custom, but there are cetain Jewish traces of such festivities. The outstanding example of such a festive rejoicing—a veritable 'saint's or martyr's Vigil'—is the 18th day of *Iyar,* the 33rd day of the counting of the pentecontade between Passah and Pentecost (*Pesach* and *Shabu'ot*) on the Hebrew calendar this is the *Lag be-'Omer* (= 33rd of the counting), when the anniversary of the death, or rather, of the 'transfiguration' of R. Simeon bar Yohai is celebrated in Meron (Galilee) by many thousands of visitors to his grave (mostly

Sephardic Jews). It is a vigil with torches, bonfires, some pre-monotheistic rites (cutting the first hairs of babies, etc.), and a good deal of folk-dancing.[29] This very popular feast is still very much alive. One must recall that even on the anniversary of Moses' death (and birth), traditionally observed on the 7th of *Adar*, the members of the 'Pious fraternity' (*Hebra kadishah*) that cared for the dead only fast during the day; in the evening a festive banquet is often arranged for that sodality.[30]

In later times, however, the martyrs were *mourned* in Judaism; the book of ritual dirges (*qinot*) contains a number of poems of penitential character, in which Israel remembers its all too many martyrs. The form of remembrance was standardized according to the pattern of the elegy of the 'ten martyrs', the sages and rabbis killed by the Romans after the revolt of Bar Kokhba in 135.[31] The form-type used for these prayers which honoured their martyrdom and that of others is the *seliha*, a poem of penitence, sometimes in the style of a litany.[32] At this point we should not ignore the question whether the prayer (for intercession) on anniversaries of martyrs and saints was not a hidden invocation of angels. For several Christian and Jewish sources seem to allude to names of angels, usually borrowed from Jewish angelology.[33]

In sad accord with Israel's long centuries of suffering and martyrdom the chain of martyrologies consists of innumerable links of names or places; nor is it easy to transmit any idea of their literary memory. As a fine example we have chosen a poem by an author who is better known as a philosopher and rabbi, the celebrated R. Saadya Gaon of Fayum. The elegy is written upon the ten martyrs massacred by the Romans. All verses open with the first words of Lam. 5:1: 'Remember, O Lord, what has befallen us.'

(1) Requite the roaring lions which trampled to death the sheep of your flock (Zech. 11:7).

(2) Yet you cover [your eyes] in times [of need] (Ps. 10:1) and you keep silence (Hab. 1:3), while they devour the scared ones.

(3) You let lie fallow our patrimonial land (Jer. 17:4) and you closed your ears, not to hear the cries of those who long for you.

(4) You shunned the city (Judg. 20:48) where all men lament the ten killed martyrs.

(5) Well did you behold the tormentors of the orphaned descendants of Jahleel (Gen. 46:14; Num. 26:26).

(6) How could you repeal your own commandment: 'Afflict not the orphans and widows' (Exod. 22 : 21); how could you tolerate that they were killed in the tower of God?

(7) You have cursed our waters (Lam. 5 : 4), and averted your countenance from us.

(8) In order not to behold the tears flowing from the eyes of Rabban Simon ben Gamaliel. . . .

(12) My God's mercy has concealed help—thus Rabbi Ismael ben Elisha was killed. . . .

(15) He once turned the fathers [of the Egyptians] into slaves (Isa. 19 : 4), but He has dissolved His covenant with them (Isa. 33 : 8), and rejected the blood-stained city [Jerusalem] (Hos. 6 : 8).

(16) And yet, my venerable Akiba was butchered while he declared 'God is One!'[34]

Fully eight centuries after the (legendary) execution of the 'ten martyrs', Saadya Gaon was inspired and moved to this composition. 'May their memory be a blessing' became a popular adage when one referred to martyrs, and in due course, to all pious defunct.[35] In this connection even the epithet 'holy', otherwise shunned and carefully avoided by Orthodox Judaism (when applied to mortals), is occasionally used. When the form was used, it designated an ascetic personality (see G. F. Moore, *Judaism*, Vol. II, p. 271).

From a strictly historical point of view the earliest reliable references to Jewish martyrdom always begin with the so-called 'Maccabean' martyrs. Postponing discussion of this instance, which is curious for many reasons, we encounter reports of martyrdom and its celebration during the first Christian century in both Judaism and Christianity. To some of them an often repeated saying was applied: 'Those [martyrs] should be privileged *to see the majesty of God in full splendour:* those who meet humiliation, but do not humiliate others; who bear insult, but do not inflict it upon others; and who endure a life of martyrdom in pure love of God.'[36] The parallel with the vision of St Stephen, the 'protomartyr' of Christianity, is obvious.

Acts 7 : 55-56:

He . . . saw the glory of God, and Jesus standing at the right hand of God; and he said, 'Behold, I see the heavens opened, and the Son of man standing at the right hand of God'.

(Rev. Standard Version)

Another instance linking Jewish and Christian literature and legends is the Ascension of Isaiah. In this apocryphal book, written by Jews of the first century C.E., and subsequently edited by Christian writers, we do not find an historical account but a biblical fairy-tale about the martyrdom of the prophet Isaiah, culminating in Isaiah's vision of the heavens and of God, and his dialogue with the Holy Ghost.[37] And, still considering the first century, the outstanding martyrs were James, the 'brother of Jesus', and R. Jose ben Joezer, both fully observant Jews.[38]

What was the theological significance, indeed the rationale of martyrdom in early Christianity? And how, if at all, did it diverge from the Jewish doctrine on this matter?

Under the title's meaning (martyr = witness, *scil.* blood witness) lies a rich stratum of theological thought. It was the binding command for every Christian to take a personal part in the 'self-sacrifice of Christ, a necessity more binding even than the instinct of self-preservation', regardless of the consequences of this act of identification.[39] In the third century the concept of perfect union with Christ through martyrdom was fully established, and with it the great hope of man's total rebirth. Another value of martyrdom was the 'blinding holiness of the open vision of God' at the moment of the martyr's death, which might alleviate and shorten the martyr's period of purification.[40] All these expectations are already envisaged in Paul's messages (esp. Phil. 3 : 8-11), 'that, if possible, I may attain unto the resurrection from the dead'. Perhaps the most beautiful as well as the most encompassing words about martyrs and martyrdom were written by St Augustine: 'If we are not able to follow them [the martyrs] by acts, let us follow them by love; if not in glory, then surely in gladness; if not in merits, then by assent; if not in passion, then by compassion; if not in excellence, then by solidarity'.[41]

In biblical and rabbinic Judaism we encounter martyrdom mainly for *ethical* considerations, only vaguely analogous to the Christian's first reason. All divine laws may be broken (according to rabbinic tradition), or at least temporarily dispensed with, if a man's life is at stake, except for idolatry, adultery and *wilful* murder (not killing).[42] The Jew is obliged to choose death rather than commit any of these three sins. This 'sanctification of the Name' (*kiddush ha-shem*) is considered the observant Jew's duty and is by no means an *opus supererogatorium,* as the Church has it.

Mystical justification of martyrdom is unusual in Judaism, if we correctly interpret the Talmudic passage quoted above.[43] Even the laughter of R. Akiba just before his death at the stake is not explained in mystical, but in strictly law-observing language. Later, and for all the pious dead (not only for martyrs) a prayer was uttered (about 1000 c.e.) 'that their souls be sheltered under the wings of the *Shechina*—in the exalted presence of the holy and the pure'.[44] The idea of rebirth, so important in Christian mystics, taken in Judaism from Isa. 25 : 8, did not play a great part in Jewish martyrdom. The main concept and reason always remains ethical, and to this our glorious era has added the ground of (enforced) self-identification. Hence Hermann Cohen, the celebrated philosopher, was not greatly mistaken when he identified rebirth with repentance,[45] and considered martyrdom, from the Jewish point of view, as 'doing one's level, quite ordinary duty'.[46] In the evaluation of martyrdom, Jewish and Christian *theologians* apparently part company.

In asserting the veneration of martyrs, early Christian literature shows a certain hostility against Jewish mores in the negation of biblical laws prohibiting contact with dead persons or graves (Num. 19 : 11, 13, 16). The *Apostolic Constitutions* nullify these principles in the words:

> Do not observe legal or natural modes in the belief that you might be contaminated by them [bodies or graves of martyrs]; nor do you need the Jewish separations, or frequent ablutions, or purifications from the touch of a corpse . . . but gather in the cemeteries . . . sing psalms for the defunct martyrs . . . and for your brethren who have been sleeping in the Lord. . . .[47]

Again, it was St Augustine who sharply replied: 'It is an insult to pray for a martyr, by whose prayer we should be commended.'[48] In similar context, he denied the value of Jewish martyrdom: 'Quid tale Judaei celebrare noverant?'

All through the centuries the two theologies were contending: 'The knowledge of God, understood as love of God, inexorably demands martyrdom. . . . In abstinence lies the basis of this highest grade of human virtue. . . . If one of the unforgivable sins is demanded, the Jew must choose martyrdom. In this case courage becomes a human virtue (not a military one). . . . For the sword of Damocles has hovered over the Jew all through history, to seduce him away from pure monotheism, or to some kind of idolatry. . . . Not our martyrs are the warrantors of our merits; only the patriarchs, and no other saints. In Christian hagiolatry, on the other hand, the "treasury of merits" is reduced to Christ and the Virgin, thereafter transferred to the Saints. . . .' These sentences, culled from Hermann Cohen's *Die Religion der Vernunft aus den Quellen des Judentums,* represent far better than a whole compendium of rabbinic sources the Jewish attitude and its variance from the Christian.[49] The Jewish masses, however, acted and felt differently.

II

The *liturgical* significance of martyrs and saints began with pilgrimages and prayers of crowds at their graves. We know today that a *logion* of Jesus, which has been overlooked hitherto, directly hints at the adoration of saints' graves. A modern scholar made Jesus's words the starting point of his investigation:
Matthew 23 : 29:

> Woe to you, scribes and Pharisees, hypocrites!
> for you build the tombs of the prophets and adorn
> the monuments of the righteous. . . .

and Luke 11 : 47, 48:

> Woe to you! for you build the tombs of the prophets
> whom your fathers killed. So you are witnesses and
> consent to the deeds of your fathers; for they killed them,
> and you build their tombs.
> (Rev. Standard Version)

In a penetrating book J. Jeremias has explored the (actual or supposed) tombs of more than forty prophets, patriarchs and kings in Palestine and its environs.[50] We shall make use of some of his results in subsequent pages.[51]

These graves, sometimes marked by synagogues above them or

in their immediate neighbourhood, were places of pilgrimage for a considerable time.[52] What persons were they supposed to shelter, and what role did they play in popular piety?

The most frequently visited graves prior to Christ and his time were those of Hulda, Isaiah, David, Joshua, Aaron, Phinehas, and Eleazar, son of Aaron, ranking after the legendary graves of the Patriarchs and the mausoleums of Rachel and Absalom, all believed to be the true resting-places of biblical persons.[53] Of post-biblical heroes the graves of the so-called Maccabean martyrs (or princes?) in Modi'in (or in Antioch?) are mentioned,[54] also the burial places of some Tannaitic sages, especially that of R. Simeon bar Yohai, and the equally legendary place of execution of the 'ten martyrs' mentioned above.[55] There are many other such places of interment of prophets or other personages renowned from Old Testament lore; and numerous places of various categories are listed in the books by Surkau and Jeremias. The first scholar to treat them systematically was probably Cardinal Rampolla, who, in his study 'Martyre et sépulture des Maccabées', set a magnificent example.[56] Soon after his pioneering study there appeared its Jewish counter-part, also a masterpiece, by Professor W. Bacher: 'Jüdische Mär-tyrer im christlichen Kalender'.[57]

Usually the pilgrimages to the graves took place on the anniver-saries of the martyrs' deaths; and the general belief has prevailed, despite rabbinic opposition, that dead persons of merit were and are effective advocates of just causes before God. Although this idea was abhorrent to many of the Talmudic sages, it is not dead even today, as witness many of the well-documented pilgrimages down to our times, to say nothing of the innumerable *kvitlech* (Yiddish = a written supplication to a martyr or saint or defunct person) on the graves.[58]

Such ideas were not entirely repulsive to some Talmudic and later scholars. Rabbi Hanina's remark seems to express more the popular feeling: 'Why does one visit the cemetery? So that the dead may pray for mercy.'[59] At one time the most popular of these sacred tombs was the mausoleum of the Patriarchs in Hebron, erected during the reign of Herod the Great.[60] Well into the sixth century reports of Jewish and Christian pilgrimages continue with rather tall tales about the splendour of these buildings.[61] We also know that during the first two centuries of Christianity Jewish and Christian visitors gathered in honour of David and James (not Jacob!) at Hebron, usually on December 26th.[62] The stories of Tannaitic graves and their pilgrimages (with or without miraculous appearances) bring us to the mid-second Christian century. Jeremias gives a fitting résumé:

> The homage to graves of biblical saints is followed by that to graves of celebrated rabbis—which would demand a special investigation. Yet we are still *before* the period of veneration of graves of *Christian* saints in Palestine. We conclude: the era of Christian relics in Palestine and their veneration, which begins in 351 . . . has ancient roots in Judaism. . . . Without exaggeration we can say that this problem of the beginnings [of early martyrolatry in the Church] must be examined *de novo* in view of the new evidence.
>
> Pilgrimage and the cult of relics are indications of the ancient adoration of graves in the popular religion of Judaism in the early Christian era. . . . Even the medieval itineraries by Jewish travellers are often nothing but long catalogues of graves visited in the Holy Land and its environs. . . .[63]

We cannot better demonstrate the continuity of that deeply rooted devotion to the 'graves of the fathers' (*keber abot*), than by quoting the opening lines of a great German-Jewish poet, written during the mass exodus from Germany in 1933-36:

> Keep as the last that is your own
> A grain of earth from graves of kin. . . .[64]

Most of these graves had their special day of celebration, on either mythical birthdays or no less mythical death-anniversaries. As they mostly sheltered the relics of *local* saints or martyrs, usually the neighbouring communities alone participated in the celebration. In general it may be said that the individual Jewish martyr is—liturgically speaking—less important and less remembered than the hundreds of entire communities which were uprooted, destroyed, or depopulated by expulsion or massacre. A somewhat flowery chronicle of these incessant persecutions of entire communities has come down to us under the title *Emek ha-bakha* (Vale of Tears), written by Joseph ha-Cohen (1496-1576?), a learned physician.

Of the many days which once constituted a kind of Jewish

martyrs' calendar, a few may be cited here. These days were, of course, never 'canonized', but persisted in the realm of popular custom, tolerated by most rabbis.

Day	Martyr	Region
(1) *Adar* 12	the ten martyrs[65]	Lydda (Caesarea?)
(2) *Adar* 14	Esther, Mordecai	Hamadan
(3) *Iyar* 14	Rabbi Meir	Tiberias
(4) *Iyar* 18	Rabbi Simeon bar Yohai	Meron
	(*Lag be-'Omer*)	
(5) *Elul* 1	Jeremiah the prophet	Fostat near Cairo
(6) *Iyar* 28	Samuel the prophet	Rama near Jerusalem
(7) *Sivan* 7	Simon the Just	Near Jerusalem
(8) *Heshvan* 25	Rachel	Burak near Bethlehem
(9) December 26	David and James[66]	Hebron

With few exceptions these days have fallen into oblivion. The exceptions are Nos. (2), (4), and the so-called Maccabean martyrs, who are celebrated nowadays during the Feast of Lights, the Maccabean festival of *Hanukka*.

These Maccabean martyrs hold a curious position in both Jewish and Christian cults. Aside from the accounts in II Macc. 6 : 18-31, II Macc. 7 : 1-41, and IV Macc. 5 : 1-30, we encounter the story only in B. *Gittin,* and then in much later midrashim.[67] How is this silence of several centuries to be explained? The hypothesis has been advanced that this restraint on the Jewish side was motivated by the 'reclamation' of the Maccabean martyrs by the Church.[68] This conjecture is hardly tenable, inasmuch as the Talmudic account of this martyrdom still *antedates* the earliest Christian references to it.[69] On the other hand, we know through Professor Oberman's penetrating studies on the sepulchre of the Maccabean martyrs that the synagogue in Antioch, built above their grave, was said to be the first one to be erected after the destruction of the Temple.[70] These martyrs were, it appears, not so forgotten after all. As well as the report in the Books of Maccabees themselves, and the fact that a synagogue once stood above their grave, we find the story of the seven martyrs in the following Jewish sources: the Talmud, in B. *Gittin* 57b, the midrash *Ekha Rabbati* (to 1 : 16) (Lamentations R.), *Pesikta Rabbati* 43 (180b), the history-book *Yosippon,* 19,[71] and *Piyutim* by Joseph ben Salomo of Carcassonne.[72] (Later midrashim and popular versions are here not mentioned.)

These sources have one thing in common: they all link the martyrology of the seven brothers and their mother anachronistically to the persecutions under Hadrian. This seems to indicate that the Christian sources come nearer to the historical truth. For the original synagogue above their grave was, according to the oldest Christian sources, replaced by a basilica in the late fourth century.[73] Their day of solemnization was August 1st, as directed in the oldest martyrologies as well as in the most recent missals; two martyrs are commemorated on August 1st: St Peter in chains (*S Petrus ad vincula*), and the Maccabees (SS Machabaei). This calendaric link must be old, since in the *Martyrologium Romanum* (of 1584) we read that the sarcophagus of the seven martyrs was brought to Constantinople and thence to Rome under Pope Pelagius I (556-561) to be interred in the Church of *S Petrus in vinculis*.[74]

The first trace in Christian *literature* seems to be found in St Jerome's expression of wonderment ('satis itaque miror . . .') over the solemnization of the Maccabees in Antioch after having seen their supposed graves in Modi'in. (He erroneously assumed that the 'Maccabean brothers', i.e., the martyrs, were the sons of Matityahu the priest.) He seems, therefore, to have known of the basilica in Antioch. Both St Augustine and St Ambrose knew of this particular martyrology and even spoke about it on the anniversary of their martyrdom, August 1st.[75] The story of that martyrdom must have stirred the world of gentile Christianity fairly early, and seems to have been widely known and respected. The oldest martyrological calendar outstanding, of Syriac origin, is dated 411, but is generally thought to be some decades older. Perhaps a plausible *terminus post quem* is the year when the synagogue over the martyrs' grave was replaced by a church, in or after 389. The Latin translation of the Syriac version reads:

> In prima mense iuxta Graecos
> Confessores, qui fuerunt ex illis, qui
> Depositi sunt Antiochae, scilicet
> In Cherateia,[76] qui sunt
> Filii Smuni, Ipsi
> Qui scripti sunt in Machabaeis.[77]
> [trans.: In the first month of
> the Greek calendar, the confessors

90

were laid to rest in Antioch, properly
in Cherateia, they are the sons of
Smuni, the very same about whom
reference is made in the book of Maccabees.]

This date was adopted by all other Christian calendars—a rare exception, because normally local saints or martyrs enjoy priority. In later centuries the Roman Church celebrated August 1st as the feast of St Peter in chains. An early Christian 'Passion' treats this matter as a special case, though whether or not this version is independent of the first entry of the Maccabean martyrs in the first extant martyrology, mentioned above, is still debated. These two sources are apparently contemporaneous.[78] In his standard work, *Les Origines du culte des martyrs,* the French scholar H. Delehaye has completely ignored all Jewish roots and sought the origin of all Christian martyrolatry in pagan models.[79] This one-sided approach has caused the neglect of a good many facts and sources, which have only now, and often diffidently, been brought to light. Aside from Jerome's astonishment and St Augustine's sermon, the first real acknowledgement of the Maccabean martyrdom occurs in the homilies spoken (or written) in their honour by St John Chrysostom between 386 and 396.[80] The irony lies in the fact that the very same Chrysostom was by all odds the most rabidly anti-Jewish Church Father of them all. Even compared with the rich bouquet of hatred of Jews and Judaism that is more or less typical of patristic literature, Chrysostom stood in a murderous class of his own. He and his attitude have been well summed up by James Parkes, who wrote:

Such was the man who, in eight sermons covering more than one hundred pages of closely printed text, has left us the most complete monument of the public expression of the Christian attitude to the Jews in the century of the victory of the Church. In these discourses there is no sneer too mean, no gibe too bitter for him to fling at the Jewish people. No text is too remote to be able to be twisted to their confusion, no argument is too casuistical, no blasphemy too startling for him to employ. . . .[81]

That in the Syriac martyrology the anniversary of the seven brothers' martyrdom was celebrated on August 1st may be due, to

91

some extent, to the influence of Jewish customs.[82] In the Jewish communities their story was originally recounted during the days of mourning for the Temple, at the beginning of the month of *Ab*. As many of Antioch's Christians were of Jewish extraction, the martyrs' memory was celebrated, following the synagogal custom, at the beginning of *Ab*, i.e., August. In the Coptic Church, August 8th is dedicated to the martyrs, corresponding to the Jewish eve of the fast-day in memory of the Temple's destruction. Perhaps the Coptic rite has preserved the original date of the Jewish celebration of the martyrs' death. The same Coptic rite has December 25th as second day of the Maccabees—again under the influence of the Jewish feast of the Maccabees—*Hanukka*. In these two cases the calendaric interdependence seems quite obvious.[83]

III

We know little about the services that were held in antiquity in honour of a Jewish or Christian martyr. The decisive question for the calendar of pericopes *outside* the Proper of the Seasons (in the Church) or within the Jewish year may be formulated in this way: Were fixed readings from the Scriptures set aside for these days, coupled with specific chants? The answer is clearly negative, with the exception of a few local customs.

The oldest of these instances is curious enough, for it demands the *omission* rather than the addition of a text. On the feast of Passover the entire *Hallel* is not recited after the first day, out of respect for the Egyptians killed at the Red Sea. Rabbinic literature explains this omission with an edifying midrash. For similar reasons all Jewish first-born males are admonished to fast on the eve of Passover. In a way one might say that the first martyrdom of which Judaism takes official note, was that of the Egyptian first-born![84] The final result might be anticipated: before Christianity became the state religion, its rationale of martyrdom, while not identical with that of Judaism, was still more or less of similar nature: it valued martyrdom in the same way, it imitated the incidents and celebrated martyrs of similar character. It mattered little if the Christian ones were martyred by the Jews or vice versa.[85]

Of the fixed days with special hymns we first mention the 18th of

Iyar or 33rd day of the *'Omer,* the pentecontade between Passover and Pentecost, called *Lag be-'Omer.* The celebration of this day is explained in various ways. Fairly early it was linked to the death of R. Simeon bar Yohai in the second century C.E.[86] This rabbi, who was once believed to have inaugurated the Kabbala, was a disciple of the martyred R. Akiba. He seems to have expressed a theory of martyrdom in these words: 'The prophecy in I Kings 20:42 was fulfilled only in that part which referred to the death of [King] Ahab. The people were saved from perdition because the one drop of blood shed by the pious [King] Jehoshaphat . . . constituted atonement for the whole of Israel. . . .'[87] It is said that 'at his death he revealed many secrets to his disciples'. The day of his death is reverently called *hillula de Rab Shimon.* This expression hints at the mystic union of R. Simeon's soul with the 'active intellect'; it is a festive transfiguration.[88] The anniversary of his death is celebrated with illuminations and fireworks, because 'at the death of Rabbi Simeon the world was filled with light. . . . A hymn . . . which consisted of ten stanzas, each stanza corresponding to one of the ten *sefirot,* is sung in many communities on that day. . . . The Palestinian Jews . . . on this day visit the traditional grave of Rabbi Simeon near the village of Meron, after which they go to the woods and celebrate the event with much rejoicing. . . .'[89] A music example reproducing a song of the Jews of the Atlas mountains may illustrate this.[90]

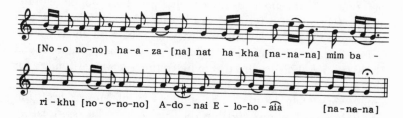

[No - o no-no] ha-a - za - [na] nat ha-kha [na-na-na] mim ba -

ri - khu [no - o-no-no] A - do - nai E - lo-ho - aia   [na-na-na]

Much later the massacres committed in the name of Christianity, the 'pious' Crusades, brought about the martyrdom of many thousands in Germany and France. From then on until the final and collective holocaust of European Jewry in our days, the German Jews used to read their martyrologies from these centuries, the so-called *Memor-Bücher,* as regular pericopes on Sabbaths, usually between Passover and *Shabu'ot* (Pentecost).[91]

As martyrdom became all too frequent during the Crusades, the Jewish authorities began to frown upon a martyr's cult more and more; they instituted a kind of 'Common of martyrs', a prayer which Ashkenazic Jews recite on certain Sabbaths during the year, and which contains the following characteristic passage:[92]

> May He in His powerful mercy turn to the saintly, the upright, the perfect, to those holy communities who gave up their lives for the glory of His Name. . . . May our God remember them for good with the other just men of the world, and avenge the vengeance of the spilt blood of His servants. . . . (Ps. 79 : 10).

Quite different is the Jewish practice of mourning for deceased *relatives.* It consists of four succeeding periods: two or three days, seven days thereafter, thirty days, and the rest of the calendar year are devoted to mourning for a close relative.[93] In addition a memorial service is held four times during the year in the regular ritual, where prayers for 'All Souls' are recited in a most solemn ceremony. There is good reason to believe that this rather late institution, commemorating a collection of members of the congregation, the community, scholars in Israel, etc., was an imitation of the Christian Common of Saints, Martyrs, Confessors, etc.[94] This service was supplemented by an older *individual* remembrance-prayer which was and is usually coupled with the observance of the anniversary of a close relative's death, called *Jahrzeit.* The name and practice are German-Jewish, but they hark back to ancient, even Talmudic times. It was then a voluntary act of piety and love, and Rashi (B. *Yeb.* 122a) claims that in olden times it was customary for the disciples of a great scholar to sit around his grave on the anniversary of his death.[95] The anniversary of Moses' death (his *physical* decease) is mourned on the 7th of *Adar,* his 'spiritual' or 'figurative' passing on the last day of Tabernacles, where it is a cause of rejoicing, and when the day's lectionary contains the story of his death (Deut. 34 : 4–5).

All such commemorations of great men of the past have, interestingly enough, a tendency to grow into festivals, sometimes of joyous and even orgiastic character.[96] Well known is St Jerome's advice to Laeta not to allow her daughter to attend the martyrs' vigils without her personal guardianship; he warns her to keep her close by her side.[97]

Surveying the rich Christian literature on the subject of the commemoration of the defunct, we come first across Tertullian's remark:

Oblationes pro defunctis, pro nataliciis, annua die facimus.[98]

This corresponds well to the old observance of *Jahrzeit* just mentioned. In the *Apostolic Constitutions* the third, ninth, and thirtieth days after burial are mentioned as days of mourning; likewise the anniversary.[99] The parallel with Jewish customs is obvious. Here the Jews may have set the example, perhaps with the exception of *mandatory* mourning on the anniversary. This last element may be linked to the collective prayer for the dead on the four days of the Jewish year.[100]

In principle, the beginnings of martyrology and prayers related to it run parallel with each other in Synagogue and Church, as Professor Lieberman has demonstrated.[101] Yet he has also shown some essential divergences, of which the most important one must be cited:

The dates of the martyrdom of the great Jewish leaders were not transmitted to posterity [we find them only in the later writings]. The Jews did not commemorate these days; there was no martyr-cult in Israel.

Let us add immediately and emphatically: not after the Crusades, the Jewish victims of which were memorialized on two Sabbaths of the year in a common martyrology. If a trend in the liturgical memorialization of Jewish martyrs is observable at all, it seems to lead towards a concentration or centralization of all martyrologies on eight days of the year: the two Sabbaths before the 9th of *Ab* and before *Yom Kippur,* on the 9th of *Ab* and on *Yom Kippur* itself, on the Three Festivals (with common prayers for all defunct) and the but recently instituted *Yom ha-shoah,* the day when the slaughter of the six million is remembered.

In Christianity the typical offices for the saints, martyrs, even the deceased, have had a fixed shape since the seventh and eighth centuries. They consist of scriptural lessons surrounded by psalmody which, in the monastic rites, extend to a full vigil with vespers, three nocturns, and the lauds at dawn.[102] Here Baumstark's question should be remembered: 'Could it be that it was first in the vigils, characteristic of the cult of the martyrs, that . . . the first models of a service—also for the layman—arose, whose structure was purely antiphonal?' The learned author is inclined to answer his own question affirmatively.[103] The old Nestorian Church seems to support Baumstark's hypothesis, at least in its characteristic use of psalmody in the offices for martyrs. There it builds up certain chanted psalm verses as 'themes'; which the subsequent prayer stanzas treat in a kind of literary-musical variation. At least nine lessons are read.[104] Thus the offices for the saints and martyrs are elaborate, and a service for one of the great saints consists of nine psalms, nine lessons, and nine responses.[105] All texts are post-biblical, with the exception of the psalms and their versicles. In the West as well as in the East the psalms chosen for such occasions sometimes belong to the cycle for the weekday. They are sometimes selected *ad hoc,* and sometimes belong to a special set or order, as in certain Eastern rites. Yet this practice is relatively late, and up to the seventh and eighth centuries each region celebrated its saints and martyrs according to a—more or less—arbitrary local tradition.[106]

After this long excursus we realize that psalmody was indeed used in the Church for the service of the saints, but relatively late; also that the distribution of the Psalter over the year is much older within the movable calendar than in the feasts of the fixed one, where no real system is recognizable. None the less the fixed calendar owes its existence to the celebration of martyrs and saints, preferably at their graves. This, as we have seen, is an old institution of the Jews, which they subsequently abandoned; perhaps because the Church thrived on it, perhaps because Judaism had too many martyrs and suffered from an *embarras de richesse* of a grim and tragic sort. We must search for yet other operative ideas behind the distribution of the psalms in the Proper.[107]

We shall renew our search, starting from the homily of Sunday or Sabbath, which habitually refers to psalms read on that very day.

THE PLACE OF PSALMS IN THE HOMILIES OF THE ANCIENT SYNAGOGUE

We have now *a negatione* established the higher age of the Sunday calendar as compared with the fixed order of saints' or martyrs' days. Yet our original question remains unanswered. Recent scholars such as G. Dix write:

> Between the lessons came the singing of psalms or other canticles from scripture (a chant known in later times as the 'gradual' . . .), a custom which must have been familiar to our Lord and His apostles, since it was universal in the synagogues of their day. . . .[108]

or A. Baumstark in his posthumous *Liturgie comparée:*

> It is true that, according to synagogue ritual, the psalmody, called *zmirot,* no longer immediately follows the scriptural lessons . . . but it is quite possible that it was the Jews, who in this have for once changed the original order of these elements. It would be the first occasion when the Christian liturgy has preserved the ancient Jewish custom better than the synagogue liturgy itself.[109]

Similarly, A. Fortescue[110] and G. Kunze[111] argue that these two chants (between the lessons) cannot have another function than as accompaniments of two non-Christian lessons. When one of the two was omitted, they contracted toward a kind of twin- or double-chant.

Even the encyclopaedia *MGG,* which incorporates the very latest scholarly findings, says in its article 'Graduale': 'Psalmody between lessons is a legacy of the Synagogue. . . .'[112]

None of these scholars can adduce truly satisfactory evidence; nonetheless they do not automatically follow each other's conceptions. Scholars of the rank of a Baumstark or Duchesne[113] depend upon their own investigations and their own judgements. So on the Jewish side did the late Jacob Mann, who stated emphatically that a regular sabbatical psalm lesson was chanted and changed in accord with the Torah and prophetic lesson.[114] It would be reasonable to conclude, if so, that this variable psalm pericope was already part of Synagogue liturgy before the Temple's fall.

It is not surprising that this possibility caught the imagination of some scholars who had learned of Dr. Mann's thesis. But instead of trying to follow in his traces, they sought for evidence of a regular psalm pericope at the earliest possible time; that is, in the Bible or intertestamentary literature itself, I have had occasion to peruse the following works: N. Wieder, *The Judean Scrolls and Karaism* (London, 1962), E. L. Ehrlich, *Die Kultsymbolik im Alten Testament* (Stuttgart, 1959), L. Morris, *The New Testament and the Jewish Lectionaries* (London, 1964), A. Arens, *Die Psalmen im Gottesdienst des Alten Bundes* (Trier, 1961), and G. G. Willis, *St Augustine's Lectionary* (London, 1962);[115] none of them reached a convincing proof *pro* or *contra*.

Since the turn of the present century hypotheses and conjectures have been ventured which connect the Triennial Cycle of the Torah-reading, as practised in Palestine, with a cyclical reading or chanting of the Psalter. The English scholars, E. G. King, I. Abrahams, and H. St J. Thackeray were in the vanguard of this investigation.[116] They did not, however, adduce any cogent reasons, not to mention definite evidence, for their hypotheses. The first scholar to do so was N. Snaith, who in 1933 boldly declared, after demonstrating that there are four *parashot* (pericopes) per month:

> We can therefore work out the portions and the psalms, four each to a month, and let the variations look after themselves. Working on this basis, we find the curious state of affairs that Exodus was begun on the 42nd Sabbath, Leviticus on the 73rd, Numbers on the 90th, and Deuteronomy on the 117th. But 1, 42, 73, 90, 107 are the first psalms in the five Books of the Psalms. This can scarcely be a coincidence.[117]

Yet Snaith was not able to prove the ordinate or corresponding numbers of the prominent Sabbaths cogently, and he completely neglected the festivals. Thus his hypothesis was refuted for lack of evidence.

Three Jewish scholars with profound erudition and deeper knowledge, have taken up Snaith's idea. They are L. Rabinowitz, J. Mann, and W. Braude.[118] All three have based their investigations upon (post-biblical) homilies for the Sabbaths. Rabinowitz started with a mild postulate: 'I maintain that the Midrash to Psalms definitely proves the influence of a triennial cycle on Psalms. . . .'

Later, after the appearance of Mann's great work, *The Bible as Read and Preached in the Old Synagogue,* he ended an essay with the remarks:

> Although naturally, to find fifty-four appropriate Psalms for the days of note requires at times a degree of homiletical ingenuity, no greater tribute could be paid to the universality of the religious spirit of the Psalms than the fact that the appropriate Psalm is always found, and never fails to heighten the religious significance of the *Sidra* (pericope) or the festival.[119]

Mann, after his inspired remarks on the subject, did not live to conclude his work, and even his editor Sonne's indefatigable hand dropped the pen when death touched it. Thus we are as yet without a systematic or cogently detailed proof of the basic hypothesis of the organic or institutional connection between the Triennial Cycle and Psalter. Yet a number of special studies and investigations have been published, and it can already be seen that the main idea is sound and will eventually be proved in detail.

Rabbi Z. D. Levy has attempted to prove Mann's thesis, using a new approach. He compared the psalm quotations of certain old midrashim for various Sabbaths of the Triennial Cycle, especially where some significant Torah lessons were read, and he found a high quota of agreement. In the various kinds of the Sabbaths examined the homilies quote the same psalms, and often enough the very same verses. He concludes at the end of his essay:

> The coincidence of parallel psalm verses occurring in the same pericope in three midrashim . . . would seem to support Mann's theory of a continuous psalm lesson once recited in the Synagogue. . . . The psalm lesson evidently had a twofold function: Liturgical and homiletic-apologetic. Yet we do not know the precise *liturgical* function of the psalms in the Synagogue. The second function, i.e., the apologetic function of the psalm lesson, would have been directed against the early Christians who gave the psalms a christological interpretation. We have already mentioned some of the numerous references of the early Church fathers to the fact that the Gradual was a direct legacy of Levitical Temple practice. This practice was introduced into the Synagogue as an *apologetic* device directed against Judaeo-Christians. . . .
>
> The high probability of Mann's theory of a psalm lesson recited in the Synagogue is amply supported by our analysis of psalm apologetics, and by the overwhelming coincidence of parallel psalm passages in the three

midrashim analysed. We have already made reference (in Ch. 1) to the system of *verbal tallies* used by Mann to link the tri-partite scriptural readings. . . .[120]

A. Arens goes one step further in his penetrating book *Die Psalmen im Gottesdienst des Alten Bundes* (The Psalms in the Liturgy of the Old Covenant). With great ingenuity he calculates the number of lessons for the 'normal' Triennial Cycle and tries to establish the months of the years during which they were read. He even attempts a tabulation, in which he points out how many months each book of the Pentateuch demanded; and his conjectures appear quite plausible. But when he has to coordinate the Penta-teuch lessons with the psalms he knows no better system than a rather mechanical one-to-one correspondence: Gen. 1, 2 corres-ponds to Pss. 1, 2, etc.[121] This system fails on all Sabbaths which happen to be New Moons, on all three 'pilgrimage festivals' (Passover, Pentecost and Tabernacles), and the Sabbath of *Hanukka* and in general on all days on which either the whole or the 'half' *Hallel* was sung. It further fails for New Year, when Pss. 47, 81, and 89, or at least Pss. 47:6 and 89:16, are mandatory.[122] All three psalms fall outside the calculated cycle unless a 'Proper of Psalms' for all festivals was introduced apart from the regular Sabbath lesson.[123]

This indeed seems to be the case, and it appears that this 'Proper' is of older origin than the psalms of the Triennial Cycle. In future studies it would therefore be useful to differentiate between the fixed psalms for the festivals, holidays and special days on one hand, and those for the numbered Sabbaths according to the ordered cycle on the other. L. Rabinowitz has taken this approach and reached some tentative results. He concludes that the Psalter should reflect the threefold repetition of the feasts (in the Triennial Cycle), and believes he has found evidence for such a structurization of the Psalter.[124] This assumption appears more than dubious to us, and until more solid evidence is presented in the nature of documents such as Mann and Sonne proffered, we must consider the problem of the correspondence of psalms on the Sabbaths of the Triennial Cycle to be still unsolved. Yet it can already be seen that the Proper with its lessons and chants had, at least in principle, its model in the Old Synagogue.[125]

THE ALLELUIA IN THE LITURGY AND THE SO-CALLED 'FREE' ALLELUIA

Until the fourth century the psalmody appears always to have been in this [performed by a special soloist] form in the church, elaborate solo and simple chorus, and never, as it is usually with us, by two alternating choruses. The earlier christian form was that which had been employed in the synagogue, where the signal for the people's refrain was the cantor's cry 'Hallelujah', whence the 'Alleluias' still found in the gradual at the liturgy. . . . The use of the psalter 'in course' (i.e., right through in regular order, and not as selected psalms to comment on other scriptures) in christian services is one of the byproducts of the monastic movement of the fourth century.[126]

Rarely in a modern work of serious scholarship does one meet such a maze of bold statements, inaccuracies, outright errors, and half-truths as in this passage by so careful a scholar as G. Dix. There is no evidence whatever for the main argument, namely, that 'the cantor's cry "Hallelujah" was the signal for the congregation's reply' in the Synagogue. His other thesis is equally untenable: The origin of chanting the Psalter *in cursu* is not only the result of growing monasticism as we know today, but goes back to the Jewish tradition and to the Christian use of psalms, or sections of the Psalter, on martyrs' days and vigils. Of the Alleluia in the Synagogue service before the lesson there is not only no trace, but it will be shown that this practice violates a basic rule of Jewish liturgy.[127]

In order to see one's way clearly in this maze of claims and counter-claims it will be useful to distinguish between three categories of Alleluias: (1) the Alleluia as integral part of a canonic psalm; (2) the Alleluia separated from its subsequent or antecedent scriptural psalm, used as acclamation; this we shall call the 'free' Alleluia; (3) the Alleluia, usually pronounced or chanted three times at the end of some psalm-verse or verses not necessarily connected with Alleluia in their scriptural context. In the Church this third category of Alleluia has the liturgical function of an organic link between the lessons.

The oldest testimony to the *liturgical* use of the Alleluia in Christianity (not in the New Testament, where it appears far earlier in Rev.) belongs to Tertullian (*c.* 200 C.E.).[128] He simply reports that

101

pious Christians add the Alleluia to their prayers, and respond to 'this sort of psalm'. The author refrains from expressly saying that the Alleluia belongs to that 'genus' *a priori* or else that it was freely added. Possibly he was aware of both practices, for shortly afterward Athanasius demands an *added* Alleluia following the recitation of three successive psalms,[129] whereas the Egyptian monks, even 150 years later, object to this observance and admit Alleluia only when the psalm bears the superscription 'Alleluia' in Scripture itself.[130] This was also the practice in the old Ethiopian Church; for the Ethiopic recension of St Hippolytus' *Apostolic Tradition* postulates that only those psalms are chanted at the *Agape* which contain the Alleluia in Scripture.[131] The West is more lenient on this point. St Benedict provides for the 'free' Alleluia during the second half of the nocturn or night-office (reg. 15).[132]

The decisive position in the controversy was that of St Jerome; and it is characteristic of his importance that letters pertaining to the Alleluia which are obviously apocryphal fabrications were attributed to him. As they play a certain role in subsequent investigations we shall quote two sentences from one of these documents, allegedly addressed by Jerome to Pope Damasus I. After an expression of consent and sympathy with the complaint of Damasus that only on Sundays could one hear psalmody between the lessons, Pseudo-Jerome continues:

Cliens precatus ergo tuus ut vox psallentium in sede tua Romana die noctuque canatur. . . . Ubi autem Deus et homo honorabili voce cantatur. Alleluia semper *cum omnibus psalmis* affigatur, ut omni loco communiter respondeatur nocturnis temporibus. [Not during the Mass?] In Ecclesia autem post resurrectionem usque sanctum Pentecosten finiatur, inter dierum spatia *tibi soli* Quinquagesima propter novitatem sancti Paschae, ut vox ita laudis canatur in Aleph, quod prologus Graece. Latine autem praefatio dicitur.[133]

(Translation): Your adherent thus asks you to let the voice of the psalm-singing [Christians] resound in your Roman see by day and night. . . . But where God and man are sung of in a worthy voice, the Alleluia may always be attached *to all psalms,* so that it be generally responded at nightly services. In the Church, however, let it be finished between Easter and the holy Pentecost, and have it *sung to you only* during a portion of the days of Quinquagesima [the pentecontade between Easter and Pentecost] because of the freshness of the holy Pascha, so that the tones of praise resound in Aleph, which stands for prologue in Greek, for preface in Latin.

From this strange letter we learn two facts, both of them negative: (1) The 'free' addition of the Alleluia was still a controversial practice at the time the letter was penned—well in the fifth century. As a chant between lessons it was probably limited to the Easter-Pentecost-tide of Western liturgy. (2) The last sentence clearly shows that the letter is a forgery. St Jerome was too good a Hebraist to assume that the Hebrew *Hallelujah* began with the letter Aleph, as did the forger, who thought only of the Latinized or Greek version *Alleluia,* and wished to display his great 'erudition'.[134]

In the Western Church the Alleluia between the lessons is testified to unequivocally and for the first time in the account of the death of a *psalmista* on the ambo, i.e., while chanting the Gradual, shortly after 427 in North Africa, notwithstanding some genuine remarks made by St Jerome which seem to indicate a free usage of the acclamation.[135]

The incident in North Africa is reported thus: During a persecution of orthodox Christianity by Geiserich, King of the Arian Vandals of North Africa, it happened apparently after Easter that a psalmist stood on the ambo and sang an enthusiastic Alleluia chant when suddenly an arrow shot through the window, and hit him in the throat so that he, 'dropping the book from which he had been singing', fell dead to the ground.[136]

The situation is different in Eastern Christianity. All pertinent testimonies are clearly and comprehensively arranged in Hanssens's monumental work on the liturgical institutions of Oriental Christianity.[137] Whereas the first documentation of the Alleluia in the Mass is not older than 715 in the Byzantine rite, not older than the eighth century in the Armenian, and not older than 903 in the Chaldaean liturgy, the Egyptian rite may claim the first *liturgical* testimony to the use of the Alleluia after the doxology in the famous Fayyum Papyrus.[138]

In general, Hanssens believes that the Alleluia with a psalm or a psalm verse between the lessons harks back to early Christianity ('magnam antiquitatem'). He concludes this from its uniform and ubiquitous appearance at the same point of the liturgy in many geographically distant rites, and stresses the fact that it was chanted whenever a greater number of lessons (from various books of the

Old Testment and New Testament) were read. At the same time he is admirably honest in stating:

> Quanam aetate Alleluia inter ritus missae orientalis admissum sit, incertum est. Mirum est enim de eo in antiquis documentis silentium vel certe in istis nequaquam ab ipsis psalmis distinguuntur. . . .[139]

Hence it is evidently possible that the Western Alleluia which was long considered a 'mos ecclesiae orientalis', was imported from the Jerusalem Church, as E. Wellesz has suggested.[140] From here it spread both east and west. All indications speak for a kind of extension of the early model, the famous psalm verse of Communion, 'Gustate et videte quoniam bonus (suavis) sit Dominus' (Ps. 34: 9), which exists in many of the oldest liturgies.[141] It was often followed by Alleluias. Even so, there still seems to be no evidence of the regular use of the 'free' Alleluia before 330 in either Eastern or Western Mass.[142]

We now turn to the role and the usage of the Hallelujah in the Synagogue. We notice immediately that it plays a far smaller part there than in the Church. As a free acclamation it was only rarely used. For the 'free' Alleluia added to or intercalated in psalms or *piyyutim,* testimony is equivocal, rare and late, and vacillates regionally and temporally. The tendency to use the Hallelujah in the Synagogue, seen historically, is certainly recessive. Before 350 the Hallelujah was responded (at least in Babylonia) 123 times during the *Hallel;* afterwards only twice—at the beginning and the end. The older rabbinic literature contains no more than vague references to 'free' Hallelujahs, except as a salutation at the end of a divine service, or as an exclamation 'of the unlearned'.[143]

During the last twenty years unexpected new sources have been discovered in the Dead Sea Scrolls. A careful study of these ancient manuscripts yields the following results bearing on our research:

The *Hymns of Thanksgiving* may be considered as late-comers to the literature of psalms and canticles. Yet they are replete with purely theological ideas, far more so than the poetically far superior Psalms. The scroll of the *War of the Children of Light* contains an abundance of references to trumpets and other signal-instruments. Both the hymns and some poetic passages of the programmatic *Manual of Discipline* frequently refer to musical instruments, to singing, to special ways of thanksgiving *(hodaya)*; the term 'Halle-lujah' is all but missing (only at the end of the 'Hymns of Triumph') in the DSS, although many other terms for praise and laudation occur. For a general survey of the musical aspects the reader should consult the specialized literature.[144]

The regular night watches at Qumran, always divided into three, engaged in readings from Scripture, expositions, study and prayer.[145] The share of psalmody and recitation in the Qumran liturgy, if one may use the term, may be briefly described: We can only surmise that some of the texts were regularly sung, others periodically recited. It is certain that the Sabbaths, the festivals and the 'appointed times, which God has prescribed' (a favourite con-cept of the Qumranites) figured considerably in the liturgy, includ-ing the night prayers. The root *h-l-l* from which the Hallelujah stems, occurs several times in the DSS. It seems that the term Hallelujah did not enjoy any special significance among the various other expressions of 'praise' or 'acclamation'.[146]

Even the scroll of the *War of the Children of Light against the Children of Darkness* does not make use of the Hallelujah in the prayer after the final victory, and the *Hymns of Thanksgiving* use a word from another root as their refrain-word, either at the begin-ning or at the end and often at both. Can it be that during the Hellenistic age the growing popularity of the Hallelujah call made the introvert and xenophobic monks of Qumran wary? Is it a coincidence that in the three Hellenistic works, Tobit 13:18, III Macc. 7:13, and the Judaeo-Christian Odes of Solomon, every song ends with it,[147] and the acclamation serves no real liturgical function? Can we detect a certain secularization here, in the begin-nings of the 'free' Alleluia? It does not seem impossible. Whatever the reasons may have been, the DSS do not mention the Hallelujah in its original meaning. The occurrence in the apocryphal Ps. 151 (as superscription) has decidedly secular overtones, like, e.g., 'A Hurrah' (in Ch. VII).

If the 'free' Alleluia was frowned upon by most rabbinic authori-ties and even in the early Church, where does the Christian Alleluia between the lessons come from? It is common to all rites. There must have been some ancient authority for so widespread and never-contested a practice. When we seek regular, ever-repeated alleluiatic formulas, we seem to find them in the Levitical songs of the so-called Hallelujah psalms (Pss. 145-50) sung at the *tamid* sacrifice of the Second Temple.[148] When regular sacrifices could no longer be offered after 70.C.E., the psalms which accompanied the daily *tamid* offering so solemnly could still be chanted, still be heard. How was this possible?

We are told in the New Testament (Hebr. 13 : 15) to offer the 'fruit of our lips' to God through His Anointed, in a continuous sacrifice of praise. This bold metaphor, borrowed from Hos. 14 : 3, contains the justification of the transition from sacrificial cult to adoration by sacred words, the 'fruit of our lips'. It also occurs in Isa. 57 : 19, as late as the Odes of Solomon and in the DSS. Indeed, the entire structure of synagogue worship rests upon this substitution by prayer, this hypostasis of the concept of sacrifice.

In the Synagogue the so-called Hallelujah psalms (145-50), each of which begins or ends with the acclamation, became a regular part of the daily morning service, and were chanted simply by one honorary precentor after having once been triumphantly sung by the Levitical chorus and orchestra of the Temple. On festivals the *Hallel* was added. It is not too far-fetched a conjecture to assume that these psalms and the Alleluia-verses, formerly rendered in the Temple as a daily part of the service, were now kept alive in the New Church. The psalm lesson was continued in both Synagogue and Church, but was eventually abolished by the former; while the Alleluia, which according to Jewish custom should not be torn from its psalms, came to serve Christianity almost exclusively. Still, it remained controversial, as we have seen, until this 'free' Alleluia was sanctioned by Pope Damasus in the West, and by the great Greek doctors of the outgoing third century in the East. Characteristically, it first took the place of the *Hallel* at Easter. To this very day Ps. 118 is distributed as Gradual over the days of the Easter week, and more than fifteen (textual) contrafacts of the melody to *Haec dies* (Ps. 118 : 24) are listed and known.[149] Curiously enough, it is also linked with the so-called *Egyptian Hallel* (Ps. 135) of the Jewish Passover tradition.

In view of the Jewish reluctance to use the Hallelujah freely in the liturgy, we comprehend the late folkloristic usage of that acclamation in a thoroughly secularized context, as recently recorded by E.

Gerson-Kiwi.[150] Indications speak for a direct Palestinian legacy, but we have seen it used outside the Synagogue. All the earlier examinations were undertaken in order to eliminate other possible customs or institutions which might have evolved a practice as general as that of psalmody between lessons, coupled with the Alleluia chant. The Temple instituted it, the Jerusalem Church preserved it and seems to have been its *spiritus rector*. Where could it have originated save in the Temple, to attain general Christian familiarity if not always recognition? The question cannot be fully settled, as there are isolated references, in the *Mishna* and in later legalistic writings, to the spontaneously inserted Hallelujah.

This same 'emancipation' of exclamatory calls or words from their scriptural context, as found in Hallelujah or Hosanna, has certain counterparts in some liturgical 'cue-words' which expanded or unfolded into whole poems. Western Christianity knows this pattern from its Great Doxology and some litanies. Byzantine liturgy established the *Kanones,* which may be viewed as 'expansions' of scriptural canticles. The Synagogue has done likewise in its *kedusha,* and the *piyyutim* based upon it.[151] As this seems to be the oldest 'expansible' cue-word, and as its nucleus has been absorbed in the text of the Western and Eastern Mass, we shall examine the interrelation of Synagogue and Church with respect to the Thrice-Holy.

CHAPTER FIVE

The Genesis of the *Sanctus* in Jewish and Christian Liturgies

DURING the last twenty years, more and more sources have come to light to indicate that the Jewish foundations of early Christian liturgies were considerably wider and deeper than had been thought previously, even at the turn of the century. Most historians have duly taken cognizance of these far-reaching discoveries, of which the Dead Sea Scrolls are only one element, albeit a significant one. Most of the musicologists, however, prefer to remain in the happy state of blissful ignorance, as far as liturgical sources are concerned, even those who deal extensively with matters liturgical. They will be reviewed in a later chapter.

Here it will be our task to trace as far back as possible that prayer, which after Eucharist and psalmody, has inspired more musicians and poets than any other: the *Sanctus*. We shall attempt to find a sort of mainstream of the text and some, if by no means all of the ancient melodies of the text. For terminological reasons we shall distinguish between the Hebrew and Aramaic *Kedusha* (henceforth K), the *Tersanctus* or Thrice-Holy (henceforth S) and the *Trisagion* or *Aius* (henceforth T), the periphrastic variant of S, which found its way into both Eastern and Western liturgies.

I

The synagogal K has a long history. Its nuclear cell, Isa. 6 : 3, has in the course of time undergone many variations. We shall not deal with these variants, as they are of peripheral importance for our quest.[1] The scriptural verse is nowhere alluded to in later books of the canonic OT; yet there are abundant references to it in the

108

apocryphal and pseudepigraphic literature between the OT and the NT. Of these numerous citations a few may be listed here: Apocalypse of Abraham 17 : 7; I Enoch (Ethiopic version) 39 : 12; II Enoch (Slavonic text) 20; Testament of Adam 1 : 4; Testament of Isaac 8 : 3.

To these long-known texts two most significant additions can now be made; they are contained in the Dead Sea Scrolls (DSS), in *Hymns of Thanksgiving,* XVI, and in the so-called *Angelic Liturgy.* All the works listed are intertestamentary, i.e., they were written in pre-Christian times, as some of them were known to St Paul. Not a few were later altered in a christological sense.[2] In all of them the Jewish angelology is fully developed.

The earliest texts of the synagogal K exist in three forms: they are all intrinsically connected with angelological conceptions. They are most evident in the *K-Yotzer* of the morning service, less pronounced in the *K-'Amida* of the eighteen benedictions, and of the same strength in the *K-deSidra* ('of the Academy'). All three have two scriptural passages in common, Isa. 6 : 3 and Ezek. 3 : 12, which are juxtaposed; the surrounding framework differs, however, quite considerably. As every K has a framework of its own, we shall quote here the essential phrases of *K-Yotzer* and *K-'Amida,* both anterior and posterior to the S itself in their ancient order. We shall underline the significant phrases.

K-Yotzer:

The chiefs of the hosts are holy beings that exalt the Almighty and *incessantly* declare the glory of God and His holiness. Be Thou praised, O our Rock. . . . Creator of holy beings. . . ; Creator of ministering spirits, all of whom stand in the heights of the Universe, and proclaim with awe *in unison* (in one voice) aloud the words of the living God and everlasting King. . . . All of them open their mouths in holiness and purity, with song and psalm, while they adore and extol, glorify and sanctify and ascribe sovereignty to—
The Name of the Divine King, the great, mighty, and dreaded One, . . . and they all take upon themselves *the yoke of the Kingdom of Heaven* one from the other . . . in tranquil joy of spirit, with pure speech and holy melody, they all respond *as one* and exclaim with awe: Holy, holy, holy. . . . And the *ophanim* ('wheels') and the holy animals with a noise of great rushing, upraising themselves toward the Seraphim, thus over against them offer praise and say: 'Praised be the Glory of the Lord from His (its?) place. . . .'[3]

K-'Amida:

True and firm, established and enduring . . . good and beautiful is Thy word for us for ever and ever. . . . Yea, faithful art Thou to quicken the dead. Praised be Thou, O Lord, who quickenest the dead.

READER: We will sanctify Thy Name in the world even as they sanctify it in the highest heavens, as it is written by the hand of Thy prophet: 'And they called one unto the other and said: Holy, holy, holy. . . .' (CONGREG.)

READER: Those over against them say 'Praised'.

CONGR.: Praised be the glory of the Lord from His (its?) place. . . .

READER (in silent prayer): Thou art holy, and Thy Name is holy and holy beings praise Thee daily. (Selah). Praised art Thou, the holy God.

The Isaiah passage early became the subject of christological interpretation, due to the threefold 'Holy'; later Church Fathers also discussed the synagogal K. The resemblances to Preface and S of the Latin rite, and to the Anaphora of the Eastern rites was likewise noticed during the Middle Ages.[4]

In the relatively recent discipline of liturgiology the question of the age of K and S has elicited a bulky literature. Of the differing views we shall record here the three main ones:

(a) Liturgically, the K antedates both S and T; the latter forms were created under the influence of K.

(b) Both S and T arose independently of K; K itself is post-apostolic.

(c) Elements of K were used by the earliest Judaeo-Christians, though not by Judaism in general in apostolic times; from these sectarian rites the Church took over the basic elements and reshaped them in various versions.

We shall examine these three conceptions and their respective arguments. Yet before doing so, we shall have to consider the angelological background of K, S, and T.

The doctrine of the angels, fairly well established in Judaism at the time of the Maccabean revolt, became one of the most beloved tenets of the people. While the aristocracy (Sadduceans and Hellenized hierarchy) frowned or smiled at these 'aberrations', the Hasideans and Pharisees fervently championed it. The idea that God delegates authority to inferior spiritual beings who may, in turn, be held responsible for mishaps as imagined by a Jewish observer, served to solve at least partly the unsolvable problem of theodicy. The scriptural verse Deut. 32:8–9: 'When the Most High gave to the nations their inheritance, when He separated the children of men, He set the bounds of the peoples according to the number of the children of Israel. For the Lord's portion is Israel, Jacob the lot of His inheritance', gave some authority to such ideas. Instead of reading 'according to the number of the children of Israel' the Septuagint (LXX) reads here, κατὰ ἀριθμὸν ἀγγέλων Θεοῦ, 'according to the number of the angels of God'—which may have been a then current variant of the Hebrew text.[5] Upon this verse and its variegated nationalistic, ethical, theological interpretations rests perhaps the entire structure of Jewish angelology until the end of the Talmudic age. The idea was again elaborated upon in Revelation, where not only every nation, but each of the Seven Communities has an angel of its own.

The picturesque idea of the interaction between the angels' liturgy and that of mortals originated in these post-Maccabean times, and has left many traces in both Judaism and Christianity. Particularly important here are the passages I Enoch 39:11–13, which we quote, and the DSS fragments of the so-called *Angelic Liturgy*.[6]

Before Him there is no ceasing. He knows what the world is before it was created, and generation unto generation that shall arise: Those who sleep not bless Thee: they stand before Thy glory and bless, laud, and extol, saying: 'Holy, holy, holy, is the lord of Spirits: He filleth the earth with spirits.' And here my eyes saw all those who sleep not, how they stand before Him and bless, and say: 'Blessed be Thou and blessed be the name of the Lord for ever and ever.'[7]

Here the second constituent element of K, Ezek. 3:12, is replaced by a short doxology from the psalms. Yet the Ezek. passage is again a vision of angelic worship, part of the immortal image of the heavenly throne-chariot (*Merkaba*). The lasting impression of that vision is best described in G. Scholem's classic book *Major Trends in Jewish Mysticism*, where *Merkaba* mysticism alone fills nearly a quarter of its contents. A characteristic portion of this angelic worship has been retained, in a relatively mild paraphrase, in the K-*Yotzer*. The apocalyptic literature of pre-Christian Judaism thrived on these passages, sometimes in a wildly phantastic spirit. Some elements of the vision entered also into Catholic theology: the four personages with the countenances of bull, eagle, lion, and the πρόσωπον ἀνθρώπου (man's countenance) became later the emblems of the four evangelists. In Judaism, that fourth enigmatic person was later identified with Metatron, highest prince of angels, and second only to God.[8]

Let us now consider the juxtaposition of the passages from Isaiah and Ezekiel in the two *Kedushot* quoted above. The strong angelological bent was characteristic of Essenic and, to a lesser degree, Pharisaic thinking during the last 150 years B.C.E. and the first century C.E. It must have been during these 250 years that the pattern of the K was set and *canonized*. That the Sadduceans, who held jurisdiction in the Temple, mocked angelology is well known also from Christian sources,[9] just as the miracle-hungry masses of Judea loved it. At least an archetype of a K must have evolved in the synagogues of that time, since a later inclusion of so significant a portion of the liturgy would not have been possible without leaving definite and argumentative traces in early rabbinic sources, such as *Mishna* or *Tosefta*. There, however, the K is already taken for granted. This is no more than an *argumentum e silentio*, but there is more positive evidence available.

The *K-'Amida* has come down to us in a Palestinian and a Babylonian version. The Babylonian redaction of the eighteen benedictions, of which the K is today an integral part, contains in its earliest form already the reference to a preceding K:

> Thou art holy, and Thy Name is holy, and holy beings praise Thee daily. (3rd benediction)

and:

> . . . unto all generations. From generation to generation we will declare Thy greatness.

This verse alludes to the preceding 'from generation to generation' of Ps. 146, which was also contained in the *K-'Amida*. The Palestinian version, on the other hand, included the recitation of the *Shma'* (Deut. 6 : 4–9), which was hidden in the *ad hoc* inserted K, because of the Roman prohibition on reading the *Shma'* in its original setting.[10] The suppression of the *Shma'* is well documented. These and other historical reasons indicate that the *K-'Amida* came into being during the persecution by Domitian and Hadrian; the total collapse of Bar Kokhba's revolt in 135 C.E. closed that period.

The case lies somewhat differently with the *K-Yotzer*. Here we are in possession of a source dating from the first Christian century, which formally states the existence of interplay between angelic and human worship:

'When the morning stars sing all together' (cf. Job 38 : 7) . . . this relates to the praises offered by Israel, and also 'when the sons of God sing' (ibid.) . . . this relates to the angelic worship.[11]

We recall the earlier occurrences of that idea in I Enoch. Thenceforth and in many variations, the idea of that interaction became a well-established tenet of rabbinic theology.

By the discovery of the DSS an older analysis by K. Kohler has been vindicated. Long before some of the pseudepigrapha were published and sixty years before the Qumran literature made its impact on our knowledge of the intertestamentary theology, Kohler had in a most intuitive study attributed the *K-Yotzer* to the liturgy of the Essenes.[12] Certain ideas reported as Essenic by Philo occur often in the DSS, thus justifying Kohler's views.

All these analyses prove the pre-Christian existence of *K-Yotzer* and the apostolic origin of the *K-'Amida*. Most modern scholars have accepted these arguments as cogent. Yet there are a few authors who continue to cast doubt on both rabbinic and DSS evidence. As they are responsible students, we are obliged to heed, and, if possible, to refute their arguments. A. Baumstark has, in two publications, discussed both K and S and their hypothetical relationship.[13] He was not familiar with the midrashic quotation above, nor could he anticipate evidence of the DSS. Thus two essential testimonies to the K in pre-Christian literature escaped his knowledge. Nonetheless, weighing all documents and arguments available to him, he reached the conclusion that a hypothetical 'primal version' of *K-Yotzer* antedated all others—this redaction might be traced to the first century. He was well familiar with Christian and many Hebrew sources. This cannot be said for C. W.

Dugmore's book *The Influence of the Synagogue upon the Divine Office*.[14] Mr. Dugmore states: 'The original form of the K has been shown to have borne no resemblance to that early Christian prayer [the S in Clement of Rome, *Epistle to the Corinthians,* 34].' The author refers here (in a footnote) to an earlier passage of his book. However, the cited pages contain no such refutation whatever. He accepts and uses the conclusions reached by L. Finkelstein, and nowhere does he go beyond these findings, let alone against them, but he ignores the most important point: the existence and higher age of the *K-Yotzer* and its connection with Essene, Hasidean, and apocalyptic conceptions and practices. Of course, he could not anticipate the evidence of the DSS; but their discovery has altered many hitherto axiomatic ideas of former times.

A much more cautious attitude is taken by J. Jungmann, S. J., in his standard work on the history of the Mass.[15] He assumes the existence of the *K-'Amida* in early Christianity, again ignoring the *K-Yotzer*. We shall return to Jungmann's point of view in connection with the relation of S, K and T.

Most recently, Kenneth Levy has felt obliged to present his views on the question of the K.[16] In his essentially solid and well-reasoned musicological essay he touches on our subject only twice in passing. Unfortunately he has not applied the same care to Jewish liturgy as to other subjects under discussion. He relies blindly upon the findings of Mr. Dugmore concerning the age of the K. While he otherwise distinguishes between S and T, no such refinement is applied to the K. Like Dugmore, he ignores the *K-Yotzer,* in general he is unaware of the existence of any new material since 1942, let alone of the DSS.

The Judaeo-Christian liturgy has been neglected for a long time, in spite of Kohler's emphasis on its importance for the formation of the Mass and the Office. This aspect was thrown into sharp focus by recent studies by E. Peterson, J. Schoeps, J. Daniélou, S.J., and most lately by D. Flusser, who has perhaps the widest command of Jewish and Christian sources. This sectarian Church amalgamated some of the Hasidean and apocalyptic ideas and practices with the new Christian theology, thus forming a liturgy, fragments of which have survived to this day. In reviewing the NT framework of S and T we shall recall that particular sect's contributions to the development of the Anaphora.[17]

114

THE CONCURRENCE OF SANCTUS, KEDUSHA, AND TRISAGION

The first literal quotations of Isa. 6 : 3, the seraphic hymn, in early Christian literature occur in Clement's *First Epistle to the Corinthians*, and in Rev. 4 : 8. Of the former document we know fairly well the date of its redaction (96–100), of the latter we have at least a *terminus post quem* in the testimony of Papias, who was Bishop of Hierapolis in Phrygia during the early part of the second century. He must have known at least parts of Rev.[18] All of this evidence points to the end of the first century as the time when canonical and apostolic authors began to make use of the seraphic hymn.

Most recently, D. Flusser has offered a most interesting, almost revolutionary hypothesis: he suggests that a certain verse of the *Gloria* (Luke 2 : 14) is virtually a paraphrase of the *K-deSidra*.[19] This conjecture would put a paraphrase of the K right into the text of the synoptic Gospels. Flusser juxtaposes the Greek with the Aramaic text of the *K-deSidra*:

Δόξα ἐν ὑψίστοις Θεῷ καὶ ἐπὶ γῆς εἰρήνη ἐν ἀνθρώποις εὐδοκίας	Holy is He in the highest heavens, the place of His divine abode: Holy upon earth, the work of His might. . . . the whole earth is full of the radiance of His glory.

Whatever one may say against this bold conjecture, the fact remains that the Targum to Ezek. 3 : 12 corresponds in its phraseology with both I Enoch and the αἰνούντων καὶ λεγόντων in Luke.[20] Yet in spite of a host of learned references and allusions, Flusser's conjecture is—to this writer—not fully convincing.

Further early references to S are found in St Ignatius, *Ad Eph.* 4 : 2 and in the Alexandrian Clement's writings. Let us compare these concrete testimonies with the liturgical function of S in early Christianity:

(1) Clement of Rome, I Cor., 34 : 6, 7:

Ten thousand times ten thousand waited on Him, and a thousand thousand served Him and cried: 'holy, holy, holy is the Lord of hosts, the entire creation is full of Thy glory', and we, guided by our conscience, gathered together in our place, cry to Him *constantly as with one voice;* so that we become sharers in His great and glorious promises.[21]

(2) Rev. 4 : 8:

And the four living creatures, each of them with six wings, are full of eyes all round and within, and day and night they *never cease* to sing: Holy, holy, holy is the Lord God Almighty (παντοκράτωρ) who was and is, and is to come.[22]

(3) Clement of Alexandria, *Stromata*, VII, 12:

. . . and let him teach his son . . . in a way . . . so that he would always praise God, just as the praising beasts do, of whom Isaiah speaks allegorically. . . .[23]

(4) St Ignatius, *Ad Eph.*, 4 : 2:

. . . this is why in the symphony of your concord ὁμονοία and love, praises of Jesus Christ are sung. But you, the rank and file, should also form a choir, so that, joining the symphony by your concord, and by your unity taking the keynote from God, you may *with one voice* through Jesus Christ sing a song to the Father. . . .[24]

(5) An allusion to the S by Tertullian:

. . . cui illa angelorum circumstantia *non cessat dicere;* sanctus, sanctus, sanctus Deus . . . proinde igitur et nos, angelorum, si meruimus, candidati, iam hic caelestem illam in Deum vocem et officium futurae claritatis ediscimus.[25]

(6) An early Martyrology (*Passio SS Perpetuae et Felicitatis*):

. . . et introivimus et audivimus *vocem unitam dicentem* (φωνὴν ἡνωμένην λεγόντων) 'Agios, agios, agios' *sine cessatione* (ἀκαταπαύστως) . . . et in dextera et in sinistra seniores quatuor. . . .[26]

In order to evaluate the elements common to all allusions to the K-S *before* the first appearance of a consistently arranged and articulated eucharistic prayer, as attributed to Hippolytus (fl. *c.* 215 C.E.), we shall add a few remarks on the standing or recurrent phrases.

ad (1) 'constantly as with one voice', occurs already in I Enoch 39 : 11, and I Enoch 61 : 11.

ad (2) 'four living creatures' cf. Ezek. I.

ad (4) 'the keynote from God' (χρῶμα θεοῦ) is another example of St Ignatius' preference for musical similes.[27]

ad (5) 'iam hic caelestem . . . vocem'. Tertullian stresses the need for preparing oneself on *earth* for the angelic adoration.

We note that in all cases the angelic choir serves as a kind of exemplary worship which all Christians ought to emulate on earth. The question arises when the OT passage of the S was understood in a christological, especially in a trinitarian sense, which the Thrice-Holy is bound to suggest. Nor was this idea neglected by early Christian authors. Origen, Jerome, and Victor of Vita, to name only three, interpreted the S in a strictly trinitarian way. The link between OT and NT, between synagogal and ecclesiastical worship was preserved exactly by the angelological framework, common to both institutions.[28]

Shortly after 200 Hippolytus' *Apostolic Tradition* was written, containing *inter alia* the first rudimentary formula of a eucharistic prayer-service. This document does *not* contain a S nor a reference to it.[29] Moreover, all allusions to angelic worship are avoided, as in general Hippolytus' angelology is negligible.[30] Closest in time to Hippolytus are the euchologion of Serapion of Thmuis (fl. 335) and the oldest strata of the liturgy of Jerusalem, reconstructed after St Cyril's '*catechesis*'.

The prayer of Hippolytus appears to represent a tradition totally different from that of the Serapion or St Cyril formulae. Not only is the S absent, but the entire angelology. The Serapion ritual and St Cyril's description, on the other hand, have quite a few standing phrases in common. If we deny the continuity of tradition running from Clement of Rome to Hippolytus, Serapion, and Cyril, we should assume that the inclusion of the S in the latter two liturgies originates in another, thus far unknown, Christian source. Or should the interplay between angelic and human worship, so characteristic of the Jewish apocalyptic writers and the first version of the K have been introduced in the spirit of catholic liturgy as late as the third century?[31] This is most improbable in view of the frequent instances quoted above, and their insistence on that very point. Moreover, both Serapion and Cyril introduce not only pertinent passages from Isaiah, but allude to Dan. 7 and to Ezek. 1

and 3. This combination of three OT passages can hardly be a coincidence.[32]

The addition of the Hosanna to the S marks the turning point in the unfolding of the eucharistic prayer. It occurs almost simultaneously in the Syrian and Greek liturgies, though one may not consider it a really new element in Christianity. Aside from the passage in Matt. 21 : 9, the Hosanna acclamation occurs first in the *Didache,* although not in connection with the S, but in a Judaeo-Christian version of the grace after meals.[33] The passage reads: 'Let grace come and this world perish [or 'pass away']. Hosanna to the Son of David.' The Hosanna in this context as that of Matt. 21 : 9 is used in an erroneous sense, as I have shown elsewhere in detail.[34] It is clear that the Hosanna had assumed the significance of a triumphal acclamation long before the fourth century. I surmise that due to its inclusion in the S the entire prayer S-Hosanna (later *Benedictus*)—Hosanna was called the ὕμνος ἐπινίκιος, the victory-hymn.[35]

Now this term ἐπινίκιος merits our attention, for it has both a classical Greek and a biblical connotation. In classical literature the term stands for a triumphal celebration or hymn, from Pindar on to Nonnus Dionysius.[36] τὰ ἄσματα ἐπινίκια are hymns after a battle won, or encomia on a victor of games; the word reaches into the Hellenistic period.[37] In this very sense Symmachus, the translator of Scripture, uses ἄσματα ἐπινίκια in Isa. 6 : 3, also for the psalm-superscription *lam'natzeah,* usually—and falsely—translated as 'to the music master' or 'choirmaster' in Pss. 4 : 1; 8 : 1 and elsewhere.[38]

Why, then, does the S carry such an almost military epithet? As far as I was able to trace this designation, it seems that St John Chrysostom used it first in a specifically liturgical sense, usually with the byword ἀκαταπαύστως—'incessantly'.[39] Thereafter it occurs quite frequently in the Eastern liturgies. Who is conquered? The epithet *epinikios* seems to allude to the Hosanna, yet Symmachus knew it for the S in Isaiah. Yet Chrysostom cannot mean the Hosanna either, for his description of the liturgy does not mention it as part of the S. Actually there are more ancient liturgies without the Hosanna than with it. Jungmann, who more or less derives the epithet from the Hosanna, is refuted by the abundance of *Sanctus* passages in early liturgies without Hosanna, yet bearing the term *epinikios.*[40] Perhaps it represents nothing but the continuation of Symmachus' byword of the Isaiah passage. Be that as it may, when we consider the next and last of our liturgies, the Anaphora contained in the seventh book of the *Apostolic Constitutions,* we are the more perplexed; for that liturgy, a Judaeo-Christian relict, neither contains the Hosanna nor uses the term *epinikios.*

A. Baumstark and J. Jungmann (and, of course, their disciples) have repeatedly stressed that the *Apostolic Constitutions* are unique in juxtaposing, just as in the K, the verses Isa. 6 : 3, and Ezek. 3 : 12. It is true: the texts, in which we observed a mixing of the two visions, were not always related to human worship. Baumstark and Jungmann emphasize the point that the verse Ezek. 3 : 12 was too narrowly nationalistic in a Jewish sense—interpreting the passage 'from His place' as the Temple in Jerusalem—and became for this very reason unacceptable to Christianity in general, to be eventually dropped altogether. However, *both scholars are mistaken,* and their explanation is untenable. For the juxtaposition of Isa. 6 : 3 and Ezek. 3 : 12 did occur at least twice, long after the spread of the *Apostolic Constitutions:* in Pseudo-Dionysius Aeropagita, and in the writings of Asterius the Sophist. We shall quote both authors *in extenso* in order to settle this matter once and for all.[41]

Pseudo-Dionysius, *De caelesti hierarchia* VII, 4:

Therefore the theology of Scripture has transmitted to us men of the earth the hymns, in which the loftiness of their illumination (ἐλλάμψεως) is revealed in a most holy manner. For like the *rushing of the waters* . . . the one group of this hierarchy exultantly exclaims:

Praised be the Glory of the Lord from His place.

The others respond in loudly sounding that often-celebrated praise of God (δοξολογία) in great piety:

Holy, holy, holy is the Lord Sabaoth,
The whole earth is full of His Glory.

I have described these supreme laudations (ὑμνολογία) of the spirits of the highest heavens according to my best ability in my book 'On the divine hymns' . . . Hence it behooves us . . . to praise the supreme divinity.[42]

119

M. Richard, *Asterii Sophistae Commentariorum in Psalmos quae supersunt:*

Ps. 18: again we encounter the juxtaposition of Isa. 6 : 3 and Ezek. 3 : 12.[43]

Most recently the studies of E. Hammerschmidt dealing with Ethiopic and Coptic liturgies show again the combination of Isa. 6 : 3 and Ezek. 3 : 12-13. They occur in the Ethiopic *Normal Anaphora* and in the Syrian *Basilios Anaphora.*[44] Hammerschmidt arrives at the conclusion that 'all elements of the preambles before the S can be traced to either biblical or late Jewish (mishnaic) concepts and phrases'. These sources and their historical interpretation definitely refute A. Baumstark's, C. W. Dugmore's and their disciples' assumption that S and K are not necessarily related to each other, because the Ezek. passage had to be dropped for reasons of universalism by the Christian authors.

Before summarizing our results, we shall briefly discuss the origin of the T. According to Brightman, the T was 'supernaturally revealed' during the pontificate of St Proclus (434-46).[45] The combination of the epithets 'holy', 'strong' (or 'unique'), and 'eternal' (or 'immortal') was already a standing formula for addressing God in the Apocalypse of Abraham, where many instances of this address occur.[46] Quite a few Jewish apocalyptic writers took over this form, and it is difficult to believe that this particular combination of epithets arose quite suddenly in the Byzantine orbit; for the doctors of that Church were in general quite familiar with the apocryphal and pseudepigraphic literature, as E. Peterson, H. Ball, and J. Daniélou, S.J., especially, have demonstrated. It seems that the T may be considered a periphrastic form of the S, interpreted in trinitarian fashion, and not very far from the character of a litany. In this sense it is still used in the Roman Church on Good Friday. We shall now summarize the main points of our evidence, in order to clarify the established or the most probable facts:

(a) The *K-Yotzer* contains both prophetic visions (Isa. and Ezek.) and elaborates upon the *Merkaba* angelology.

(b) The *K-'Amida* contains mainly Isa., and uses only one verse from Ezek. (3 : 12).

It is certain that (a) existed in pre-Christian times; (b) was introduced into the Synagogue during the first Christian century. Both formulae have roots in Jewish apocalyptic literature.

(c) All Christian Prefaces (except Hippolytus) contain S with angelology, and many of them add verses from Dan. 7.

(d) Most of them mention the interplay between angelic and human worship; this concept is also rooted in pre-Christian Judaism.

(e) In many cases we find a continuous parallelism, which turns from *Dignum et justum*

> to Angelology
> to *Sanctus*
> to Hosanna-*Benedictus*-Hosanna[47]
> to Holy art Thou

the last-named being the incipit and close of the Hebrew benediction of the *'Amida* after the K.

(f) Many Prefaces contain the angelological doctrine of the 'never sleeping' spirits and their 'incessant' exaltation of God. Both conceptions are already well-established in I Enoch and in early rabbinic literature.[48]

(g) Elements from Isa. and Ezek. are usually combined in the preface and S. The verse Ezek. 3:12, however, is omitted in most of them (Roman, Byzantine, Egyptian, Syrian); it is retained in the liturgy of the *Apostolic Constitutions* VII, the Ethiopic Anaphora, and in quite a few angelologies of the Church Fathers.

(h) The Ezek. verse (3:12) does not lend itself to a trinitarian interpretation, while Isa. 6:3 invites it and has been so understood from the second century on. It is suggested that this fact was the real reason for the omission of Ezek. 3:12.

THE MUSICAL TRADITION

I have but a few observations to add concerning the musical tradition of the S; this topic has been frequently and extensively discussed during the last forty years.[49] Little is known about the early practice in performance of the K. We know that it was chanted responsorially in a kind of simple recitative; this was necessary because the Thrice-Holy was always sung by the congregation.

This fact is amply testified to in Talmudic literature.[50] No notation of the old synagogal tradition has come down to us that was written before the eighteenth century, if we set aside the K-parody in the form of a three-part motet, which was perhaps written by a Spanish Marrano in Italy about 1460.[51] If I persist in the task of tracing an ancient tradition in spite of such formidable obstacles, it is due to the method as set by Prof. Wellesz, that blazed a viable path of investigation and has established a pattern and pace to follow.

We shall, therefore, resort to much older, indeed to truly primary sources: to Clement of Alexandria, the Apocalypse of Moses, and to those numerous angelologies, where, as in Rev., psalmody is coupled with the chant of the S.

Clement of Alexandria:

> For this reason also we raise the head and lift the hands towards heaven, and *stand on tiptoe* (τὰς πόδας ἐπεγείρομεν) as we join in the closing outburst of prayer, following the eager flight of the spirit into the intelligible world: and while we thus endeavour to *detach the body* from the earth by lifting it upwards along with the uttered words, we spurn the fetters of the flesh and constrain the soul . . . to ascend into the holy place.[52]

Clement refers here to a peculiar *gestus orationis,* which was well known among the Jewish mystics of antiquity: the lifting of the feet and almost jumping on tiptoe three times exactly timed with each 'Holy' of the K. This custom is practised even today among certain hasidic groups. The question arises here whether Clement also alluded to the S; he says 'as we join in the closing outburst of prayer' (κατὰ τὴν τελευταίαν τῆς εὐχῆς συνεκφωνήσω), which seems to indicate at least a *congregational* response, spoken or chanted.

It is all but impossible to state what was the last congregational response in the Alexandrian Mass during the second century. Yet, if we may trust the sources that have come to light thus far, one may conjecture that it was either the S or the acclamation: 'One is holy . . .' (Εἷς ἅγιος, εἷς κύριος, κτλ).[53]

If the S was the last public response, we may apply Clement's remark about the tiptoeing to it, and understand it as an observation on a more or less familiar gesture, which originated with the Jewish mystics, perhaps even among the Egyptian Therapeutae, who paid considerable attention to dance-like movements in prayer, as we know from Philo.[54]

We recall also that in Rev. and in the Apocalypse of Moses the S is coupled with, or surrounded by psalmody and Alleluia-singing. It was the same Alexandrian Clement who gave us, in his *Paedagogus,* a valuable description of the practice of psalmody among the Jews of Egypt. This is a lengthy, well-known passage, wherein he suggests that the mode of the Jewish psalmody was a variant of the *Tropos Spondeiakos.*[55] Plutarch offers in his book on music a technical analysis of the *Tropos Spondeiakos,* so that we may—however roughly—reconstruct the skeleton of that mode.

I have closely examined this mode and Plutarch's analysis of the *Tropos Spondeiakos,* also its identity with the mode mentioned by Clement, in four previous publications. I may, therefore, refer to those without repeating the details of my investigation. It will suffice, if I briefly summarize the conclusions I reached many years ago.[56]

(1) The mode of psalmody mentioned by Clement is the *Tropos Spondeiakos.*

(2) This mode consists of a hexachord based on E, whereby either the F or C, yet never both at the same time, are omitted. Sometimes a subtonal D is added.

(3) To the same mode belong many melodies of the oldest strata of Gregorian chant, especially the S in the *Te Deum,* the *Gloria* XV, and passages of *Gloria* XIV, also the psalm verse of the Antiphon *Postquam surrexit Dominus* on Maundy Thursday.

(4) A number of Byzantine tunes belong to the same mode; also ancient prayer-tunes of the Yemenite Jews, e.g., their *Sh'ma',* which is almost literally identical with the S of the *Te Deum.* The mode is also known in Nestorian and Syrian chant.

(5) The Doric Spondaic mode or *Spondeiakos* mode originated in the Hellenistic world of the Near East; its solemn ethos was acclaimed by numerous Hellenistic writers, such as Dionysius of Halicarnassus and Plutarch, to name only two eminent authors.[57]

(6) The mode is common to early Jewish chant of the first Christian centuries, as well as to the early Church; its origin in all cases lies in the Mediterranean orbit.

(7) The *Sh'ma'* forms an integral part of the *K-'Amida;* and the oldest Jewish traditions (Yemenite, Babylonian, and to a lesser extent Kurdistani) maintain the tradition of chanting the K in the *Tropos Spondeiakos.*[58]

THE SACRED BRIDGE II

TROPOS SPONDEIAKOS.

ABBREVIATIONS : HUCA = Hebrew Union College Aunnal.
LU   = Liber usualis.

HUCA 1947, *p.* 427-428

(1)

or

(4 a) (b)

Ue-ba-ne-he- ha. Sof pa-sug. 'At-nah. Te- bir, Tar-ha; Kadma v'asla'; Sof pasug.

(6)

V' ha- ko- ha- nim   v'- ha- 'am ha- om- dim ba- 'a- pa- na etc.

'af hu' hayā   mitz kad ven. *etc.* ve' o- mer la kem utharm.

(7)   *etc.*

Niš-mat col hay t'varech *etc.*

min ha- 'ó- lam   'ad ha- 'o- lam 'at- ta 'el.

(11) Cp. with ♯ 1, 2 a, 6, 4 6, 7, 8, 10.   HUCA 1947 *p.* 428

Καὶ ὢν ἐν κόλ- ποις τοῦ Πα - τρός....

ἱ- λάσ- θη- τι ταῖς ἁ- μαρ- τίαις ἡ- μῶν.

Te Deum (first verses)

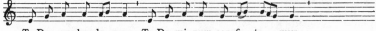

Te De- um lau-da- mus, Te Do- mi- num con-fi- te- mur,

(later verses)

Ve- ne- randum tu- um ve- rum Tu Patris sempi-ternus es Fi- li- us.

124

Gloria (LU p. 55)

Glo- ri- a   in excel- sis De- o...   Qui tol- lis   pec-ca- ta mundi,

etc.

su-sci- pe de-pre- ca- ti- o- nem nostram.

Yemenite Sh'ma (IT vol. I p. 71)

(a)   *etc.*

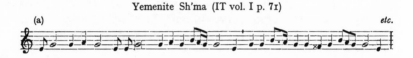

Yemenite Thora-cantillation (IT vol. II)

(b)

As for the Gregorian tradition, the *Sanctus* XVIII is usually considered the oldest version.[59] It seems, in its present form, to be related
to the *Tropos Spondeiakos,* though the *finalis* is different, and the
emphasis upon the B is alien to the Greek mode. The final notes of
the phrases of the *Te Deum* close with G before the verse 'Tu rex
gloriae,' and end with E thereafter. This trait shows close proximity
to the Mozarabic *Pater noster,* to which I have drawn attention in
former publications.[60] Peter Wagner had already noticed this resemblance and concluded: 'Occasionally such types of recitation connect themselves with the Greek tetrachords. In this case the (Greek)
Dorian is represented as E–F–G–A. . . . I hold these speculations to
be entirely mistaken. In our tune (*Pater noster*) the Dorian tetrachord
is exceeded already in the first part; and the same objection is valid
for other types of recitation. This practice of recitation has nothing
in common with Greek music; it comes directly from the Jewish
and Christian liturgies of the Near East. . . .'[61]

In comparing the formulae of the Anaphora with the Mozarabic
Pater noster, the *Gloria* XV, the *Te Deum,* etc., K. Levy reaches
conclusions which somewhat differ from those of P. Wagner: he
successfully parallels the various occurrences of the tune under

examination in the Byzantine Anaphora with Latin traditions. Moreover, he adds to his list of parallel formulae the *Exultet,* which seems dubious to me, and the Lamentations, which already P. Wagner had compared with a Yemenite tradition quoted by Idelsohn, and which I had included in my list of Hellenistic formulae.[62] The formula for the *Flectamus genua* E–G–A–B–A–A is again an all but identical variant of the ancient tune of *Nishmat* which I had included in my own list.[63] It runs: E–A–G–B–A–G–A. *Satis superque!* It can be seen that Mr. Levy, approaching the problem from quite different premises than I had envisaged, has attained exactly the same results as I did. He even assumes a 'broad pre-octoechic modal area that combines aspects of the modes on E and G'.[64]

Let us now survey the field covered: musically speaking, the oldest tradition of K–S can be traced back to the second century C.E., and there is a good probability, to judge from the widespread and the invariably ancient texts connected with the tunes of the *Clementine Spondeiakos,* that that particular tradition had its origin in or around Alexandria. The stability of the texts, the mixture of angelologies from Isaiah, Ezekiel, and Daniel (which Mr. Levy did not mention), the position of the S before the *anamnesis*—the most memorable place of the liturgy!—the many biblical and some post-biblical Hebraisms, the possibility of trinitarian interpretation of the S, of christological significance of the Hosanna, the *gestus orationis* in K and S, common to Jews and Christians: all these factors let us believe that indeed the musical tradition of the S was established early in Christianity. The identity with the psalmody of Alexandrian Jews of Clement's time, with the primitive Yemenite tradition, with Byzantine and Gregorian patterns make it more than likely that we have succeeded in tracing an important case of liturgical and musical interdependence between Church and Synagogue.

CHAPTER SIX

Two Hymns for Passover and Good Friday

I

THE mythology of all nations is replete with bloody fables of patricide, matricide, and fratricide; in those cases where gods are involved, the slaying of a relative was, of course, a deicide. The archetypes of Tammuz, the Cretan Zeus, Attys or Osiris-Apis seem to be as old as mankind itself. Indeed the stories of deicide of an animistic or crudely polytheistic civilization were often but a reflection of posterity's shock at earlier lawlessness. Small wonder that already in antiquity the most famous of these tales were interpreted allegorically, that is, as astral, solar, or generally, as calendaric myths. Thereby they lost, as disguised sun-myths, most of their horror—in fact, they were viewed as poetic visions of the seasons, or of the eternal cycle of life and death.

Not with such harmless fables are we concerned, but with a grim and pseudo-historical element in the doctrine of Christianity. We are all familiar with this Christian concept of deicide, and while in the last Council's *Schema Concerning the Jews* it was considerably modified, it remained in essence unchanged. It is also well known that the first insinuation of deicide occurs in the Johannine gospel, and it seems superfluous to waste many words on this topic.

It is less well known that the articulate accusation of deicide has given birth to a literary work of art, which up to this day is solemnly recited and chanted in the Catholic liturgy for Good Friday. As this liturgical poem, due to its artistic excellence, has had a great impact upon all means of communication, especially upon the pictorial arts and on music, its anti-Jewish effect has been more massive and more violent than the Gospel story itself, which is read in Latin and not very loudly.

127

The poem referred to here is called *Improperia,* meaning 'Reproaches', and describes in poetic language the accusations levelled by the dying Jesus on the cross at his people, the Jews. How strong its influence was upon the men who shaped the liturgy can be seen from the fact that the most hateful anti-Jewish passage of the entire Catholic liturgy followed upon the *Improperia.* This passage, composed by St Augustine, was eliminated by Pope John XXIII together with the expression 'Perfidi Judaei', and is no longer a part of the service, whereas the *Improperia* were permitted to stay:

Non dicant Judaei. . . .
Let not the Jews say: we did not kill Christ. For they submitted him to Pilate as judge, so that they seemed almost absolved from his death. For when Pilate said to them: you kill him, they replied: we are not permitted to kill anybody. They wanted to shift the infamy of their foul deed to a human judge; but did they deceive God, the divine judge? Whatever Pilate did, and wherein he was committed, he was to a degree an accomplice; yet in comparison with them, he was much less culpable . . . etc.
(Transl. E. W.)

And now we shall quote, with but a few explanatory remarks, the text of the Latin *Improperia* in translation. Of other Churches, both the Byzantine and the Georgian rituals contain similar, though somewhat cruder and more primitive texts of the same content. Actually, the oldest MS of the *Improperia* was published by Kekelidze as part of the Georgian Kanonarion in Tiflis in 1912. This earliest extant variant seems to have originated in the seventh century. The following is the present Roman version:

(1) My people, what have I done to you? And in what way have I saddened you? Answer me!
Because I led you out of Egypt: you have prepared a cross for your Saviour.
(1a) [Here the choir falls in with the bilingual *Trisagion*]
Agios o Theos—Sanctus Deus
Agios ischyros—Sanctus fortis
Agios athanatos, eleison imas—Sanctus immortalis, miserere nobis.
(2) Because I led you through the desert for forty years and fed you with manna, and introduced you into a very good land: you have prepared a cross for your Saviour.
(2a) Bilingual *Trisagion.*
(3) What should I have done for you that I did not do? I have planted you as

my most precious vine: but you have become all too sour: for with vinegar you have quenched my thirst: and with a lance you have pierced the body of your Saviour.

(3a) Bilingual *Trisagion*.

(4) Because of you I have slain (*flagellavi*) the Egyptian through his first-born sons: and you have delivered me flogged (*flagellatum*).

Refrain: My people, etc.

(5) I led you out of Egypt after having drowned the Pharaoh in the Red Sea: and you have delivered me to the princes of the priests.

Refrain: My people, etc.

(6) I have opened the sea before you: and you have opened my body with a lance.

Refrain: My people, etc.

(7) I went before you in the column of the fiery cloud: and you have led me to the tribunal of Pilate.

Refrain: My people, etc.

(8) I fed you with manna in the desert: and you fell on me with slaps and whips.

Refrain: My people, etc.

(9) To drink I gave you the water of grace (*aqua salutis*) from the rock: and you gave me gall and vinegar to drink.

Refrain: My people, etc.

(10) I have hit, for your sake, the kings of Canaan: and you have hit my head with a stick.

Refrain: My people, etc.

(11) I granted you the royal sceptre: and you granted me a crown of thorns.

Refrain: My people, etc.

(12) I have exalted you with great strength (*virtute*): and you have hanged me on the gallows of the cross (*in patibulo crucis*).

Refrain: My people, etc.

Most of these motifs will be very familiar to the Jewish reader; they sound like an anti-Jewishly twisted version of the enumeration of God's benefits to His people as recited on Passover under the name *Dayenu* (It would have sufficed). Indeed, if we were to seek a name for this strange form, we might call it a midrashic litany on God's benefits and on the Passion of Christ interwoven with each other. Strictly speaking, it is a parody, in the classical sense of the term, of the *Dayenu* of the Passover ritual. Let us now compare the list of motifs: verse (1) is identical in content in both versions; the Latin verses 6–10 correspond, though not quite literally, with the Hebrew verses 3–9. In order to enable the reader to compare the

129

two sources in question, we quote here the *Dayenu* litany in its entirety, though in English, in the usual translation.

(1) What abundant favours hath the Almighty conferred upon us! For had He brought us forth from Egypt, and had not executed judgment upon the Egyptians: It would have sufficed.
(2) For had He inflicted justice upon them, and had not executed judgment upon their gods: It would have sufficed.
(3) For had He executed judgment upon their gods, and had not slain their first-born: It would have sufficed.
(4) For had He slain their first-born, and had not bestowed their substance upon us: It would have sufficed.
(5) For had He bestowed their substance upon us, and had not then divided the Red Sea: It would have sufficed.
(6) For had He divided the Sea for us, and had not caused us to pass over on dry land: It would have sufficed.
(7) For had He caused us to pass over on dry land, and had not plunged our oppressors into the midst of the sea: It would have sufficed.
(8) For had He plunged our oppressors into the midst of the sea, and had not supplied our needs in the desert for forty years, and had not fed us with manna: It would have sufficed.
(9) For had He fed us with manna, and had not given us the Sabbath:
                           It would have sufficed.
(10) For had He given us the Sabbath, and had not brought us nigh unto Mount Sinai: It would have sufficed.
(11) For had He brought us nigh unto Mount Sinai, and had not given us the Law: It would have sufficed.ʻ
(12) For had He given us the Law, and had not brought us to the Land of Israel: It would have sufficed.
(13) For had he brought us to the Land of Israel, and had not erected for us the House of His Choice [the Temple]:   It would have sufficed.
(14) Had He erected the House of His Choice, and not given us a High Priest: It would have sufficed.
(15) How much, therefore, are we indebted for the manifold favours the Almighty hath conferred upon us? He brought us forth from Egypt; executed judgment on the Egyptians, and on their gods; slew their first-born; gave us their substance; divided the sea for us; caused us to pass over on dry land; plunged our oppressors into the midst of the sea; supplied our needs in the desert for forty years; gave us manna to eat; gave us the Sabbath; brought us nigh to Mount Sinai; and gave us His Law; brought us into the Land of Israel; and erected for us the House of His Choice [Holy Temple], wherein to make atonement for all our sins.

The Latin text has twelve regular verses, the first three of which close with the bilingual *Trisagion,* together fifteen verses. It stands to reason that this number has not been chosen arbitrarily, for the *Dayenu,* its *Vorlage,* also consists of fifteen verses, according to Finkelstein's revision of the text.[1] In the Hebrew text, however, no motif is repeated, as happens in the Latin and even more in the Byzantine text; this fact suggests that the repetitions were made in order to attain the necessary number 15. In the Catholic ritual fifteen candles are kindled at the beginning, and after each verse one is extinguished; only the last one remains aflame. Fifteen is the numerical value of the characters *Jod-He,* the abbreviated Name of Deity. This significance of fifteen was surely known in the early rabbinic literature.[2]

Without further ado I shall now state my thesis, which I shall try to prove in the subsequent exposition: the Latin *Improperia* represent an old anti-Jewish parody of the *Dayenu* of the Passover-Haggadah. Even in the high Middle Ages the vicinity of the Hebrew tradition seems to have been felt by some Catholic authorities. Thus we read, not without wonderment, in the *Rationale* of Durandus, one of the foremost source-works of Catholic liturgy, written during the thirteenth century (about the *Improperia*):

> . . . quod versu sequitur: Parasti salvatori tuo crucem. . . . Cantat autem sacerdos quasi *hebraice* in persona salvatoris; acoliti cantant *graece* Ayos atheos [sic!] quasi in *persona graecorum:* chorus respondet: Sanctus, sanctus, in persona latinorum. . . .[3]

The first traces of a list of God's benefits to Israel are found in the following passages of the Bible: Ps. 135 : 8-12; Ps. 136 : 10-22; Ps. 78 : 12-16. When compared with the later Hebrew source, we see that some motifs are still missing: the killing of the first-born, the giving of the Law on Mt Sinai, the feeding of manna, and the erection of the Temple. The order of succession of the motifs is also different.

The strong resemblance between the two texts is quite obvious; but it does not originate in the biblical sources. We should first establish the age of the Hebrew *Vorlage,* and shall thereafter attempt to trace the genesis of the *Improperia.* According to E. D. Goldschmidt, L. Finkelstein and other scholars, parts or even the entire concept of the *Dayenu* were already familiar in the Tannaitic age. The reference to the erection of the Temple and to the High Priest, as well as the absence of a supplication for the rebuilding of the Temple give us a sort of *terminus ante quem,* as in most prayers after the Temple's destruction a plea for its rebuilding would hardly be lacking. Finkelstein draws attention to the fact that neither Moses nor Jerusalem is mentioned in our text. He suggests certain reasons for these omissions, well known from rabbinic literature, and reaches the conclusion that the 'litany of benefits' originated in the second century B.C.E. As the *Improperia* are in form and style much nearer to the post-biblical, midrashic type of the 'benefit litany' than to the biblical patterns, we must now seek for the transition of motifs from rabbinic sources to the sphere of Christianity. One of the earliest traces of it may be found in the apocryphal Acts of Pilate and its continuation, the so-called Gospel of Nicodemus. There we read:[4]

And Pilate was wroth and said unto the Jews: Your nation is alway seditious and ye rebel against your benefactors. The Jews say: Against what benefactors? Pilate saith: According as I have heard, your God brought you out of Egypt out of hard bondage, and led you safe through the sea as by dry land, and in the wilderness he nourished you with manna and gave you quails, and gave you water to drink out of a rock, and gave unto you a law. And in all these things ye provoked your God to anger, and sought out a molten calf, and angered your God. . . .
(Translation by M. R. James.)

Some scholars, such as K. L. Schmidt and W. Michaelis, have conjectured that parts of the apocryphon came from the circles of Judaeo-Christians; this may be upheld only for a rather small part, chapters 12-19, which may indeed indicate heterodox ideas.[5] The age of this compilation—it is actually not more than that—is uncertain; it is generally assumed to have originated at the end of the fourth or early in the fifth century; the fictitious author, Hananya, calls himself later Aeneas, and seems to have been a contemporary of Emperor Theodosius II.[6] During the latter's reign, a rather strange event seems to have taken place: a plague struck Byzantium and an earthquake excited the population so much, that at an *ad hoc* arranged service something like the *Improperia* seems to have been recited. The story is intentionally kept obscure, because the sacrifice of a child seems incidentally to have taken place, which is but poorly camouflaged in the sources.[7] This is the first reference to a public liturgy where some early form of the *Improperia* is documented. Speaking of sources, the evidence for the inclusion of the *Improperia* in the liturgy is not conclusive before the seventh century. According to Dom Martène's list of MSS outside Rome, which dates from the middle of the eighteenth century, we should find the text of the Latin *Improperia* already in a *Pontificale ecclesiae Apamiensis* in Syria, and in an ancient MS of the Colbertina. Both MSS are said to have originated before the sixth century, according to Martène. None of these sources has ever been found or seen since. Moreover, it is well known that Martène's datings are to be viewed with the utmost scepticism.[8] Yet from the seventh century onwards, the Latin text is fully documented, even in the Mozarabic version.[9]

II

We shall now analyse the structure of the Latin text. It begins with a verse, which goes on as refrain through the entire piece. It is, as many others, kept in OT phraseology, and we encounter paraphrases of the subsequent biblical passages: Mic. 6 : 3-4; Deut. 8 : 2; 8 : 3; 8 : 7; Isa. 5 : 4; Jer. 2 : 21; Ps. 69 : 22. The first part, the so-called Great *Improperia,* consists of three verses, three times interspersed with the bilingual *Trisagion.* The following verses, or Small *Improperia,* consist of nine *stichoi,* always interspersed with the refrain, which is our first verse, 'Popul. meus, quid feci tibi?' etc. . . . . Our particular attention is directed to the conspicuous parallelistic verbs which permeate the Latin text; thus, for instance, if the first clause has:

Ego propter te *flagellavi* Aegyptum, etc.,

the second has:

et tu me *flagellatum* tradidisti.

or:

Ego ante te *aperui* mare: et tu *aperuisti* lancea latus meum. . . .

This identity of verbs occurs six times in the nine Small *Improperia;* sometimes we find only similar expressions, such as this one:

133

Ego te exaltavi magna virtue: et tu me suspendisti in patibulo crucis.

This sounds like a bad pun in Latin, for 'exaltare' means 'to set' or 'make high', the Hebrew *romem* or *godel,* whereas 'suspendisti' signifies 'hang high'. Actually, such and other forms let us believe that the Latin text is a paraphrase of an originally Syriac or even Hebrew text. There are other indications to suggest this. Verses 1 and 2 both contain the word 'eduxi'; verse 3 introduces quite unexpectedly Isa. 5, the Song of the Vineyard. This makes no sense in Latin, but if we translate the last preceding line 'parasti crucem Salvatori tuo' into Hebrew, the operative word, that for 'parasti', is the same as that for 'fecisti', and this leads quite naturally to the quoted Isaiah passage in the words: 'Quid ultra debui facere tibi, et non feci?', but in Latin the link with the foregoing 'parasti' is weak and unrecognizable. There are other such cue-words: the word 'tradidisti' connecting verses 4 and 5; the 'ante te', linking 6 and 7; the 'Salvatori tuo', verses 1-3. We sense here traces of the original Syriac or Hebrew anadiplosis or developed parallelism, familiar to us from the psalms of ascent (Pss. 120-134) the prayer-book and the *piyyutim*. Investigating now not only the parallelism of the verses, but also of the verbs, we arrive at the following list. In the order of verses (which do *not* show, in the Latin text, verbal identity) we have:

(5) Ego eduxi te de Aegypto, demerso Pharaone in Mare rubrum: et tu me tradidisti principibus sacerdotum.

If we translate the 'eduxi' with '*hozethi*', the opposite 'tradidisti' (periphrastically 'traditus sum' to save the parallelism) is rendered by the Huphal-form of the same verb, as it occurs in the meaning of 'tradere' in Jer. 38 : 22:

Ecce omnes mulieres quae remanserunt in domo regis Juda *educentur* ad principes regis Babylonis.

It is even possible that the Latin redactor had this very verse in mind, for the Vulgate uses here the word 'educere', and the *Vetus Itala* has here 'tradere'. The English translation is:

134

Behold, all the women left in the house of the king of Judah were being led out to the princes of the king of Babylon and were saying:

> Your trusted friends have deceived you
> and prevailed against you;
> now that your feet are sunk in the mire,
> they turn away from you.
>
> (Rev. Standard Version)

(7) Ego ante te praeivi in columna nubis: et tu me duxisti ad praetorium Pilati.

Here the two opposite words are 'praeivi' and 'duxisti'. Translating, according to the Pentateuch text, the 'praeivi' with '*Hithalachti*', the 'duxisti' becomes simply '*holachtani*', as in II Kings 24 : 15. In English:

And he carried away Jehoiachin to Babylon; the King's mother . . . he took into captivity (*holich*) from Jerusalem to Babylon.

(8) Ego te pavi manna per desertum: et tu me cecidisti alapis et flagellis.

'Pavi manna' stands against 'cecidisti'. Here there are two ways of re-translation: (a) with '*yarod et ha-man*' (as in Num. 11 : 9); then the 'cecidisti' corresponds to '*oridem*' in Hos. 7 : 12, 'to fell', 'to bring to fall'; or (b) metaphorically, as '*he-echilanu eth ha-man*', as in the *Dayenu* text, and the idea of eating the sword or the whip (*herev t'uchlu*) in Isa. 1 : 20 and similar passages, establishing the root *ochal*.

(12) Ego te exaltavi magna virtute: et tu me suspendisti in patibulo crucis.

We spoke about this unintentional pun; here '*romamti*' is set against '*yarim*' (as in Job 39 : 27, or metaphorically in Num. 17 : 2 and similar passages).

Sometimes the redactor of the Latin text chose the same word and verb, although it did not fit quite correctly. Thus we have:

(10) Ego propter te Chananaeorum reges percussi: et tu percussisti arundine caput meum.

The 'percutere' of the antecedent clause signifies simply 'to destroy' or 'to annihilate', or 'to conquer'. Yet the succeeding clause uses 'percutere' in the sense of 'to hit', 'to beat', 'to pierce'. If we for a moment think of a Syriac *Vorlage*, the first 'percutere' corresponds with *qtal*, the second with the noun *q'tilin* or *qtalya*, which is nothing else but the *arundo* of the Latin text, a band for the forehead.

We summarize: All verses of the *Improperia* begin with the same word 'ego'.
All verses of the *Dayenu* begin with the same word '*Ilu*', the number of verses is the same—15—in both cases.
Cue-words are amply used in both texts.
The literary motifs are mostly identical.
The parallelism of verbs and of sentences make us believe that the original text of the *Improperia* was Syriac or Hebrew.

These premises suggest a conjecture that the author was (a) familiar with Semitic languages, possibly with rabbinic texts, and (b) that he knew, in particular, the text of the *Dayenu*. Yet all attempts to locate the author in the circle of the redactors of the Acts of Pilate, or of the Gospel of Nicodemus have led nowhere.

Hitherto we have bypassed a source which in our opinion is the real origin, *the* main source, *fons et origo,* of both the theological concept of deicide and of the text of the *Improperia*. This source is the *Homily on the Passion* of Melito, Bishop of Sardes.[10]

He lived about 120-185 C.E., which makes him a contemporary of Emperor Marcus Aurelius, to whom he also addressed an *Apology*. He was probably the first truly erudite man to visit the holy places of Palestine, where he lived for some time. Unfortunately his fragmentary travelogue is lost, as are most of his other writings. He was interested in questions concerning the Canon of the OT, and his contemporaries and immediate successors considered him a great scholar as well as a most effective orator; Tertullian called him 'elegans et declamatorium ingenium', an elegant and most eloquent spirit. In his dogmatic attitude he took a rather orthodox, rigidly anti-Marcionite, anti-gnostic stand; yet he belongs not to the Pauline tradition, but to the Johannine. For later historians he was interesting less for his writings, which soon fell into oblivion, than for his championship of the quartodeciman movement. Since the

Council of Nicaea Easter must fall on the first Sunday after the full moon of the spring equinox. This was not always so. In the province of Asia Proconsularis the Christians celebrated Easter together with the Jewish Passover, that is on the 14th of *Nissan,* following the report of the Johannine Gospel. This meant that on that evening—coincidental with the Jewish *Seder*—Good Friday and Easter Sunday were celebrated together; the death and the resurrection of Jesus were put on the same day as the memory of the Exodus from Egypt. The Asiatic Christians championed this custom and stuck to it until the Council of Nicaea in 325, which set the canonical Easter dates. We need not enter here into a minute description of that long and casuistic struggle, as it is sufficient to know that Melito was one of its most effective and important protagonists.

About fifty years ago, fragments from a codex in the British Museum, from the library of Mr Chester Beatty, and from the library of the University of Michigan were put together by Prof. Campbell Bonner, and, behold, they together added up to the hitherto lost *Homily on the Passion,* or in Greek, Εἶς τὸ πάθος by Melito, Bishop of Sardes in Asia Proconsularis, the ancient Lydia. The MS is in Greek, but many Syriac fragments of the same text have come down to us, and it is an open question in which language the homily was first written. Today some scholars are inclined to believe that the original was Syriac; we shall see that even the Greek text contains certain Semitisms.

Yet before dealing with these aspects, we should add a word about the relationship between quartodecimans and Jews. In their dogmatic ideas the quartodecimans emphasized, perhaps more than any other Christian sect, the differences between the OT and the NT, between the new religion and its mother. For they were anything but Judaeo-Christians, most of them being gentiles through and through, and striving to be good Roman citizens, as we saw from Melito's address to Marcus Aurelius, and to be good Christians. The crucial part of our problem, the origin of the *Improperia,* is to be found in the following passage (I follow the translation of the first editor and discoverer, Prof. C. Bonner; see n. 10 above):

Melito, *Homily on the Passion,* No. 87:

Come hither, Israel, and plead thy cause against me
  concerning thine ingratitude.
What value didst thou set upon thy making by his hand,
Upon the finding of thy fathers, upon thy going down into
  Egypt and thy nurturing there by the good Joseph?
How didst thou esteem the ten plagues?
How didst thou value the pillar by night, and
  the cloud by day,
And the crossing of the Red Sea?
How didst thou value the gift of manna from heaven,
The gift of water from the rock,
The making of the Law in Horeb,
And the land of thine inheritance and the gifts there?
Of what worth to thee were thy sufferers, all of whom
  he healed,
Himself coming to them,
And the withered hand, which he restored to the body?
Honoured by the lame, honoured by the blind, and by
  the sick. . . .

Here we encounter the first extended 'welfare-litany' with the anti-Jewish twist. The number of benefits mentioned here are fourteen, in the Syriac fragment fifteen. Is it possible that Melito emphasized the number 14, because he was a quartodeciman, stressing the 14th of *Nissan?* It is hard to decide. What distinguishes this piece of harangue or diatribe from the *Improperia,* is the person of the speaker: here it is not the dying Jesus, but the homilist, pure and simple. The verbal parallelisms are absent here, although they occur in other parts of the homily, for instance in the dramatic statement:
No. 96:

He who hung the earth in its place is hanged,
He who fixed the heavens is fixed upon the cross,
He who made all things fast, is made fast upon the tree,
The Master has been insulted, God has been murdered,
The King of Israel has been slain by an Israelitish hand.

Here we have both: the parallelisms together with the accusation of deicide—by no means the first one of the homily—and one more thing, interesting to the philologist: suffix-rhymes in the Greek text. I quote a few lines from this passage:

138

Two Hymns for Passover and Good Friday

ὁ κρεμάσας τὴν γῆν κρέμαται . . .
ὁ στηρίξας τὰ πάντα ἐπὶ ξύλου ἐστήρικται . . . .

Even more sharply:

ὁ Θεὸς πεφόνευται,
ὁ βασιλεὺς Ἰσραὴλ ἀνήρηται.

Now, suffix-rhymes are totally alien to Greek poetry; they are a legacy of Syriac poetry, where they, as in Hebrew, play a considerable part. Even stronger are the suffix-rhymes in the title of the homily; there they appear together with the old Semitic device called isosyllabism: two or three lines have the same number of syllables, regardless of their accents. Yannai and other early *paytanim* employed this device; in my opinion it can be traced back to the quotations from the lost Book of the Lord's Wars (*sefer milhamoth hashem*) and the Book of the Just (*sefer hayashar*), which all lean towards isosyllabism. As for the beginning of the homily in Greek:

ἡ μὲν γραφὴ τῆς Ἑβραϊκῆς ἐξόδου ἀνέγνωσται,	(16 syllables)
καὶ τὰ ῥήματα τοῦ μυστηρίου διασεσάφηται,	(16 syllables)
πῶς τὸ πρόβατον θύεται	(8 syllables)
καὶ πῶς ὁ λαὸς σώζεται.	(8 syllables)

translated:

The Scripture of the Hebrew Exodus has been read,
and the words of the mystery have been explained
how the sheep is sacrificed
and how the People is saved.

Shortly before the beginning of the diatribe quoted above, Melito anticipates it in more narrative style, and again the list comprises fourteen benefits, namely: the Patriarchs; guidance to Egypt; pillar of fire; shelter by a cloud; division of the Red Sea; destruction of Pharaoh; manna from heaven; water from the rock; the Law from Mt Horeb; inheritance of the land; issuing of prophets; raising of kings; healing of sufferers; raising of the dead.

Before we discuss some special points, we are bound to ask about the influence of this seemingly forgotten work upon the doctors of the Church. Prof. Bonner has, in his lucid introduction, given a rather full list of the authors who stand under Melito's influence. Instead of repeating his findings I shall give now only a brief list of the most important authors: Apollinaris; Hippolytus; Pseudo-Cyprian; Pseudo-Origen; Ephrem Syrus; the Jewish apostate, Romanus of Byzantium, greatest poet of the Greek Church; Proclus; Epiphanius, and, naturally, the most vicious enemy of Judaism in the long list of Church Fathers, St John Chrysostom. From this it is pretty clear where the Byzantine and Latin authors took their invectives, their poetry, and their rhetoric from—it all can be traced back to Melito.

III

It is easy to shape a conjecture such as this one on a *prima facie* evidence, but a serious scholar is obliged to trace every link of the chain, if possible. This is a stern postulate, but a just one. I shall not claim to satisfy it completely here, but I shall attempt to trace back the most important elements of Melito's homily to Jewish, biblical and extra-biblical sources.

As the homily says, the Greek or Syriac text of Exod. 12 : 1-15 was first read at the celebration of the Passah. Melito calls it one of the two mysteries, of which the Passion is the second. This typology is not his idea, but occurs first in Justin's Dialogue *Contra Tryphonem*. Melito goes on to his christological and exegetical interpretation of Exod. 11-35. His extremely dramatic description of the ten plagues and especially of the killing of the first-born may be traced back to the Wisdom of Solomon, where we find similarly gloomy pictures of the same scene, esp. 71 : 1-18. Yet in one extremely important detail Melito deviates from Scripture as well as from the Wisdom of Solomon and even from Philo's *Life of Moses*. He says (and I quote Bonner's translation):

No. 16:

> When the sheep is sacrificed, and the Passover is eaten,
> and the mystery is fulfilled, and the people is made glad,
> and Israel is sealed, then came the angel to smite Egypt. . . .

Most emphatically, Melito addresses the angel:

Two Hymns for Passover and Good Friday

No. 31-32:

. . . the death of the sheep became the life of the people, and the blood abashed the angel. Tell me, angel, what stayed thy hand, the sacrifice of the sheep or the life of the Lord? . . . Therefore didst thou not smite Israel, but madest wretched Egypt childless.

Here Melito deviates sharply from both the scriptural and the haggadic text, which both insist that it was the Lord Himself who slew the first-born. Here the homilist was in a dilemma; he wanted to show the suffering Jesus whom he, in orthodox christological fashion, identified with God, as the force that brings life, not death. This is eloquently stated; the passage is fortified by the device of rhyme and isosyllabism, of which I give a brief sample:

No. 32:

λέγε μοι, ὦ ἄγγελε, τί ἐδυσωπήθης,	
τὴν τοῦ προβάτου σφαγὴν	(7 syllables)
ἢ τὴν τοῦ κυρίου ζωήν;	(7 syllables)
τὸ τοῦ προβάτου αἷμα	(7 syllables)
ἢ τὸ τοῦ κυρίου πνεῦμα;	(7 syllables)

In stressing the archetypal analogy between the Passover and the Passion Melito was, as far as I know, the first author to stress the conventional christological relation between OT and NT. He does it in a clever parable, which reads like a genuine midrash, but which I cannot reproduce here. I shall, instead, emphasize certain characteristic details, which may permit conclusions about the origin of Melito's thinking. I have singled out, for this occasion, six points and passages of the homily, which, to a certain extent, show the way to further investigations.

(1) No. 82:

But thou wast not Israel, for thou didst not see God, thou didst not perceive the Lord.

This refers to the passage Gen. 32:31, which was misunderstood already by Philo,[11] whereas Melito bypasses silently the interpretation of Gen. 32:32. As the former version *p'niēl* from *seeing God* was often repeated, we suggest that it was included in the Books of

141

Testimonies, which conveyed a good deal of rabbinic and midrashic material to the Hellenistic world. If this was unintentionally mistaken, the following error was quite intended:

(2) No. 46:

What is the pascha? It is so called from that which befell; that is Passover (i.e., Pascha) from 'suffer' and 'be suffering' (*pathein, paschein*).

Melito had been in Palestine for a considerable time; he certainly mastered Syriac, if not as his first, then as his second tongue; he was an erudite man, and interested in the Canon of the OT. Yet the pun Pascha-Passion is totally unintelligible in Syriac, and far-fetched in Greek; it sounds tolerably well in Latin, but that was not the vernacular in those parts of the Empire. Justin's reference to the Passion (*Dial.*, 40 : 3) omits any hint of the Passover, and could hardly have served as *Vorlage* for Melito, as Prof. Bonner suggests. In my opinion Melito used this intentionally wrong etymology because he wanted to avoid every unnecessary Hebraism; Dr J. Blank is probably right in remarking on this: 'One may observe in the quartodeciman texts, and especially with Melito, that the all too close vicinity of the Jewish Passa created an anti-Jewish polemic among them, because one wished to avoid any suspicion of Judaizing.'[12]

Melito concludes his vision of God's master-plan (the *Heilsgeschichte*) with the archetypes of Christ, of which more later on. When he has done with the OT and its christological interpretation, yet without letting Jesus appear concretely, he opens the new chapter on his mystery, that of the Passion, with the following Greek words:

(3) No. 66:

(ἀμὴν) οὗτως ἀφικόμενον ἐξ οὐρανῶν ἐπὶ τὴν γῆν διὰ τὸν πάσχοντα. . . .

In English:

Now many other things were made known by many prophets concerning the mystery of the Passover, which is Christ, to whom be glory for ever and ever. Amen. When he had thus come (ἀφικόμενον) from heaven to earth for the sake of suffering man. . . .

The word '*aphikomenos*', which means 'arrived', 'to come to', has a similar sound as the '*aphikomon*' in the text of the Passover Haggadah. The word 'ἀφικόμενος' comes from ἀφικνέομαι, and occurs mainly in poetic works, in Homer, Sophocles, Euripides, much more rarely in prose writers. And while the style of the homily is certainly rhetorical, it is not exactly poetry. Why did Melito use this rather recherché expression? It is my belief that he wanted to mimic the Passover *halachah* instead: 'One does not dismiss after the Passover the *aphikomon*'. This enigmatic passage was already formulated by Melito's time and, with or without the framework of the midrash of the 'four sons', constituted an integral part of the Jewish ritual. It seems to me suspicious that at the end of Melito's midrash on the Exodus he uses that very expression which characterizes the reply to the faithful Jew, the *hacham*. However that may be, I think we might reconsider the customary interpretation of *aphikomon* in the light of the Hellenistic *aphikomenos*; in this case the *halachah* should read: 'We do not dismiss the guest after the Passa-meal'.[13]

The method of constant analogizing of the Exodus (mystery of the Passah-lamb), and the Crucifixion (mystery of the Passion) affords Melito ample opportunity to distance himself from Jewish conceptions and tenets. This contrasting juxtaposition, so to speak, of the Jewish part in the Exodus and in the Passion has two purposes: to set the New Testament sharply against the Old Testament, and, while doing so, to prove it to be the fulfilment of the Old Testament archetypus. By this stratagem Melito opposes Marcion's doctrine of the abolition of the Old Testament, while at the same time he constitutes the hermeneutic relationship between Old Testament and New Testament.

Here he follows mainly Justin, whom he rhetorically embellishes and paraphrases.[14] Thus, the following passage is directly inspired by Justin, *Dialogue, 95 : 2-3*:

No. 74-76:

Come, he says, Israel, thou hast slain the Lord. Why? Because he must needs die? Thou errest, O Israel, in reasoning thus falsely upon the slaying of the Lord. He must needs suffer, but not through thee. . . . He must needs be hanged upon the cross, but not by thee and thy right hand. Thus, O Israel, shouldst thou have cried to God: 'O master, even though thy son must suffer, . . . let him then suffer,˙but not at my hand; let him suffer at the hand of the Gentiles, let him be judged by the uncircumcised, let him be nailed to the cross by the oppressor's hand, but not by me'. . . .

Yet while Justin, debating against the Jew Tryphon, continues in the noble sentiment of 'You are our brothers! Recognize, then, God's truth. . .', Melito stresses and stresses *ad infinitum* the accusation of deicide:
No. 79:

Thou didst bind the beautiful hands with which he shaped thee from the earth; and his beautiful mouth, the mouth that fed thee with life, thou hast fed with gall, and thou hast slain thy Lord in the great feast.

Identifying Jesus with the world's creator, Melito strikes out against Marcion; accusing the Jews of murdering their Lord and creator, incarnate as man, he succeeds at the same time in formulating the Christian concept of deicide. The high point of this method—against Marcion, at the same time against the Jews—is reached in the harangue, quoted above in Greek, and anticipated in No. 96, climaxing with the memorable words: 'God has been murdered, the King of Israel has been slain by an Israelitish hand!' A further instance of utilizing Jewish material against the Jews—a method that goes through the ages up to this very day—is an old midrash of apocryphal origin, of which Melito avails himself:
(4) No. 98:

> For though the people trembled not, the earth trembled;
> though the people feared not, the heavens were
>   afraid;
> though the people rent not their garments, the
>   angel rent his.

To what angel does Melito allude here? As the author speaks of the hour of the Crucifixion, we have no doubt that the 'rending of the garment by an angel' hints at the rending of the veil of the Temple, according to Matt. 27:51. Yet this idea is pretty old; it has been pointed out that the second Baruch has almost the very same idea, this time alluding to the imminent destruction of the Temple by Nebukadnezzar.[15] Interpolated passages in the Testaments of Benjamin (IX : 4) and of Levi (X : 3), to which already Prof. Bonner refers, convey the same legend, this time with clearly christological tendentiousness. It all goes back to a famous passage in Josephus, *De Bello Jud.* VI, 5 : 3, which lists some bad *omina* before the Temple's fall, in particular a vision of cohorts of angels appearing over the Temple, and of people hearing words like 'Let us depart hence'. This legend has made the round in Christian homiletics; a good list is found in Bonner's introduction, pp. 41 ff. Most interesting, from our point of view, is the paraphrase of Isho'dad of Merv, a Syrian Church Father: 'The veil of the Temple was rent; which was a type that was annulled; first, because it could not bear the suffering of its archetype; second, to show that the Divine Shekina had withdrawn from it and the grace of the Holy Spirit.'[16] Another variation of the same device is the type of scolding or threatening speech, known to us from the prophets, such as Micah 6, the refrain of the *Improperia*; Isa. 3 : 13; Jer. 2 : 4 ff; Mal. 3 : 5, and, of course, the prototype in Hos. 4 : 1. If we leave out of this account the Gospels—and there is no evidence that Melito knew even *one* Gospel in its totality—there remains actually only *one* apocryphal '*Din Tora* (i.e., litigation) between Adonai and Israel' to bridge the period between the OT Canon and Melito's own time (for Pauline literature, which Melito knew, does not contain this type of fictive divine speech against Israel): this apocryphal speech is found in IV Esdras 15 (= V Esdras I). The origin of this chapter is highly controversial, and there are some scholars who ascribe it to a Judaeo-Christian interpolation, calling it the Fifth Esdras. This chapter contains the only full list of God's benefits to the people Israel in intertestamentary literature, but this time as an indictment, not, as in the *Dayenu,* as praise from Israel, but as a divine argument. It must have been the immediate *Vorlage* of Melito, both in its literary contents and in its chronological vicinity. This text, as well as the *Dayenu* itself, has been overlooked by all Christian commentators on Melito. The pertinent text reads:

(5) IV Esdras 15 : 7-24 (= V Esdras I):

(7) Did I not take them out of Egypt, the house of bondage? But they angered me and abused my counsels.
(10) For their sake I unseated kings, conquered Pharaoh with his knights, with his whole army.

(11) Because of them I destroyed their enemies scattering in the East; the people of two provinces, of Tyre and Sidon. . . .
(12) Thou talk to them; thus saith the Lord:
(13) I led you through the sea, and gave you secure ways through impassable land.
(14) I gave you Moses and Aaron as your leaders: I gave you light through the pillar of fire, and did great things for you, and marvellous ones.
(15) The quails served you as a sign; I gave you a camp for shelter, but you continued to grumble.
(19) I pitied you because of your sobbing and your sighs; I gave you manna as your food; and you ate the bread of angels.
(20) Did I not open the rock, when ye suffered from thirst? Against the heat I protected you with branches full of shadow.
(21) And I distributed fat land among you, drove away from you the Canaanites, the Pherezites, the Philistines. What more shall I do for you that I have not done as yet?
(24) What else shall I do for you, Jacob? Thou wouldst not obey, Judah; I shall go to other nations, I shall grant them my Name, so that they may heed my precepts. . . .

With the last verse we find ourselves in the immediate neighbourhood of the *Improperia,* for both in the Byzantine and the Georgian versions the last verse has been taken over almost literally.

We remember, further, that Sardes was one of the seven Christian communities mentioned in the Book of Revelation (I : 11), that there the Jews enjoyed all the privileges of *cives Romani* (Josephus, *Antt.,* XIV, 10 : 17), that Sardes leaned toward the West, not the East, especially to Smyrna and Ephesus, that Melito was familiar with stoic ideas, indeed had addressed both emperors Marcus Aurelius and Antoninus Pius on their own terms, and was also familiar with the phraseology of Hebrew prayers, as indicated by the following passage:

(6) No. 68:

This is he who rescued us from slavery to freedom, from darkness to light, from death to life, from oppression to an eternal kingdom, and made us a new priesthood and a chosen people for ever.

The oldest Hebrew prayer-book, the *Siddur R. Amram,* has, for the reading of Scripture on weekdays, the following passage:

146

May the all-present have mercy upon them: Bring them forth from trouble to freedom, from darkness to light, from subjection to redemption. . . .

The Hebrew text has three 'stages', the Greek (in Melito) four; it adds the Christian 'from death to life'. There can be no doubt that the Hebrew text is the original, as its phraseology is strictly biblical.

Let us now resume and summarize: Melito was familiar with both the *Dayenu* litany, and its subsequent perversion in IV Esdras. He knew Hebrew, as he was active in the study of the OT Canon. He presented for the first time the conception of a murdered God, whereby he, like ancient mythology, considers the God mortal. He was a fervent anti-Marcionite, and stressed, whenever he had a chance, the unity of Son and Father even before the trinitarian controversy. He was familiar with Philo and some of the testimony-books, also with apocryphal literature.[17] Being a quartodeciman, he leaned towards certain Jewish practices without wishing to appear as a Judaizer. The conception of the archetypal significance of Passover and Passion is basically a Stoic idea; similar archetypes were conceived by the rhetors Cleanthes and Chrysippus, whose main writings Melito seems to have known. He was a gifted, yet demagogic poet, synthesizing both Hebrew and Greek patterns. As a theologian, he followed the Johannine trend, especially in his emphasis upon the pre-existence of the archetypes. This then was the man who introduced the accusation of deicide into monotheistic religions, and the poet who was responsible for the *Improperia,* which made the accusation popular, attractive, and poetic.

His way of reasoning, while superior to that of the Syrian Apostolic Fathers, shows a curious resemblance to the Syriac *Didascalia,* which, like Melito, are sharply anti-Jewish, anti-Marcionite, and even opposed to Judaeo-Christianity. Indeed, the attitude of the *Didascalia* towards Judaism is almost identical with that of Melito. It was A. Marmorstein who first recognized the true tendency of the *Didascalia,* which hitherto were generally considered a Judaeo-Christian compilation: 'The Syrian *Didascalia* preserved a number of the most hostile attacks of the "Catholic Church" against Jews who believed in Christ, but would not sever their Jewish connections.'[18] On the other hand, the author of the *Didascalia* was opposed to the doctrine of the quartodecimans, as he warns Christians not to fall into this sinful practice of celebrating Easter according to the Jewish calendar. Just as Melito does, the *Didascalia* fight the Jews as well as the anti-Judaism of Marcion, as Harnack has demonstrated.[19]

However interesting Melito may appear to a historian of the Church, in the history of Judaism his name will retain a most sinister sound.

CHAPTER SEVEN

Art Music and Folklore in Ritual

SACRIFICE AND LOGOS

THIS theme is difficult and delicate. To comprehend it in depth, one must go *ad fontes* of organized ritual—well into the third millennium B.C.E.

Definitions: Professor Yerkes has coined the classic description of ritual. He says: 'All religious rites are primarily *doing* something with something, either to a deity or to worshippers, or both, by way of accompaniment or explanation of what was done.'[1] In this fundamental statement, applicable to all ritual, there is already an allusion to the basic antinomy between the ritual *deed* and the ritual *word* or *sound*. We shall term the former approach a sacrifice, and its symbols sacraments. The verbal approach to deity, on the other hand, has given birth to the far-reaching concept of the *logos* and the worship based upon it, i.e., upon the sacred word.

It stands to reason that these two fundamentally different approaches represent also opposing attitudes in the relationship of the celebrant (priest, singer, preacher, minister, shaman, etc.) to the worshipper. We claim that this essential variance reaches into the ancillary arts of ritual, i.e., poetry and music, and we shall try, in the following pages, to give a detailed account of the liturgical image as shaped by the differing demands of the two approaches. It will be our task, in particular, to demonstrate a sort of correspondence or parallelism between the two liturgical principles: sacrifice and *logos*, on the one hand, and the two musical *Gestalten*, art music and folklore, on the other. Specifically, we suggest the following correspondence between them:

The institutions of sacrifice and hierarchy normally inspire art music.

149

The categories of *logos* worship and of rudimentary democracy normally tend to sponsor folklore and folk-song.

We are, by habit, accustomed to distinguish between art music and folk-song, but the difficulties that arise from the various meanings and interpretations of these terms—dependent upon varying aspects of time, location, social conditions, *et al.*—are considerable. Only a few *general* criteria or necessary conditions can be stated that spell the difference between art music and folk-song without raising some controversy or other. Yet these conditions are by no means *sufficient;* such distinctions must be sought and established anew in each case. It is, therefore, necessary to separate the concepts of art music and folklore from their habitual aesthetic evaluation.

(a) If the concept of art music is to be of general validity, the fact that each such work aspires to one and only one *Gestalt* is most relevant; whereas in folklore the *Gestalt* of the individual work is neither important nor always recognizable: it is replaced by an archetype that serves for an entire class of individualized variants.[2]

(b) A corollary of this argument is the fact that in art music one, or at most two, versions are singled out, preferred and canonized by the author or composer, while in folklore many variants of the same item coexist with equal authenticity with each other. They are either results of the gradual *zersingen* of the piece during long spans of time, or they represent various aspects of the archetype, as it was generated under different ethnic or social conditions.[3]

(c) Often, the distinction between art and folklore coincides with that between written and oral tradition, but by no means always. Thus we find that instrumental art music of the modern Near East has not been notated, while the contemporary folk-song of the same region has been written down. Nor does the norm of the notated art music place it automatically on a higher level than the oral tradition. One of the few scholars who has been able to say something original on this subject is Charles Seeger. In his article 'Oral Tradition in Music', he observes:

. . . it may be remarked that in this study of folklore in general the term 'oral tradition' is used a bit loosely. Three separate meanings in common use may be distinguished: (1) an inherited *accumulation* of materials; (2) the *process* of inheritance, cultivation and transmission thereof; (3) the technical means employed. This is not an unusual semantic complication and does not confuse us unduly as long as we remain in the field of folk music. But it may confuse us when we attempt integration of the folk and the fine arts of music. . . .

A fourth consideration bears upon this misunderstanding. Popularization of European fine art of music has itself achieved such cultlike devotion, that oral tradition and folk music are very generally regarded, by professional musicians, as a low form of musical life. Almost universal adoption has been given to a theory of unilinear evolution, whereby the art of music progresses ever onward and upward from primitive, through folk and popular, to the fine art. The possibilities that estimable qualities may be lost as well as gained, that the order of historical development may have been different in different places, and that the whole hierarchical conception may be unwarrantably subjective, have apparently been little explored.[4]

Similar caution, coupled with equally profound considerations, was first systematically advanced by the late Curt Sachs, and pressed strongly in his posthumous book, *The Wellsprings of Music*. Such counsel will guide us in the subsequent historical investigations. In considering the various rituals, the distinction between these two antithetic practices will serve as our guidepost. At the end of the chapter, a new exact criterion of folk music will be offered.

While it is necessary to stress the dichotomy between the sacrificial and the verbal or spiritual approach to deity, it is all but impossible to establish a rationale common to all kinds of sacrifices. We shall have to trace our steps back to the prehistoric age, when magic conceptions guided and often determined human behaviour. From ancient sources we know of many different ways of approaching a supernatural, presumably *friendly* power, or else of fending off a hostile one: (1) the sacrifice; (2) the sacred *connubium*: (3) the sacred pantomime and similar pageants; (4) totemistic veneration; (5) various forms of the *unio mystica*; (6) countless apotropaic rites, by which real or fancied antagonistic powers would be either propitiated or chased away; and many other cultic arts. With the emergence of monotheism this syndrome of variegated rites was gradually reduced to two polar attitudes and their derivatives. They are:

The sacrifice in whatever form, to whatever purpose—a *deed*. The *logos* worship—being the promulgation, reproduction and veneration of the sacred *word*.

The sacrament—in its most general form representing a symbol or visible sign of a *deed* or *action*.

The order, institution, study and examination of pericopes, i.e., of portions of sacred writ, including fixed and 'canonized' *prayers*.

Of the various theories and conjectures on the original function of the sacrifice, we shall mention, in passing, only the most significant. The most recent bibliographies on the subject may be found in Roland de Vaux's monumental work, *Ancient Israel* (2nd ed. London, 1965) and in Otto Eissfeldt, *Old Testament, an Introduction* (4th ed. New York–Oxford, 1968).

The oldest of these theories, the 'gift-hypothesis', advanced during the nineteeth century, does not explain sacrifices which were eaten by the worshippers; the theory of the common banquet with the gods, suggested by W. Robertson Smith, cannot account for the burnt sacrifice;[5] Jastrow's interpretation of the sacrifice as a divination ritual is inadequate in view of certain Hebrew and Roman meal-offerings;[6] the general idea of 'do ut des' has been discredited by modern anthropologists.[7] Following Freud's thesis, some scholars see in totemistic practices the origin of bloody sacrifices. Examining the classical Greek term for sacrifice, *thysia*, we find that etymologically it is derived from the root *thy–*, 'smoke'; *thyein* would mean 'to produce smoke', and *theoi*, the gods would signify the 'receivers of smoke'. If one eats the god in the form of a bull, the worshipper might believe that he had eaten the god, the *theos*. In fact, the expression 'a *theos* in man' or 'a man in a *theos*' was the old word for the partaker of a sacrificial meal. This is in Greek '*entheos*' and the frenzy during which one became '*entheos*' was described as '*enthusiasmos*', 'being engodded', our recently secularized enthusiasm.[8]

Quite different from Hellenic spirit and practice is the old Roman rite of self-sacrifice, called *devotio*, from which our words devout, devoted, etc., originate. It was a battle-sacrifice, and in its mildest forms an *ex voto* sacrifice, a vow-offering. In the military form a soldier 'devotes' himself to the gods, i.e., to being killed, so that the gods would grant victory to the Romans. A consul had the right to devote himself or some other 'devotee', who normally was proud of obtaining the privilege. We find a similar type of sacrifice in the vow of Jephthah and his daughter. This vow-offering occurs in many civilizations.[9]

Yet another category includes the Phrygian mystery rite of *taurobolium*, the slaying of a bull above the worshippers' pit. The worshippers would be immersed in the bull's blood and so invigorated and cleansed. It was one of the many blood-rites with which not only paganism, but also ancient Judaism, were replete.[10] In Judaism the blood was sprinkled on or around the altar, which, by the way, is called *mizbeah*, that is, 'slaughtering-place'. The Hebrew generic term for sacrifice is *qorban*, which means 'approach, coming close'; there are also more than a dozen specific terms for sacrifices with special significances, such as the *omer* (the offering of sheaves of grain), the *olah* (burnt offering), the enigmatic Pascal sacrifice, about whose full meaning we are still in the dark, and many more which cannot be discussed here. All sacrificial ritual was restricted to the Jerusalem Temple, Israel's central sanctuary. With its fall the sacrificial ritual lost its function and significance.[11]

Verbal (or logocratic) worship, emphasizing the sacred word, on the other hand, was developed by the synagogal liturgy of Judaism. Yet this new approach comprised the prophetic ethics, the observance of civil laws, and some symbolic reminiscences of the sacrificial cult in a truly unique synthesis. Prophetic utterances[12] have always resisted the domination of the sacrificial cult.[13] The OT prophet demands as proof of adherence to Yahweh's covenant not sacrifice, not ritual, but ethical actions: feeding the hungry, doing justice, speaking truth, loving one's neighbour, etc. Ethical action replaces or at least completes ritual action. When, long before the fall of the Temple, the reading of Scripture was instituted, the new form of synagogal word-worship was established upon the firm foundation of prophetic monotheism.[14]

At the emergence of Christianity both forms of worship were still practised in Judaism, as the Temple still stood at the time of St Paul and the other apostles. Indeed, the Church has availed itself of both forms. The Mass, the *sacrificium missae*, was originally the eucharistic worship pure and simple, emerging from the domestic Passover ritual of the Paschal lamb, as enacted by Christ. *Eucharistia* and *agape* were united during the first century, while the sacrificial element still remained manifest. Later these two types of worship assumed different functions. As a close examination of early Christian worship would exceed our scope by far, we cannot proceed

153

without a certain amount of simplification.[15] Suffice it to say here that the principle of transubstantiation finally established the Mass as a sacrifice of the great type of the *unio mystica*. Thus, Mass is still considered the '*logikē thysia*', the spiritual sacrifice.

The proper functioning of the Church was not possible, however, without the sacred word and its worship. Naturally, this liturgy followed the pattern of the Synagogue, as we have seen in many early chapters of the first volume. When Christianity began to make proselytes, it had to instruct the neophytes in its doctrine, history and observance. For this purpose the original separation of sacrificial and verbal worship had to be abandoned: the *missa catechumenorum* (of the still unbaptized proselytes) preceded the 'Mass of the Faithful', and scriptural lessons and instructions were instituted in this first part. As this section does not contain the Eucharist, but many biblical quotations and references apart from the formal reading of Scripture itself, it resembles closely a Sabbath morning service of a traditional Jewish house of prayer. This holds true only for the Western liturgies of Christianity. Eastern Christianity has evolved quite different forms and symbols, as was shown in the first volume. Still, the two institutions, mass and office, reveal the basic difference.

PROPHETS, PRIESTS, AND PSALMISTS

We return to the thesis suggested at the opening: sacrificial rituals show an affinity for and a tendency to art music. All solemn cult music was invariably sponsored by a hierarchy, usually bound to an arcane discipline; hence its professional performers had to be priests *de jure*. Worship by virtue of the Sacred Word, on the other hand, tends to folk music and congregational singing in the vernacular, and to the simplicity that necessarily goes with popularity; it also leans to democratic forms of representation. To prove so far-reaching a theory would fill a book; here we shall search for traces of this polarization in the cults of the ancient Near East.[16]

The status of the performers and their functions will be examined first; in some instances it will be possible to draw tenable inferences as to the purpose and nature of the music to be performed.

Our knowledge of Sumerian and Babylonian cult music—about

the Hittites we know next to nothing[17]—is, of course, severely limited; yet their ritual certainly contained a good many songs, hymns and dirges, as well as processionals and dance music. We know also that a kind of genealogy of many of the professional musicians was kept rather carefully in the archives of the temples, not unlike the biblical genealogies of returning Temple-singers and musicians.[18] From the epithets that accompany the names it is assumed that they were well-trained, dynastically reared muscians. They held the rank of priest of three different degrees. At one time there was even a special Temple dedicated to sacred song (es-sir).[19] They appeared mainly at the occasion of rituals accompanying the various sacrifices. The main function of these musician–priests seems to have been the performance of a widely variegated repertoire of ritual songs, which H. G. Farmer quite arbitrarily terms 'cantillation', songs of lament (er) and hymns of praise and prayer. The last-named category was preponderant on the chief holy day, the feast of New Year, when the sacred marriage ritual was staged and actually consummated by the King and the hierodule appointed for that task.[20] On the fourth day the ancient epic of the world's creation was solemnly intoned. Some of the ancient titles seem to indicate that the offices of the hymn-singer and of the singer of dirges were separated.[21] This specialization implies the professionalism of trained soloists and their services, excluding spontaneous mass-singing by excited crowds. For a crowd—and an illiterate one to boot—was certainly not familiar with the intricate and often changing, often esoteric texts and forms of the ritual. Stephen Langdon, who knew these liturgical texts perhaps best, used to say that in quantity they equalled a Roman Antiphonale plus Breviary, plus Lectionary—and they had to be memorized!

The juxtaposition of sacrifice, totemistic ritual and music is clearly visible in recent literature (see notes 18 and 21).

We may concluded that the hierarchy of the ancient Orient, bent upon maintaining its esoteric doctrine and practice, eschewed all active participation by the people. Even if its music was not yet art, the trend in this direction is unmistakable.

The personal union of priest and professional musician was typical in the cults of Egypt, Babylonia and ancient Israel. This was not always so in ancient Greece. A position between the sacrificing priest and the champions of the divine word, whether seers, soothsayers or prophets, was held by the non-political bard or singer who was still respected and regarded as god-inspired and god-protected.[22] It seems as if the Greek priest was less concerned with music than his oriental colleagues. The prayer of Chryses, priest of Apollo (*Iliad*, I, 37-42), mentioned as his acts of devotion to the god, 'thighs full of fat of bulls and of she-goats', also new roofs of the god's Temple, but no singing or teaching. The ritual shouting and wailing during a sacrifice, performed by women and children (cf. *Odyssey*, III, 450 f; or Euripides, *Medea*, 1170-7), was uttered without music; we shall return to this organized wailing, which is still well known in the Near East.

The bards and minstrels, often considered god-inspired, as De-modokos (*Odyssey*, VIII, 44; 73; 498 ff) or Phemios (*Odyssey*, XXII, 346-48, etc.) held themselves aloof from political strife and were, in general, not associated with priestcraft.[23] The orphic Mousaios, whose family, the Eumolpides, shared with him the legacy of certain mysteries, linked to the Eleusinian rites, was not a priest, but rather a seer, probably a soothsayer; and many hymns and paeans were attributed to him.[24] Ritual priests and diviners, on the other hand, collaborated often, as we see in the case of the Delphic oracle. It was first stammered by the Pythian seeress; then her utterances were polished and reformulated, often in ambiguous terms, by the attending priest. The bards, while god-inspired, were probably a 'genus irritabile vatum' as Horace calls them; they cultivated the word, not the sacrificial deed. In classical antiquity, 'professional choirs were trained to lead the singing, but never to perform it as a substitute for the worshippers', as Guthrie repeatedly emphasizes.[25]

By contrast, the priests of the Egyptian cult of the dead, the musical liturgists of Babylonia, the *kalu*, the Levites at the Temple and the court musicians of King Hezekiah demanded as tribute by King Sennacherib of Babylonia, were all professionals, i.e., they aspired to artistic standards. The training time of a Levite who functioned as musician amounted to no less than five years; as Josephus tells us, they were fully occupied with regular rehearsals and preparations for the poetry and music to be performed.[26] The more instruments were employed in the service, the stronger became the professional-artistic element, the esoteric *'reservata'* art music.

Art Music and Folk Song in Ancient Israel

Although there is ample evidence in the OT of both professional and popular musical performance, clear indications of the distinctions between the two categories are found but rarely. David's famous elegy on the death of Saul and Jonathan is, as the text demands, 'to be taught to the people of Judah' (II Sam. 1 : 18), thus eliminating, at least textually, all possibility of variants. The instrumental music of the Temple was in the hands of trained professionals, and the frequent heading *'Lam'natzeach'* (falsely translated as 'to the choirmaster' or 'musicmaster', etc.) testifies to it.[27] From the Song of the Well (Num. 21 : 17) to the popular ditties embedded in the Song of Songs, from the colourful incipits of old folk songs in the Psalter, e.g., 'The dove far away' (Ps. 56), 'The tune of lilies' (Ps. 45), to the 'hind of the morning dawn' (Ps. 22), etc., we find many quotations of, and allusions to, folk tunes in the Old Testament. We hear of songs improvised on the spot, such as 'Saul has slain his thousands, David his tens of thousands', of the ancient song of Lamech (Gen. 4 : 23). Similar results of spontaneous improvisation were the mocking-songs, a genre which survived the destruction of the Temple; they and the songs of women seem to have been moulded in an old established pattern, like the simple tunes that once accompanied the processions of pilgrims to Jerusalem, or the monotonous reapers' calls in the old Palestinian idyll, called the Book of Ruth.[28] To this well-known treasury of priestly and popular lore has now been added the rich evidence of the Dead Sea Scrolls with their sectarian theology and literature.

The originally sharp contention between the hereditary hierarchy and the prophets, considered the champions of God's word and will, once clearly profiled in visions of angelic choruses or vulgar songs, seems to have moderated in the course of time. In consequence of this softening of the opposing sides a middle ground seems to have emerged in old Israel between the sacrificial ritual of the priests and the logocratic worship sponsored by the prophets. More than fifty years ago, A. C. Welch saw in this development the

157

solution of many problems inherent in the use of the Psalter in sacrificial worship. He wrote:

> A parallel may be drawn between their action [of the religious leaders in Israel] and the attitude of the Presbyterian Communion, which has always held firmly by an approach to God ministered to men through word and sacrament, not through sacrament alone, nor through the word alone, but through the combination of the two . . .[29]

This attitude is still close to that of Mowinckel's assumption of 'cultic prophets' which, in fact, preceded Welch's argument:

> With the organized Temple prophets inspiration is rather what we should call an official, occupational inspiration, a permanent charismatic equipment belonging to the office itself.

Elsewhere, Mowinckel considers these Temple prophets as the representatives and leaders of the lay worshippers.[30] With this reasonable assumption three parties emerge instead of the two: the priests, the Temple prophets, and the non-cultic, highly individualistic, 'independent' prophets.[31] Mowinckel and other scholars believe that after the building of the Second Temple the cultic prophets were absorbed by the corps of its Levitical singers, who assumed with their old function also the oracular service.[32] This conjecture is confirmed by the chronicler's remark: 'David and the chiefs of the service also set apart for the service certain of the sons of Asaph, and of Heman, and of Jeduthun, who should *prophesy* (Hebr. *ha-n'bi'im*) with lyres, with harps, and with cymbals.' (I Chr. 25 : 1).

The scholarly arguments pro and contra are deep, intricate, and often in too technical a vein to be of general interest. An important aspect of this discussion, however, must not be lost sight of, namely the distinction between supposedly 'popular' songs and the products of 'professional' poets in the Psalter. Many scholars have addressed themselves to this thorny question, but none as strongly and convincingly, *before the discovery of the Dead Sea Scrolls*, as S. Mowinckel. He elucidated and expounded several disputed concepts about the psalmists, their function and status.[33] In the following, a few important results of that author's lifelong occupation with the psalms will be gleaned:

There is a close connection between the psalm poets and the temple prophets. The temple prophet had a definite task in the cult liturgy and he was also to a certain extent a psalm poet. . . . A description of the different types of psalms. . .will certainly demonstrate to what great extent the whole of this poetry is bound by tradition. The content, the formal language and the thoughts are determined by purpose and custom. To write poetry was, one may say, to put together the details, thoughts and phrases which were presented by tradition, in the form which according to custom and tradition, corresponded to the purpose.

This shows the close analogy to the practice and structure of musical composition in the Near East up to this very day as has been shown repeatedly in this work.

The creating of the psalms differ also in another way from what we moderns instinctively expect from poetry. The experiences and emotions that the psalms give expression to were not only those of an individual, but common events, general experiences and feelings. . . . But this does not necessarily imply that the personal element was lacking. To the old Israel personality with the quality of originality and uniqueness was neither an ideal nor a reality. . . .

According to Mowinckel, most psalms originated among the Temple singers. The 'I' expression, so frequent in the psalms, is put 'on the lips of the worshipper. . .who was to present it in the Temple'. The intrusion of the so-called wisdom literature into the psalms would not produce more individualistic traits in the poetry.

Through the influence of the wisdom style in the psalms of the learned admonition and reflexion brought about a dissolution of the old styles of writing, because the poets no longer had the support which was offered by the connection with definite cultic situations. This led to an uncertain and styleless mixture of the old types of composition . . .34

Most of these arguments, however well-reasoned, were hypothetical; with the discovery of the DSS many of the hypotheses were proved, others refuted. Later we shall realize how well Mowinckel had assessed the influence of sapiential literature upon the psalms, before ever knowing about the *Psalm-Scroll* discovered only recently, where this trend is quite manifest. The weakening of the originally firm link between sacrificial ritual, hierarchy and art music (by professionals) becomes quite evident in these post-biblical poems from Qumran, especially in the *Damascus* (*Zadokite*) *Document* (*Zad.* hereafter) and the *Manual of Discipline* (*Man.* hereafter).

Yet priests were very much in evidence in the Qumran community (*Zad.*, XIV : 3-6; *Man.*, VI : 1-6), also the Levites; according to their social system, the Third Estate was that of the 'accepted layman', to be followed by the 'accepted proselyte'. In the same source one encounters concrete references to priestly sacrifices (*Zad.*, XI, end). Yet it is also assumed of priests and Levites that they are familiar and knowledgeable in biblical exegesis (*Zad.*, XII: 23-24).

While, however, priests and sacrifices are closely associated in the *Zadokite Document*, this is not the case in the *Manual of Discipline*; there the priets bless and instruct the community, also sometimes act as judges, but their sacrificial duties are hardly mentioned at all. Although the Qumran priest may have worn the vestments of their confreres at the Temple in Jerusalem, they had practically abandoned all sacrificial rites and duties. It was only because the Law demanded a certain adherence to the Jerusalem Temple, that the Qumran community did not openly reject it. The fulfilment of the Law's precepts was rendered possible by a transfer of meaning, from the carrying out of blood sacrifice to the living of a life according to the precepts of the Law, thus making a 'sacrifice of deeds and lips'.[35] The real Temple in Jerusalem was considered desecrated and therefore useless for the atonement of the people's sins. As its substitute served the spiritualized Temple of the community; it consisted of the life of the community which 'lived in perfect obedience to all the precepts of the Law'. This idea finds its clearest expression in 4 *Qumran Florilegium*, I, 6 f: 'And they purposed to build Him a sanctuary of men, in which should be offered sacrifices before Him, *the works of the Law.* . . .'

After the fall of Jerusalem in 70, the old trend toward the Law and its study was finally realized as the most vital element of the Jewish religion, a trend which had begun much earlier.[36] The spiritualization of sacrifices, preceding the same process in Christianity by more than a century, took place under permanent and tradition-bound priestly supervision. Here the priests held a mediating position as instructors, pastors, and spiritual leaders of the community—a position that anticipates that of the presbyter and even of the bishop in the ancient Church.[37]

The sacrificial banquet, however, was still much in evidence, to judge from the problematical Ps. 154 (apocryphal) that belonged to the Qumran lectionary.[38] We cite a part of it:

Ps. 154:

> For to make known the glory of the Lord
>   is Wisdom given,
> and for recounting His many deeds
>   she is revealed to man:
> to make known to simple folks His might
>   and to explain to senseless folk His greatness,
> those far from her gates,
>   those remote from her portals.
>
> For the Most High is the Lord of Jacob
>   and His majesty is over all of His works.
> And a man who glorifies the Most High,
>   he accepts as one who brings a meal offering
>   as one who offers he-goats and bullocks,
>   as one who fattens the altar with many burnt offerings,
>   as a sweet-smelling fragrance from the hand of
>   the righteous.
>
> From the gates of the righteous is heard her voice
>   and from the assembly of the pious her song [wisdom's].
> When they eat with satiety she is cited [spoken of],
>   also when they drink in community together.
> Their meditation is on the Law of the Most High
>   their words on making known His might.
> How far from the wicked is her word
>   from all haughty [Hebr. zedim] men to know her . . .

This part of the 'Ode to Wisdom' needs a good deal of elucidation. The Hebrew expression for 'simple folk' carries a less sympathetic overtone than its translation, an expression of humility, seems to imply. It is, on the contrary, an epithet, spoken 'from the high horse'.[39] On the other hand we find, in the last verse quoted, a condemnation of 'haughty men'—how is this contradiction to be explained? Perhaps thus: the Hebr. zedim may mean 'haughty', but also 'heinous' or 'shameless', in good parallelism to the 'wicked' in the antecedent half-verse. The four 'as' of the translation (stanza B) correspond faithfully to the Hebrew prefix ke- = like, as, as if; and in the subsequent verses the poet speaks of Wisdom's 'song', heard at the banquets of the pious. Moreover, the last two verses of stanza C are clearly metaphorical.[40] We might therefore conclude, *per analogiam*, that the preceding allusions to sacrifices should likewise be taken as a poetic metaphor. Far more serious than these questions of literary interpretation is the usage of an almost gnostic conception of wisdom—*sophia*—which we encounter here and in the Qumranite version of Ecclesiasticus. We also remember Mowinckel's criticism of the intrusion of sapiential thoughts into the poetry of the psalms. The real or apparent contradictions, the emergence of semi-gnostic thinking, the unclear metaphors, all these mar the style of the psalm.

Nonetheless, this is obviously a poem by a literary artist, not by a man of the 'simple folk'. In the *Hymns of Thanksgiving* (*Hodayot*), another creation of Qumran poets, one frequently encounters metaphorical references to musical instruments, as was shown in Ch. II. In the more 'learned' *Zadokite Document* an ancient popular song, quoted from the Bible, is subjected to allegorical (midrashic) treatment:

Zadokite Document, VI: 2-6;

And He. . .raised from the priesthood and from the laity men of wisdom, and He made them hearken to Him. And those men 'dug the well'—that well whereof it is written, 'Princes digged it, nobles of the people delved it, with the aid of a *mehoqeq* [Hebr. 'staff', also 'lawgiver'], (Num. 21 : 18). The 'well' in question is the Law. They that 'digged' it are those of Israel who repented and departed from the land of Judah to sojourn in the 'Land of Damascus' . . .

There we learn that the 'princes' of the dynastic aristocracy are to be understood as called by God 'because they went in search of Him' and 'because their glory was never gainsaid' (?) by any man's mouth.

The trend towards allegorization of sacrifice, hierarchy, and aristocracy indicates a certain mixture of democratic rule and hierarchic authority.[41] No less puzzling are the remnants of arcane discipline, by which the measurement of time, the calendar and the 'appointed feasts' were fixed; these were distinctive tenets of the group, by which the Qumranites identified themselves. Their calendar of feasts, based upon the pentecontade system of groups of fifty days, is now clearly established beyond any doubt, and the hypothesis stated in the first volume of this work, according to which the psalmodic *octoechos* is linked to the pentecontade and Jubilee calendar, has been fully confirmed, both in the *Psalm-Scroll* quoted from, and even more in the quite recently discovered so-called *Temple Scroll*.[42]

The *Psalm-Scroll* contains two poetic pieces which are quite contrasting in style and spirit, and which seem to address themselves to different listeners (or readers). While the contrast is not sharply defined, one senses easily both the 'folksy', ballad-like tone of the first, and the paean-like exalted language of the other. The first one is the newly discovered Hebrew text of Ps. 151, whose existence was known through its Greek (LXX) version and the Syriac translation. Now we have perhaps the original text, and, lo and behold, it turns out to be a popular religious ballad! What's more, it reads like a midrash upon I Sam. 16 : 1–13 in the form of a ballad.

Psalm 151:[43]

A Hallelujah of David the Son of Jesse

(1) Smaller was I than my brothers
          and the youngest of the sons of my father,
   So he made me shepherd of his flock
          and ruler over his kids.
(2) My hands have made an instrument [Hebr. *'ugab*]
          and my fingers a lyre [Hebr. *kinnor*];
   And (so) have I rendered glory to the Lord,
          thought I, within my soul.
(3) The mountains do not witness to him,
          nor do the hills proclaim;
   [But] the trees have cherished my words
          and the flock my works.
(4) For who can proclaim and who can bespeak
          and who can recount the deeds of the Lord?
   Everything has God seen,
          everything has he heard and he has heeded.

(5) He sent his prophet to anoint me,
    Samuel to make me great;
    My brothers went out to meet him,
        handsome of figure and appearance.
(6) Though they were tall of stature
    and handsome by their hair,
    The Lord God chose
        them not.
(7) But he sent and took me from behind the flock
    and anointed me with holy oil,
    And he made me leader to his people
        and ruler over the sons of his covenant.[44]

There are no less than ten slightly differing versions of the poem in Syriac, also a few in Greek, which indicates the popularity of the text.[45] The easy-going tone of the poem, which reminds us a little of a biblical ballad or a Franciscan 'laude', especially verse 3, shows little of Orphic austerity and intentional darkness, as suggested by the editor. In sharp contrast to this fairly simple and popularly phrased poem stands the highly artistic, but less natural 'Apostrophe to Zion'. This poem is written as an alphabetical acrostic, which is always an indication of the poet's artistic aspirations. We quote here only one characteristic stanza:

> Purge violence from thy midst;
>   falsehood and evil will be cut off from thee.
> Thy sons will rejoice in thy midst
>   and thy precious ones will unite with thee.
> How did they hope for thy salvation,
>   thy pure ones have mourned for thee.
> Hope for thee does not perish, O Zion,
>   nor is the promise of thee forgotten.
> Who has ever perished (in) righteousness
>   or who has survived in his iniquity?
> Man is judged according to his ways
>   every man is rewarded according to his deeds:
> All around are thine enemies uprooted, O Zion,
>   and scattered are all that hate thee . . .[46]

And he continues:

> Praise of thee is pleasing, O Zion,
>   cherished throughout the world;

> Many times do I remember thee for a blessing,
> With all my heart
> I bless thee.

Even in translation the contrast between young David's ballad and this solemn ode to Zion is quite marked: the popular tone of the first poem is just as evident as the exalted, hymnic style of the second. As formal blessing was a priest's prerogative, it is quite reasonable to assume that a learned priest was the author of the 'Ode to Zion'; a priest, we might add, who was quite familiar with the last chapters of Isaiah. Nor is it too bold a conjecture to imagine a pious layman as the author of young David's song.

In sum, it seems that even before the destruction of the Temple in 70, and certainly thereafter, the pure hierarchical and professional art of priestly musicians and poets waned and the more popular style of singers and especially of late imitators of classical poetry became preponderant. An isolated sect like that of Qumran was an ideal nurturing place for such a mixture of hierarchic and democratic style, since there, and only there, priests, Levites, and the community of the brethren lived closely together. The didactic sourcs of the sect speak of the (priestly) teacher or moral guide, who counsels and teaches the 'many', i.e., the pious community.

We shall now try to interpret a number of related facts in the light of our theory. If it is correct, it should be possible to establish historical evidence for the link between sacrificial worship and art music; and since of all forms of monotheistic worship the Catholic Mass has best preserved its sacrificial and hierarchical character, we shall examine its development first, however summarily.

Until the Council of Nicaea (321–325) the celebration of the Eucharist seems to have been a communal event, fully understandable and to a certain extent actively performed by the adherents of the new Church. Soon after we hear only little of community singing to accompany the solemn action. The priestly office becomes more and more an arcanum, and after 800 we encounter mainly complaints about the lack of participation by the community.[47] The development away from the Latin language accelerated this development. Caesarius of Arles (542) seems to have been the last outright champion of congregational singing during Mass.

With the exception of a few calls, such as *Kyrie eleison,* and acclamations like Amen, Alleluia, *Sanctus,* etc., the singing participation of the laymen declined and eventually vanished silently. It is only today that the vernacular liturgy is being established in order to revitalize active lay-participation.[48] The chants and songs were usually performed by the schola or (in the cathedrals and collegiate churches) by the chapter. Popular chants found their way into the liturgy by memorized formulae, as in the doxology, or in some songs, which were mixtures of Latin and the vernacular. Plain psalmody could not have been sung by the people, due to their lack of Latin, and the popularity of martyrs' vigils became proverbial for reasons not exactly theological.[49] Not the Mass, but the offices and the martyrs' feasts, were the main outlets of popular piety, the representatives of logocratic worship. By contrast, the service proper, based upon the sacred word, as exemplified in Protestantism, was from the very beginning inclined to community singing, and its champions Luther and Calvin successfully encouraged the introduction of simple, popular tunes.[50] For both of them prayer, praise and thanksgiving represented the natural functions of communal chant. Both considered the folkish stanza-form best suited for congregational songs; while Luther still reckoned with a clerical or scholars' chorus, i.e., with some polyphony, Calvin favoured a strictly laicistic service, i.e., unison chant. Luther tried to preserve at least the shell of the Mass, Calvin restricted the communion service to four (or twelve) days during the year. The more the idea of sacrifice retreats, the more dominant becomes the word, be it as lesson or prayer or sermon, or as hymn. And with the word go simple, straightforward, popular songs, and vice versa: when during the counter-reformation the hierarchic powers and the emphasis upon the sacrifice in the Mass gained ground politically and ideologically, the polyphonic art music flourished anew.[51] The two trends coincide in the art of the great Heinrich Schütz.

These all too brief explanations—their detailed enumeration would fill a big and dull book—seem to justify the hypothesis stated at the beginning; but we must also bear in mind that the democratic ideal, in worship or in politics, has really conquered only the souls of Protestants, and is just beginning to make inroads in others— with many a relapse into authoritarian rule. Hierarchy, sacrifice, and art music flourished together in the Catholic and in the Anglo-Catholic (cathedral!) liturgies. Even the Protestant collegiate churches such as the Thomas-Kirche in Leipzig or the Kreuz-Kirche in Dresden, to name but two, must not be forgotten here. In all such cases, at least a shell of sacrificial worship (Mass) was maintained by the clergy, however transformed in substance and spirit.[52]

The foregoing deliberations do not amount to a strict proof of our thesis, and are valid only when confined to Western civilization. Yet the concomitance of hierarchy and art music seems to be incontrovertible, while the link between democracy and folksong is by no means so clearly established.

EASTERN AND WESTERN FOLK MUSIC

The pagan antecedents of popular, non-priestly cults were ceremonies performed by non-initiated laymen, usually accompanied by traditional cries, sayings and gestures. Some of them are known to us, as they have come down from the Graeco-Roman as well as from the ancient Semitic civilizations. But we know very little about ritual music of the Mycenean age aside from Homer's 'stylized' descriptions. For when poets or historians spoke of music, they meant already a skilled art. And while art music was regularly employed at solemn religious occasions, the line between the religious and the secular was differently drawn when compared with ancient Semitic practice. 'In the *Iliad* music has already the status of an art over and above a mere ritual; and the Greek tradition remained humanistic, anti-liturgical, swiftly sensitive to social and mental change.'[53]

Bordering on the realm of 'traditional folk music' there were also institutions such as popular laments, musical magic and the like. To the first category belongs the *ololygē,* a stylized wailing with clearly apotropaic function, often exclaimed at a private, *non-priestly,* sacrifice.[54] Magic-therapeutic purposes were achieved by incantations, sung by laymen, to still the blood of the wounded Odysseus (*Od.* XIX, 457). The wailing and sobbing for the fictitious Linos was, as the *Ailinon*-song of the harvesters, common to Greeks, Phoenicians, and probably Hebrews.[55]

We encounter a clear outline of the rite of the lament for the dead

Hector (*II, XXIV*, 720 f), where professional singers, Andromache, his wife, Hecuba, his mother, and Helen, his sister-in-law, appear as dirge-singers. The wailing of the attendant women is repeatedly mentioned; it sounded almost like a refrain, exactly as is still customary at the funerals of Arabs or Oriental Jews. We are here in a realm far from any artistic aspiration; simple sayings, probably simple tunes, spontaneous execution—all this places these songs in the category of folk music.

To the same word-bound, popular, and strictly secular category belong the mocking-songs, so often mentioned in the OT, especially in Job and in the *Hymns of Thanksgiving* (in the DSS). In Rome they were known as *carmina famosa* and some authors of the most insulting ditties were punished by deportation.[56] The distinction between genuine folk-song and popular mocking-songs was felt by the Romans, who speak of 'songs of vulgar poets' and of 'learned songs', whereby the epithet *doctus* does not imply pedantry or presumption, but artistic form and aspiration—just as in the French term of *musique savante,* used for art music par excellence. How contemptuously Horace places himself above a tavern singer, when he writes: 'Odi profanum volgus et arceo' (*Odes,* III, 1, 1), or when he warns against the vulgarization of the silvan deities: 'Do not ascribe to fauns, the gods of the woods, language befitting the plebs of the slums or the dandy who strolls in the forum' (*Ars poetica,* 244).

In the liturgies, street-songs or popular ditties seem to have been rare, but decidedly lascivious and obscene songs belonged *de jure* to the correct ritual of some goddesses, e.g., to that of the Bona Dea and Rhea Kybele.[57]

Once more it is proper to ask for an acceptable and tenable distinction between art music and folk-song. In the past as well as in the present, the indiscriminate usage of terms like 'primitive', 'traditional', 'popular', etc., has clouded rather than clarified the basic diversity. A good deal of learned studies by ethnomusicologists have done more harm than good, due to the lack of uniform terminology and method. We shall, in the following pages, try to find criteria which by-pass the customary categorical distinctions, such as notation *v.* oral tradition, one version as against many, anonymity of author, etc., and other similar conventional devices.[58]

An attempt has been made to single out certain unifying features of 'primitive' and 'folk music', which set these closely related types apart from art music.[59] Yet it cannot be said that the investigator is convincing in proving his thesis, e.g., when he claims that iso-rhythmic structures, common to both primitive and folk music, are rare in art music. The author has evidently reinterpreted the term 'isorhythmic' to suit his purpose; for it means, as C. Sachs explained so elegantly, the repetition of a rhythmic motif; 'There were different notes in the new phrase, to be sure; but these notes were forced into a Procrustean bed: in their time values they had to fit the durations that their counterparts had had in the initial phrase'.[60] All this refers to polyphonic art music, whereas B. Nettl applies these very terms to 'primitive' songs of the Comanche Indians. He frequently stresses the trend toward unification in it. Well, what else was the purpose of *Ars Nova* isorhythmics, if not to establish some unifying factors? Turning to much newer music: in many of Grieg's compositions (cf. his sonatas for violin and piano, also the piano concerto), we encounter such isorhythmic phrases, sometimes *ad nauseam,* and the same holds true of Tchaikovsky and other adher-ents of the nationalistic schools. Now it may be said that these occurrences are symptomatic of the 'primitiveness' of the folkloris-tic raw material of nationalistic composers, but I think rhythmic monotony is not necessarily characteristic of folk music.[61]

Much more fruitful for our search seems the concept of the *res facta,* a term which has caught the fancy of many writers on music, in spite of the clear and strenuous warnings against such use by the scholar who has treated this elusive designation *ex professo,* Dr. E. Ferand. The learned author convincingly demonstrated that the term *res facta* was possibly 'the result of a confusion with *cantus fractus,* because of the similar sound of the Latin terms. This confusion comes to light in the version *res fracta,* of which a single instance is known from 1550'.[62]

Nonetheless, the idea of a *res facta* = *chose faite* seems to approxi-mate many of the properties of art music, and was so understood—and opposed—by John Calvin.[63] So interpreted, the old *chose faite* has certain features in common with the modern concept of *Gestalt.* This fruitful principle of aesthetics and psychology may enable us to consider an even more serviceable criterion to distinguish between art music and folk music: *Gestalten* have, in music, the significance of 'non-consummated symbols'.[64] How concrete such an abstraction can appear in real music, may be seen in the variations of *Gestalten* as they emerge in the folk-songs collected by Bartók.[65] What this great student of folklore termed *Urgestalt*, corresponds roughly to the concept of archetype, not to that of *Gestalt*. As R. Lachmann pointed out long ago, an imagined, not concretely existing archetype of a music line corresponds to the Platonic idea of a melodic pattern.[66] *Gestalt*, on the other hand, is a tangible quality of an individualized work of art, not a general pattern applicable to many variants of a given folk melody. Archetypes are 'idealizations' of melodic patterns ('modes'), convenient to the scholar for purposes of classification, whereas *Gestalt* is the image evoked by experiencing an individual work of art.

To be sure, these concepts can hardly be applied to the music of the ancient Near East, simply because we know much too little about it. The esteem for creative imagination, especially that for originality, is of relatively recent date in Western art music, and—since Beethoven—its value has often been overrated by naïve music critics, down to the appraisal of the musical clowneries of Mr John Cage. In contrast, folk music esteems most highly 'tradition', which in this case stands for a collective familiarity, at least one or two generations old, with a motif or a melody, within a given region. Common to both art music and folk music, to oriental and occidental music, *was,* but is no longer, the postulate of discernible *coherence* of musical substance and its utilization.[67]

As for the performers, those of art music normally belonged to a higher class than the popular musicians, at least in the ancient Semitic civilizations. In Judaism the status of the trained priest-musician declined drastically with the abolition of sacrifices; the cantor of the Synagogue, however, is in no way comparable to the hierarchically protected priest; he was an appointed (and paid) singer with no priestly function whatever.

Encouraged by his social equality with the main level of his community, the latter did his best to stimulate congregational responses and in so doing developed the tradition entrusted to him. Moreover, the lay-singer or precentor saw in spontaneous improvisation, in the 'outpouring of the soul' the only *theologically as well as aesthetically* approved chant, sanctioned by the Rabbis and generally accepted. It became also the common practice in early American lay congregations, both white and black.

The principle of modally bound improvisation upon 'traditional' (in this instance popular) melos is the distinctive characteristic of oriental Synagogue chant; just one singer, an appointed layman, of whom in olden times no musical training whatsoever was required, led the synagogal service, without priest or sacrifice, also without pomp and usually without art. The chant of the ancient Synagogue developed upon the lines of popular songs, and it was only much later, and only in the European orbit, that it absorbed certain elements of art music, e.g., tunes of minnesingers, or of the virtuoso style of the late eighteenth- and early nineteenth-century Italian opera.[68]

Even when these rather peculiar circumstances are taken into careful consideration, the distinction between certain types of folk music and certain borderline cases of art music remains in the twilight of conflicting reports and divergent manuscripts. For important questions such as the stability or fluctuation of oral tradition during longer time spans, and the relationship of one folk-song's many variants to each other, are still very far from any trace of a rational, that is, *measuring,* solution. For comparisons of folk-songs which originated in different parts of the world at different times, some systematical method is urgently needed, in order to obviate typical errors which have crept in repeatedly, whenever Eastern and Western, or old and new tunes were compared.[69]

Yet here we enter the battle-lines of many conscientious scholars of ethnomusicology. Not unlike the partisans in the conflict between Baconians and Aristotelians in the physical researches of the Renaissance, two opposing groups appear: those concerned with minute details maintain that it is senseless to search for encompassing laws of comparative folklore, because the simplifications necessary in any such search would invalidate them. The scholars on the other side of the dispute, some with a fine mathematical and anthropological background, remind their opponents that Galileo could never have discovered his celebrated laws if he had used ultra-precise instruments; for in physics, as in all natural sciences, the risk of a certain (exactly determinable) degree of simplification or 'idealization' must be taken, if one aims at arriving at any semblance of natural laws.[70]

While precise and minute *description* of any individual phenomenon is indispensable, it does not in itself constitute an essential advance in science. Only by comparison with other phenomena, leading to their generalization, will ethnomusicology emerge from the unmapped jungle of specialized and exotic observations, however exactly measured.

In the following pages, a mathematical principle, which might be applied to a practical evaluation of the variants in oral tradition, will be stated and explained. It will, under certain circumstances, constitute a criterion by which to distinguish between art music and folk-song.

STATISTICAL FEATURES OF FOLK-SONG

One of the most characteristic elements of folk-song is the co-existence of many and often equally well transmitted variants of a 'traditional' melody. This fact has an important corollary: it is normally not possible in orally transmitted folk-song to single out one variant as 'authentic', unless specific historic data can be adduced—a rare occurrence indeed. The co-existence of many variants is comparable to the equivalence of many differing measurements of one given phenomenon in the natural sciences, or in statistics. If the brightness of a star is measured fifty times during the same week, fifty results will be obtained, each one differing from the others, however slightly.

From the mathematical point of view all such variations may be regarded as deviations from a hypothetically 'true' or 'correct' value; in the realm of folklore this hypothetical value may be considered equivalent to the hypothetically 'authentic' version of the melody under consideration. In order to render such variants of melodies accessible to the same mathematical treatment as different data in the natural sciences, we assign numerical values to each of the existing variants, x, x_2, x_3 . . . . x_n. By applying the so-called Theory of Error we should obtain important insights into the relationship of the variants to each other.

The numerical value of a variant may be obtained by representing some of its characteristic properties through well-chosen parameters: e.g., (1) the number of discrete tones of a variant (NT); (2) the quotient of the sum of ascending intervals by the sum of descending ones (IQ); (3) the quotient of the sum of syllables by the number of tones (NS)/NT; (4) the quotient of the interval-range of the variant, minus omitted or singular tones, divided by the number of the interval-range (R—ST)/R; (5) the quotient of the number of tones, minus the number of melismata, by the number of tones (NT—M)/NT; (6) the interval between the final note and the highest note, divided by the entire range (I max.—fin.)/R. All these parameters are chosen arbitrarily, and could just as well be replaced by others. My experience has shown, however, that the parameters chosen represent well some of the variants' properties.[71]

As most oral traditions are connected with words, it is useful to distinguish a syllabic treatment of the text from a melismatic one. Mathematically speaking, the number of syllabically and melismatically treated syllables differs from variant to variant. There are also extreme cases: the total number of syllables divided by the total number of tones NS/NT yields 1 in a strictly syllabic melody without any melisma, but becomes smaller than 1 in any other case, and very small in a prevailingly melismatic melody, as e.g., in an Alleluia. The more parameters are used, the more exactly will the resulting curve describe the relationship between the variants. If such a curve is plotted on graph paper, it will usually have the shape of a long-stretched S.

This curve and another, the famous 'bell' curve of Normal Distribution, emerge as results of purely empirical applications of existing data. Yet it has been shown by rigorous mathematical methods that, whenever a number of coexisting variants (i.e., 'errors' in the mathematical sense) of a hypothetically 'true' melody, or, what amounts to the same thing, a number of differing measurements of one and the same phenomenon, are plotted according to their frequencies, the resulting curves will be of the same nature and property as those obtained by a simple arrangement of empirical data. These curves, the methods which lead to them, the study of their equations and properties constitute the starting point for the mathematical Theory of Error, an integral part of the Calculus of Probability.[72]

173

The curve of Normal Distribution demonstrates well the dispersion and the importance of the mean value: it lies in or near to the middle of the curve, and is the highest point of it, i.e., the maximum, as the majority of variants approach it more or less closely. The curve is obtained by plotting in the ordinate y the relative frequency of the observational data (in this case, the numerical values of the variants), i.e., the percentage of observations which correspond to each x.

An important condition for the validity of all these calculations of error-function is that $x—x_1$, $x—x_2$, etc. (that is, the deviations v_1, v_2, . . . v_n from the arithmetic mean $\bar{x}$) must be much smaller than the mean itself. In the variants of a melody this condition is usually satisfied.

The mathematical approach to the study and the theory of folksong enables us to solve two problems which have puzzled the folklorists for a long time. The first one is concerned with the identity of a given tune: occasionally some of the variants diverge so widely from the majority of the versions, that one is led to question the identity of the 'strange' variants with the tune as it appears in more 'normal' variants. Here the theory of statistics helps us to decide the case. If the variants of the melody are 'distributed

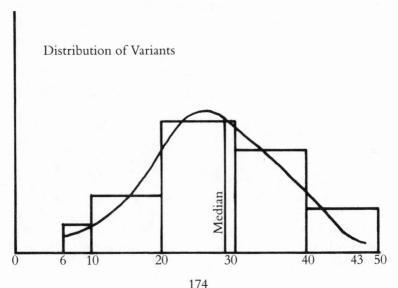

Distribution of Variants

Median

0   6   10   20   30   40   43 50

normally', and their numerical values are contained in the central 68 per cent of the area of the curve of Normal Distribution, they belong with a high grade of probability to the tune under consideration; only if they lie outside that area are their case and their identity questionable. Usually, all melodies of genuine folk-song are represented in variants which are distributed normally; this is a criterion of most European and Near Eastern folk-songs. This statement is not reversible; it cannot be said that any group of melodic variants, grouped in Normal Distribution, constitute *ipso facto* proof that they spring from genuine folk-song.

Much more could be said on these and related matters that are of great importance to the foundation of an exact method, so eminently desirable in the study of folk-songs! Yet any further step in this direction would considerably transcend the scope of this book. Very much within the scope of this book is, however, the study of those forces, ideas or persons, who by their stylization of the musical tradition, be it 'popular' or 'artistic', effected the liturgico-musical interdependence of Church and Synagogue.[73] We are still far from penetrating the cultural and personal intricacies of the forces and persons that transposed the traditions in either direction. In examining this aspect we shall have to focus our attention on the historical problem of rising and declining cultural values; this phenomenon is intrinsically linked with the quest for the transferrers of tradition in the past.

CHAPTER EIGHT

Tradition, its Trustees and Transmitters between Synagogue and Church

A TERMINAL ESSAY

ACCORDING to the dictionary, a tradition is handed down by a *traditor,* a word which has the meaning of a traitor as well as instructor. Indeed this double meaning is justified when the role of transmitter of tradition between Church and Synagogue is being examined: in handing over the customs of the older institution he was, in fact, surrendering them to the newer—he was both prose- lyte and apostate. This feeling of guilt may have hardly been conscious to the first Christian generation, but there can be no doubt that it existed, however disguised and rationalized by such concepts as that of the 'New Jerusalem', the 'Old Law and the New', even by constant reference to Christ's sacrifice as the fulfil- ment of numerous OT prophecies.[1] A badly veiled sense of guilt is evident also in the *Didascalia Apostolorum* (of the late second cen- tury). It admonished Christians to mourn, even to fast, over the loss of Jerusalem and its Temple: '. . . for their sake [of the Jews] we ought to fast and mourn, that we may be glad to take our place in the world to come . . . so we ought to take pity on them . . . and to fast and to pray for them. . . .'[2]

The following inquiries will not exceed the first millennium in the search for the persons and circumstances through which musical tradition was interchanged between Judaism and Christianity. In the first volume of this book a number of forms, concepts, musical modes and archetypes were traced, common to Church and Syna- gogue. A short list will recall the most significant items:

Psalm Tones, *octoechos,* Cantillation, Response and Antiphon; Punctuat- ing Melismata; Ecclesiastical Calendar and its Pericopes; Attitude to

Instrumental Music; Psalmodic Formulas and Intonations such as *Neannoe,* etc.

This list represents part of the liturgico-musical cargo that traversed the Bridge, alluded to in our title, during a score of centuries. The aforementioned designs were no less airy than the great theological concepts that travelled the same road. And yet there was a difference between the two categories: unlike theology or philosophy, whose ideas during a period may be 'in the air' forming part of the *Zeitgeist* and its forces, melodies, rhythms and forms corresponding to those intangible ideas are *not* 'in the air'. They constitute part of the various established traditions of a group and were invented, performed and handed down by individuals known or unknown— by persons, not by the written sound or word. For the period under discussion did not have any musical notation. It will be our task to trace, and if possible to identify those persons or groups of persons who acted as bearers of liturgico-musical tradition between the institutions of Judaism and Christianity. (Some of them were singled out in Vol. 1, pp. 54, 345.)

Judaism of the second century had lost its heritage of art music, for the Temple, the only institution where professional musicians rehearsed and performed regularly and conscientiously, was no more, its musical splendour destroyed, the authority of priests and Levites abrogated! The Synagogue, on the other hand, a logocratic and democratic institution, turned to lay-performers and to folk music. The question of a continuity between Temple and Synagogue has often been raised and indeed answered in this work (Vol. 1, pp. 23 f).

What were the tunes of the Old Synagogue? Apart from psalmody, the foremost heritage of the Temple, orally transmitted, learned and taught from generation to generation of precentors, they were mainly folk tunes that were stylized ever and anew over the centuries. If we are to believe the rabbinic sources, they were mostly love songs, working songs, women's ditties. Their evaluation is not easy. It would be a bad mistake to assume that these were songs of a primitive civilization, or even songs of a backward group within an advanced civilization. Any study that fails to differentiate between folklore in a high culture and that of a primitive civilization, will founder because of the incommensurability of their basic premises. J. G. Herder, otherwise an ingenious and penetrating thinker and researcher of folklore—he coined the word *Volkslied*—committed just this error. Unaware of the disparate elements that constituted his society, he sincerely believed that all poetry of the 'common people' represented the status and quality of the quintessence of a nation (*Grundsuppe einer Nation*): this was a far-reaching concept and has all too often been misused by nationalistic propagandists and politicians who interpreted Herder's cautious phrase in the sense of an 'immutable prime essence of a nation'.[3]

Three main theories emerged in the studies of folk-song during the nineteenth century when the subject was most eagerly pursued by German and English romanticists: (1) All folk-song is the residue of decayed or decaying art, which has 'sunk down' to the level of popular imitation (*Absinkendes Kulturgut*). (2) Most art music has its roots in folk music; through many channels the 'folkish' element rises until it is sublimated by a good composer, knowingly or unknowingly (*Aufsteigendes Kulturgut*).[4] (3) Between the two, a third category of 'modification of values' seeks to erase certain contradictions in either theory. This concept of quasi-simultaneous rising and declining values was most eloquently championed by R. Wagner who in his programmatic essay, *Oper und Drama,* castigated the exploitation of the 'manna' of genuine popular song and, at the same time, expressed his contempt of *'ekelhafte Opernmelodien'* which nonetheless assumed wide popularity. All folk-song was precious to him, yet he was unable to distinguish between the genuine article and the dubious popular ditty. His *Meistersinger* embodies in its libretto his folkloristic convictions; musically they are all but contradicted therein. . . . In the following, a concrete example of such a descending and at other times ascending process of a concept in art, science and folklore will be given, pertinent to our subject matter.

THE OCTOECHOS IN ORAL AND WRITTEN TRADITION

The long history of the eight Psalm Tones' scheme was outlined in the first volume of this work; there the hypothesis of the original calendaric connection between *octoechos* and the pentecontade calendar was offered and elucidated.[5] To the author's satisfaction many scholars were inclined to accept this interpretation.[6] Meanwhile documents of the DSS have more and more confirmed the hypothesis and the most recently discovered *Temple Scroll,* not fully published, seems to prove it. The origin of the pentecontade calendar has been traced far back into the second pre-Christian millennium, as Babylonian priests and astronomers were familiar with it; it seems that the system antedated even them. It was then the closely guarded and esoteric secret of scholars and priests. Yet in the Bible it was not only priests who were privy to it, and in the psalms the transition to more or less familiar patterns of folklore was completed.[7] This 'descending' process will be sketched here, a development from priestly arcanum down to a popular concept well known to the Christian monks of the fourth century.

The earliest references to eight modes seem to occur in one or two Hittite cuneiform tablets.[8] Certain psalms bear a heading which was early interpreted as 'on the eighth mode'; all these veiled references might be considered the last remnants of an old priestly *musica ficta* or *reservata.* Yet when the Rabbis explained and divulged this to the people, the 'descent' had begun, the more so, as the explanations were given in the vernacular Aramaic or Arabic.[9] This system of eight modes was practically implemented by the Jews of Baghdad as we learn from the travelogue of R. Petachya.[10] In the earlier Middle Ages, principle and practice of the eight Psalm Tones seem to have been familiar to the Oriental Jews, not only to their Rabbis, and the system became part of their folklore.

A similar process had taken place with some variations in the entire Near East, both Christian and Moslem. It will remain A. Baumstark's lasting merit to have pointed out the evasive and multifarious nature of the term *octoechos* in its full scope during the Middle Ages. The Arabs no less than the Persians accepted the *octoechos* in principle and even tried to integrate that Greek term into their languages.[11]

In Near Eastern Christianity the idea of the 'holy Eight' originated in heretic circles and we can trace these elements back to the gnostic Valentinians. The wild Hebrew-Greek-Christian syncretism of this literature is replete with references to *Ogdoas* (the great

179

Eight) who was identified with *Achamot* (Hebr. wisdom, Greek *sophia* as in Prov. 9 : 1), the mother of *Hebdomas* (the divine Seven).[12]

Tertullian's description of the Valentinian gnosis does not shed much light upon this syncretistic maze, yet it contains the calendaric term *Sabbatum* for the hebdomadal nature of the demiurge's abode and *Ogdoas,* the demiurge's mother, is still identified with *Achamot*.[13]

This is a set of metaphysical phantasmata, to be sure, yet when it 'descends' to the popular level, it assumes quite concrete aspects and a supposedly practical value: the vulgar counterpart of these cosmological phantasies are not so much the magic papyri, but a step lower, the magic amulets as the practical application of the syncretistic ideas.[14] The magic amulets and other superstitious fancies grew out of this gnosticism as popular traditions emancipated from their theological framework.

We notice, on the other hand, the phenomenon of *ascending tradition* when a great book of hymns assumed the title *octoechos* and, even more so, when composers of Western art music intentionally made use of the intonations characteristic of the various Psalm Tones.

Numerous similar instances are known. The great scholar, Moses Gaster, has collected a number of such 'descending' or 'ascending' motifs; and the motifs common to Buddhism, Byzantine culture, Slavonic literature, Judaism and Christianity are much less rare or far-fetched than one would expect.[15]

In our search for the intermediaries of tradition between Judaism and Christianity the views of past generations of thinkers and scholars should not be disregarded; they reflect the philosophies of earlier centuries. Hence we shall offer here a brief survey of the most representative views of the problem at hand.[16]

Two contradictory answers were given to the main question: Did the Primitive Christian Church borrow originally Jewish tunes? If so, from whom? We shall first consider some of the negative answers and their authors. The original question had to be modified, to be sure. In view of the mounting evidence of similar melodies, identical Psalm Tones, resemblances of archetypes, the suggestion of a common 'Mediterranean style' has been offered,

championed mainly by J. Handschin. Of that style, Greeks, Hellenized Asiatics, and Hellenized Jews were said to have partaken in
equal measure. Yet there is hardly much evidence of such a style; the
Oxyrhynchos Hymn, which is said to represent it best, contains
many more Hebrew than Hellenistic elements, especially the punctuating melismata.[17] Yet another evasive solution was suggested: if
the entire Mediterranean music was diatonic and tetrachordal,
occasional resemblances would occur for reasons of mathematical
probability. Obviously the scholars who suggested this way out of
the dilemma did not know enough about probability. They simply
thought: there are only eight tones in a diatonic octave, hence the
chance of a complete identity of two rows of tones is not too poor;
in fact, it amounts to more than $1/10^8$.[18] Yet they completely forgot
that in our case we are not concerned with a simple but with a
compound and iterated probability, complicated by tunes with
ranges above and below an octave. We do not deny, however, that
identities of 4–6 tones are bound to occur. What does this fact
mean? It would be easy to 'detect' similar 5–6 tone identities in the
music of Bach, Lehár and Schoenberg. What would be the resulting conclusion if the rhythm is disregarded in toto?

Among the authors who chose a clearly negative answer to our
question, we find many fine and critical scholars of the eighteenth
and nineteenth centuries. No longer willing to accept uncritically
the authority of the Church Fathers, they could not believe that the
chants which they heard in the assimilated Western Synagogues of
their times were of the same substance as those which many
centuries before had inspired young Christianity. They looked for
other models and were inclined to believe that ancient Greek music
provided the best solution in view of the considerable remnant of
Greek terminology among the early European music theorists.
Among them we encounter polyhistors like A. Gevaert, an outstanding expert in the field of ancient Greek music, or teutonic
perfectionists such as J. N. Forkel, who summarized his conclusions
in these ringing phrases:

> In short, even under immediate instruction by divinity [Christ] the
> culture of that nation [the Jews] remained so backward, that it is not to be
> counted among the number of cultured nations.[19]

Later on, he does not entirely negate the possibility of a direct transfer of the modes of psalmody.

An enlightened Austrian, the prudent and cautious R. G. Kiesewetter, found another solution which became rather popular for a time and was borrowed by G. Schilling and other writers:

> But that Grecian, or, as some authors have supposed, Hebrew melodies should have found their way into the assemblies of Christians, seems altogether impossible. . . . They [the Christians] evinced an equal anxiety also to separate themselves from the Jews; and their object was, in fact, more especially to found a peculiar art of song distinct from that of any other religion. . . .[20]

His forerunner, K. C. F. Krause, advanced the strange hypothesis of a *creatio ex nihilo,* in distorting a quotation from Eusebius' *History of the Church:*

> Only in 260 was chant admitted *(aufgenommen)* to the Oriental Church. The bishop Nepos composed melodies for the psalms, but instrumental music remained still prohibited. The Christians were obliged to start the art of music *de novo* and had to find a radically new way which would separate the Christian music from the pagan one. . . .[21]

J. Handschin likes ancient authors whom he sometimes quotes, sometimes not. He found an original answer to our question; it might have been uttered by G. A. Bontempi of the seventeenth century.[22]

> If St Paul often recommends to the faithful the singing 'of psalms, hymns and spiritual songs', we must not assume that he meant to impose upon them [in Antioch] some tunes which might have been as strange to them as missionary chorales to Africans. . . .[23]

It is but natural if a great scholar such as A. Gevaert does not mention the possible influence of ancient Jewish chant upon Christian liturgy, for which he in his time (1828–1908) could not have any evidence.[24] Yet the obstinacy with which Handschin wilfully ignored any evidence he must have come across which might have contradicted his prejudices, is hard to comprehend from a strictly scientific point of view.

The affirmative answer has at least four variants: (1) The older historians who considered biblical and patristic statements tantamount to historical evidence, cemented these notions by theological arguments. By far the most original author among them in this respect was Michael Praetorius (1571–1621). Being a fine humanist, he was familiar with the rudiments of the Hebrew language and grammar. According to him, it was the Holy Ghost who served as link between the sacred tradition of the Jews and the customs, prayers and chants of the nascent Church. In the dedicatory epistle of his *Syntagma Musicum,* he views the Old Testament oracles, the enigmatic *Urim* and *Thummim,* as instruments directed by the Holy Ghost. In his opinion there was a perfect continuity between the Temple and the New Church. He refers also to Jewish converts who had given him valuable information on these and other questions. Quite erroneously he derives the word 'Mass' from the Hebrew.[25]

To the same category of the learned humanists belongs W. C. Printz, who correctly observed that the 'hymn-singing' mentioned in Matt. 26 : 30, refers to the great *Hallel* of the Jewish Passover.[26]

(2) The scholars of the century of Enlightenment appear more critical; even a devout Catholic priest, G. B. Martini, examined the question rather independently and rationalistically, as suited the spirit of his times.[27] He too assumed continuity from the Synagogue to the Church and he believed that the Apostles themselves, and certainly the first faithful Christians served as the bearers of traditions from Judaism to Christianity.

This conception, well elucidated, was rationalistic as well as loyal to the tenets of the Church, and full of profound humanistic learning. Padre Martini was rather tolerant toward certain 'progressive' views of his time, as compared to his contemporary and correspondent, the Abbot Gerbert.

Gerbert, no less a polyhistor and *peritissimus* than Martini, and pioneer historian of medieval writers on music, eludes any general categorization: (a) he was no 'man of progress'. Quite to the contrary, he believed that sacred music had reached its highest point at the time of Palestrina and had since declined. (b) Being closer to ancient sources than his contemporaries such as Charles Burney, he remained a strict traditionalist, opposed in principle to instrumental music in the Church. He even championed the return to severe and monophonic Gregorian chant.

He too assumed an organic continuity from the Synagogue to the Church, which is the Synagogue's heir *de jure* as well as *de facto*. He even quoted a layman such as Hugo Grotius to the effect that ancient Jewish psalmody 'which St Paul had so strongly recommended, remained for a long time the custom of the ancient Church'.[28]

A similar but much stronger position was held by Arthur Bedford, two generations before Gerbert. He shows a surprisingly high degree of solid knowledge of Hebrew language and literature. His book, *Temple Musick,* has long been forgotten; yet, if his methods were often dubious and his conclusions absurd, he had a better and deeper insight into the problem than many of his successors. As his book is rare and unavailable, I shall quote a few pertinent observations from it:[29]

> I shall lay down this Hypothesis: that the Musick of the Temple did very much resemble that part of our Cathedral Service which we call the Chanting of the Psalms, esp. where Men and Boys sang the same Part without a Bass; not excluding the other Variety of Responses, which we find in our Litany, and also in our Morning and Evening Prayer. (p. 61)

> This was the Method used by the Primitive Christians in the most Early Ages of the Gospel, and this they borrowed from the Jews. When the Apostles were sent to convert the lost Sheep of the House of Israel, they took a particular care not to separate from them in any thing which was lawful, lest by this means they might frustrate their great Design. (p. 62)

Thus he considered the Judaeo-Christians as the main bearers of liturgico-musical tradition, a surprisingly modern theory, favoured by most archaeological and palaeographic evidence. Bedford reasons along these lines:

> There are some, who take an Occasion to express their Dislike of our Method in Singing at the Cathedrals, because it resembles the Practice of the Jews, in the Time of the Old Law, and therefore they think it must be abolished at the Coming of Christ. This Argument hath been sufficiently confuted by Mr Dodwell, as it related to Instrumental Musick, and his Reasons are as strong in Relation to Vocal. St Paul exhorts the Ephesians to speak to themselves in psalms and hymns, and in spiritual songs. . . . And

St James (5 : 13) commands us that 'if any man is merry, he should sing psalms.' . . . This without Doubt, they sang according to the Direction of the Apostles, and according to the Practice in Singing used among the Jews, unless we will suppose that they invented a New Method; which, I think, will be very hard to prove. (p. 236) . . . When the Apostles exhorted us to sing Psalms, they could certainly have forewarned us at the same time of the Manner of their Singing, if it had been unlawful: but since in this, they made no Alteration from the Jews, we have no Reason to make Alteration from them. . . . Now the Singing under the Law was a *Type,* not of the Gospel, but of the Saints in Heaven; and accordingly St John alludes to this, when he tells us (Rev. 15 : 3) that they sang the Song of Moses, the Servant of God and of the Lamb. . . . And as She [the Church] hath always paid a due Regard to the Customs of Her Forefathers: and as She hath in Her Divine Musick adhered to the Custom both of the Jews and of the Church of Rome: so we may hope. . . .

The purpose of Bedford's book was to justify and to defend the traditional plainchant psalmody in the English cathedrals, which was then under attack from both the non-Puritan gentry and from the simple folk, who preferred the few metrical hymns of their song-books or the English metrical psalms to Merbecke's *Booke of Common Praier Noted* (1550). Bedford fought valiantly against all dilution of psalmody but in vain, at least in his time. The tide of fashion ran against him. Only at the end of the nineteenth and the beginning of the twentieth century did the old plainsong regain some, if not all, of its former ground in the Church of England.[30]

The 'two musical friends' of Dr Johnson, Hawkins and Burney, were personal antagonists and held opposite views on the question of the musical legacy of the Synagogue to the incipient Church. One could hardly expect a profound understanding from a man like Burney:

The value of Gregorian Chant corresponds to the low level of barbarians, i.e. the First Christians. They had no sense for the fine poetry of the Greeks, for they used for their melodies the prose-texts of Scripture—in so doing rhythm and metre were lost. Indeed, these chants bear nearly the same proportions to a marked and elegant melody as a discourse drawn from Swift's Laputan Mill would do with one written by a Locke or a Johnson.[31]

He thought little of Hebrew music for he actually believed that the Hebrew language 'contained no vowels, and therefore was very unfavorable to music' (in antiquity its vowels were not written).[32] Certainly, for Burney, 'a marked and elegant melody' was preferable at any time to ancient psalmody. Had he not defined music as 'an innocent luxury, unnecessary, indeed, to our existence, but a great improvement, and gratification to our sense of hearing . . .'? Thus his final conclusion concerning our quest reads like a stifled yawn:

That some part of the sacred music of the Apostles and their immediate successors, in Palestine and the adjacent countries, may have been such as was used by the Hebrews, particularly in chanting the psalms, is probable; but it is no less probable that the music of the hymns which were first received in the Church . . . resembled that which had been many ages used in the Temple-worship of the Greeks and Romans. . . .[33]

The distinction between psalmody and hymnody is well taken, but Burney was really interested in neither. For his conception of musical history implied a firm belief in infinite progress, and it was unthinkable for him that at the beginnings of recorded history, or rather history of culture, nations as uncouth as the Jews should have left valuable music.[34]

His rival and contemporary, John Hawkins, judges quite differently. He also believed in progress but thought that 'a change in the public taste, whenever it takes place, can hardly fail to be for the better'. In his *General History of the Science and Practice of Music* he is convinced that: 'it [music] was intended by the Almighty for the delight of His rational principles and a deduction of the progress of the science. . . .' which sees in music more than an 'innocent luxury'; thus Hawkins intends to demonstrate that music 'was always supposed to serve higher aims than those of the excitement of mirth'.[35] This appears to suit modern conceptions of music and musical forms much better than Burney's 'elegant melodies'. If Hawkins was less of a musician than Burney, he was more of a scholar and a scientist; his mathematical-acoustical ideas are more lucid than those of Burney. Nor did he hedge in the question of the interrelation between the chant of the Synagogue and Church but took a rather firm, slightly dogmatic point of view: he claimed Jewish influence on the basic ecclesiastical melodies for the first centuries and even for later times, though without citing any evidence. In his manuscripts in the British Museum are found a number of additional 'footnotes' of which those on Church music and psalmody are quite original and interesting.[36] The axiom of progress so dear to the eighteenth century was strengthened by the theory of evolution dominating the nineteenth century. As biblical composers, excepting perhaps King David, were anonymous, the danger of an historical approach with the emphasis upon Great Men never permeated the discussion of biblical music. Even the naïve rationalistic approach had to yield to evolutionist ideas, and music history is indebted to them for some glorious and inspired chapters.

(3) In 1859 Charles Darwin published his *Origin of Species* applying the postulate of progress to biology. The consequences of this work were, as is well known, immense; nor did music history remain untouched.

The three great music historians of the nineteenth century were, without exception, adherents of the theory of evolution: F. J. Fétis, A. W. Ambros, and H. Parry; next to them stand two solid but non-philosophic authors, A. von Dommer and Franz X. Haberl. Of these scholars it was Fétis who had occupied himself most eagerly with oriental music; indeed one may consider him the father of ethnomusicology. Consequently, he was successful in applying the morphological-analytical and the historical method to our problem. He recognized psalmody as the oldest common ground between Hebrew and Christian chant and 'especially ornate psalmody, which came from the ancient Hebrews'.[37]

Stressing the similarity of Byzantine and Oriental Hebrew psalmody, he tentatively identified the proselyte Judaeo-Christians as the transmitters of synagogal chant to the Church; he was the first scholar to recognize the *structural* importance of the *octoechos*.[38] His familiarity with the chant of the Near East is no less admirable than his power of intuition which anticipated some findings of scholars of our time, especially those of C. Sachs and of R. Lachmann.

Compared with Fétis's prophetic insight, his two younger contemporaries, Ambros and Sir H. Parry, could not measure up to this specialist's knowledge of the Near East and its music. Ambros mentions the two contradictory attitudes vis-à-vis our main problem, but refutes some of his uncle Kiesewetter's arguments against Jewish influence. He concludes with the concession

187

. . . that the Apostles . . . intoned the psalms in the melodies with which they were familiar, and that the first Christian community in Jerusalem certainly must have used the old and accustomed tunes for their chant of the psalms.

He ends with the suggestion of Jewish chant in *Palestine* which was transformed for the Hellenized Diaspora into Greek-Jewish *popular* chant.[39]

In contrast to Fétis we hear a great deal about Arabic music in the writings of Parry, but it appears that his knowledge of that branch of Near Eastern folklore did not stand up to serious examination. He speaks of 'the Old Arabic system, which was not pentatonic—whereas the seven-note systems are mostly characteristic of the Caucasian races, and the five-note scales of the somewhat mixed but probably kindred races of Eastern Asia.' Here the reader encounters such a mixture of truths, half-truths, hypotheses, and sheer non-sense, that he must resign all hope of understanding. In his provoca-tively titled *Evolution of the Art of Music,* Parry is quite sure (he is often 'quite sure' in his rhetoric emissions) that after having prac-tised Hebrew psalm singing, 'the early Christians adopted the principles and some of the melodic formulas of the ancient Greek system. . . .'[40]

(4) At this point we might stop and wonder if perhaps Jewish scholars, to whom the problem was not strange after all, contrib-uted to its solution. It was only after the Emancipation at the beginning of the nineteenth century that Jews obtained access to regular university training and, what is more, to the free use of the great libraries. Therefore we can name, for the nineteenth century, only four scholars of respectable knowledge who concerned them-selves with our problem: S. Naumbourg (1815-80), A. Ackermann (1867-1912), J. Singer (1841-1911), and J. L. Saalschütz (1801-1863). He was the first scholar to investigate the possible interrela-tion between Greek and Hebrew chant.

They all tried to analyse the problem of musical tradition com-mon to Jews and early Christians during the first centuries of our era. S. Naumbourg, chief cantor of Paris and friend of Vincent d'Indy, relied not upon historical sources, but upon the morpholog-ical similarity between ecclesiastical and synagogal chant.[41] He was the first to construct or reconstruct certain modes (not scales) which can be found in Church and Synagogue alike. This was also J. Singer's method.[42] In his book, *The Modes (Tonarten) of Traditional Synagogue Chants*, he showed some interesting parallels with Gregorian chant, but failed to reach any conclusions. A. Ackermann,[43] a philologist and historian more than a musician, was thoroughly familiar with the Jewish aspect of the problem and relied for his conclusions on the results and theories of Ambros and Fétis, which he strove to harmonize with his own studies of Hebrew sources.

The next generation of Jewish scholars, however, actually collaborated with the best contemporary musicologists in the discussion of the problem. They had studied at universities, they had established personal contact with the best scholars in the field, and they all stressed the importance of primary historical sources and spade-work in Near Eastern folklore. Their best representative was E. Birnbaum (1855-1920), a profound researcher whose correspondence with H. Riemann and Romain Rolland touched upon our subject. In his publications he concerned himself mainly with the High Middle Ages and the Renaissance.[44] A. Z. Idelsohn (1882-1938) cultivated both the historical and ethnographic aspects of Jewish music; his studies on the system of the Arabic *maqamat* introduced a new concept and a new terminology to the examination of Near Eastern music.[45] In his monumental *Thesaurus of Hebrew Oriental Melodies* (1912-32) he collected in ten volumes a veritable treasury of Jewish and Judaeo-Arabic folklore and tradition. P. Wagner, the great explorer of Gregorian chant, while studying the first of Idelsohn's volumes, discovered obvious similarities and drew the attention of scholars to them. In contact with H. Kretzschmar, C. Sachs, and G. Adler, Idelsohn set the pace for subsequent generations of musicologists as far as comparisons and morphological analyses alone could establish any evidence. His historical training, however, left a good deal to be desired, and *au fond* Idelsohn was not really interested in history.[46] A. Nadel (1872-1943?), collector, rather than scholar, musical writer, rather than researcher, was particularly interested in the Jewish folklore of Eastern Europe; hence there was no reason for him to express his opinions on the origins of Christian chant.

Involved in this controversy were all the outstanding musical scholars of the twentieth century and their positive answer to the

189

basic problem, supported by musical, historical, liturgical and anthropological arguments, appeared strong indeed—yet this conclusion was resisted for almost an entire generation by Nazi racists and their doctrinaires: Not a few musicologists were among the latter!

H. Riemann considered the problem almost solved, and felt sure that the entire Christian psalmody originated in the chant of psalms in the Temple.[47] He hardly argued the case, but simply referred to his extensive bibliography. In G. Adler's *Handbuch der Musikgeschichte* (2nd edition, Berlin, 1930), the chapter on early Christian music and Gregorian chant was written by Peter Wagner, whose sovereignty appeared both in his historical reasoning and in his analytical comparisons.[48] For him the Jewish origin of psalmody and of melismatic chant was certain beyond any doubt. In similar manner W. O. E. Oesterly, in the *Oxford History of Music,* Vol. VII, Oxford, 1929, wrote:

> But if Jewish music was influenced by Greek music, it is on the other hand in the highest degree probable that the music of the Synagogue influenced that of the early Church. 'The forms of liturgical chant', says Hadow, 'on which our Church music was largely founded probably came, in the first instances, from Jewish sources'.[49]

This statement was made without any documentation either historical or analytical. In the same general vein wrote A. Einstein,[50] while R. Lach's and C. Sachs's judgements were founded on minute and detailed comparisons.[51] Even H. Besseler could not argue against obvious evidence[52] and when an entire group of French specialists on Gregorian tradition, A. Gastoué, D. Pothier, A. Dechevrens, S.J., F. Combarieu, D. Mocquereau, O.S.B., and others, emphatically stressed the Jewish roots of plainsong, the case was clear, and the first question answered. Yet the second one—concerning the bearers of the tradition—was not even examined. Or so it seemed. For there remained, or reemerged, new sceptics who stressed, like J. Handschin, a 'common Mediterranean tradition of melodic contour', or, like G. Wille, disregarded any possible Jewish element in favour of Roman chant; he quoted St Arnobius (of the late fourth century!) as his first and foremost authority.[53]

With the exception of P. Wagner, none of the authors mentioned had offered a possible answer as to the identity of the transmitters of the tradition. This was mainly left to the new generation of Jewish scholars in or outside Israel who emerged after the Second World War and of whom we shall mention only H. Avenary, E. Gerson-Kiwi, I. Adler, P. Gradenwitz, and the author of this book. Dr Gerson-Kiwi comes from ethnomusicology and treats our question through comparisons alone; the others with the help of literary as well as historical and liturgical tools.[54]

At this point the interrelation between 'specialists' and 'general historians' bore ample fruit indeed. G. Reese made full use of the work of the specialists in his outstanding book on the music of the Middle Ages; E. Wellesz, who had always maintained a keen interest in and a profound knowledge of the musical history of the ancient Near East, utilized their findings for his monumental study on Byzantine chants; H. Anglès, being most interested in the Jewish tradition of Babylonia and Spain, returned most generously the contributions by Jewish specialists in his comprehensive works on Spanish music; and the very same give and take relationship prevails between K. G. Fellerer and B. Stäblein (the outstanding experts on Catholic Church music) and their counterparts in Synagogue music.[55]

The 'best-selling' textbooks on music history in America appear not as well informed as this high-level literature or as appreciative of the consequences of the interaction between the two groups of scholars mentioned above: distortions, ignorance, inaccuracy are rampant. By far the best representation, however brief, occurs in P. H. Lang's *Music in Western Civilization,* although at the time of its publication (1941) most of the decisive evidence, such as the Dead Sea Scrolls (DDS) or the great archaeological findings had not come to light as yet.[56] D. Grout's massive textbook is, as far as our question is concerned, not quite up to date and often ignores ancient sources such as the DSS as well as modern findings.[57] Some items of the pertinent terminology leave a good deal of preciseness to be desired.[58] We fare no better with other English or American textbook authors; this judgement, of course, does not apply to great encyclopaedic works such as *NOHM,* or *MGG,* where most chapters or articles were written by specialists.

191

THE TOPOGRAPHIC AND HISTORICAL APPROACH

After this survey of changing or fluctuating opinions on the subject of this chapter, we venture to scrutinize it *de novo*. If we attempt, in a mental experiment, to think of a history of music excluding the Bible and its exegesis, we should meet with a strange discontinuity in the flow of documents: from Egyptian, Babylonian, Greek and Roman testimonies we would have to jump to Christian statements about music in Palestine, Gaul, Spain, Byzantium, etc. We would constantly encounter quotations from, allusions to, and discussions about biblical remarks, which we could then hardly comprehend. Such a 'jumping' sort of selection of historical sources has indeed been undertaken.[59] Its discontinuity testifies strongly to the continuity of music's road from East to West, if only *per negationem*.

The apostolic and post-apostolic teachers of the early Church, such as Clement of Rome, Origen, the Judaeo-Christians, Hegesippus and Symmachus, the orthodox Epiphanius no less than heretics such as Paul of Samosata and the unjustly banned Nestorius, were all familiar with Jewish doctrine and lore, perhaps through the 'testimony-books' to be mentioned below. In spite of all rivalry, it is still amazing how close some of their fellow Christians felt to Judaism as late as the fourth century, as may be seen in a brief excerpt from Eusebius' *Martyrs of Palestine,* which we quote in its Syriac version.

16 February, 310:

Having harassed the spokesman of them all with these trials, he [the Roman judge] first asked him who he was; then, when he had heard, instead of the man's proper name, that of some prophet—for this was what they all did: in place of the names which their fathers had given them (names, perhaps, belonging to idols) they called themselves by others: for instance, you might have heard them assuming names such as Elijah and Jeremiah and Isaiah and Samuel and Daniel, and thus manifesting, not only by deeds but by the literal sense of the words they used, *the Jew which is one inwardly* (Rom. 2 : 29) and the genuine and pure *Israel of God* (Gal. 6 : 16). . . . The judge (he cannot have been very learned) asked the martyrs where they had come from; and they all said 'from Jerusalem', a place of which he had never heard (at that time the Romans called Jerusalem, Aelia Capitolina), yet the martyrs again quoted St Paul who had said, 'The Jerusalem

192

that is above is free, which is our mother' (Gal. 4 : 26), this they cited as their hometown—to the great perplexity of the judge.[60]

Only where primitive Christians and Jews lived in proximity, or where the existence of proselytes *en masse* is well established, is the first and necessary condition for the transition of customs and ideas fulfilled; yet it is not sufficient. For quite frequently both the Jewish and the Christian traditions have been lost in the turmoil of the centuries. Such a case is Armenia, whose close relations with ancient Judaism were demonstrated in the first volume. We must look for communities which survived the storm of the people's migration, which maintained their literary, liturgical, and linguistic identity until their tradition was firmly established.

Of the five ancient centres of Christianity, viz. Jerusalem, Antioch, Byzantium, Rome and Alexandria, the last named city fell out early because of the massacres of Jews during the third century, organized under the instigation of St Cyril and climaxing in the subsequent edicts by Emperor Theodosius. By the Council of Chalcedon (451) the power of the Patriarch of Alexandria was seriously diminished; the Monophysite Church arose and opposed the Byzantine State Church. When the Arabs conquered Alexandria, many Christians greeted them as liberators. By that time, there were but a few Jews left in Alexandria.

Somewhat more favourable appeared the case of Jerusalem. After the revolution in 135 under Bar Kokhba, the Jews were forbidden to enter Jerusalem or to dwell therein, a state of affairs still true at the time at Eusebius (313).[61] Nonetheless a number of ossuaries containing bones of Jews and Judaeo-Christians dating from the second to the fourth centuries have been found in the Valley of Yehoshaphat.[62] The Byzantine emperors after Constantine seem to have extended some privileges to the Jews in or around Jerusalem that were not granted to Jewish subjects elsewhere.

The Jerusalem Synod complained about the presence of Jews during the *missa catechumenorum,* referring to them as 'Jewish serpents and Samaritan imbeciles listening to the sermons in church like wolves surrounding the flock of Christ'.[63] Later, the Byzantine emperors did whatever they could to harass the Jews under their jurisdiction. In 429, Theodosius abolished the Jewish patriarchate which had been vacant since Gamaliel VI, of the House of Hillel, who died without sons. This decree assumes a somewhat shady aspect if we attach any value to the gossip related by Epiphanius, probably a Jewish convert himself. According to Epiphanius:

> The patriarch Hillel II on his death-bed sent to the Bishop of Tiberias and was absolved by extreme unction in form of a medical treatment. Feigning bashfulness and commanding all others to leave him alone, the patriarch was then initiated [into Christianity] by holy baptism and divine mysteries.

Epiphanius' source was the well-known apostate Joseph of Tiberias, a tale-bearer of the first rank, much beloved by Epiphanius, Eusebius, and even Emperor Constantine, who elevated him to the rank of *comes*. The entire story is a fabrication, for Gamaliel V, son of Hillel II, continued as patriarch after his father's death. But the story might have given Theodosius a nice 'legalistic' reason for abrogating the patriarchate.[64]

Justinian tried to undermine the liturgy of the Synagogue by his laws, especially by the *novella* 146, which was discussed in our first volume.[65] When in 614 the Persians conquered Jerusalem, the Jews helped them, hoping for liberation from the hated Byzantians; after a short interlude due to Emperor Heraclius, the Arabs conquered the city in 638, when the Jews again gave assistance.

The entire period beginning with Theodosius was replete with violence and murder, sacking and rape, arson and vicious destruction. It was a war of all against all and the Jews sought to survive by force or ruses. How deeply rooted the hatred was between Christian and Jew can be seen in the numerous massacres that took place there in the sixth and seventh centuries.[66] Even worse feelings than these must have stirred those who left Judaism in fear believing the story that Sophronius, Patriarch of Jerusalem, and Kaliph Omar had come to an agreement that the Jews were forbidden to live there.[67]

Even less peaceful is the history of religion with respect to Antioch. A rich and powerful Jewish community was comfortably ensconced there during the West Roman rule.[68] Yet it was always surrounded by hostile forces. From prehistoric times, Syria had been a mongrel mixture of various races, religions, languages and customs, and the centrifugal forces were often stronger than those that held Syria together. Yet the hatred of the Jews was old and well established. From the time of the conquest by Joshua until the day when Syria became an independent state after 1945, that is for almost three millennia, this country was rarely ever united or autonomous. The rule of the Seleucids was actually the only successful period in its history. The Maccabean Wars against the latter indicated the deep-seated conflict between Jews and Hellenized Syrians—and even the Hellenization of Palestinian Jewry under the Hasmoneans and under Roman rule could not neutralize the ancient antagonism. The best characterization of the Syrian problem can be found in a book on Christian liturgy by an author of exceedingly penetrating judgement. We cannot do better than to reproduce some of his descriptive observations.

> Syria was an older underlying patchwork of races, languages, traditions and religions, with a recent and different patchwork of hellenism and the surviving native cultures superimposed upon it. The underlying patchwork is *local,* but the only line of division one can draw between hellenism and the oriental traditions is purely *cultural.* By A.D. 300 a man might be a Syrian (which could mean racially a mongrel of half-a-dozen different strains) and yet as hellenised and westernised in speech and mind and habit of life as an inhabitant of Athens or Alexandria or even Rome. And his next-door neighbour might be equally Syrian by blood and remain as completely oriental in culture and language and thought as his forefathers a thousand years before. Or he might be bilingual, with some sort of footing in both worlds. . . . Apart from a whole succession of obscure and fantastic popular movements . . . we have to reckon, first, with the great East Syrian revolt against Antioch in the fifth century, which adopted the banner of the Nestorian heresy; and secondly with . . . the West Syrian revolt of the sixth century which called itself Monophysite; and thirdly, with the Maronite schism in the Lebanon of the eighth century, which took the excuse of Monothelitism. We need not here concern ourselves with the doctrinal pretexts. The real dogma of all the rebels was 'anti-Byzantinism' or 'anti-hellenism', as the 'orthodoxy' of Antioch was always in practice 'Caesaropapism.' Between them the royalist patriarchate and the nationalist schisms shattered Syrian christianity as a living force. . . .[69]

And yet, this seething cauldron of sects, religions, nationalities, customs, races and ruling cliques, facilitated the active exchange between Jews and Christians. There were many reasons for this

195

intercourse. First and foremost the language: Aramaic together with Greek were the two languages which in Antioch every Jew and Syrian mastered. Even typically poetic forms had transcended all national boundaries: the biblical psalm, the Syriac hymn form, the Syriac metre of isosyllabism were common properties. Unless the isosyllabic system can be proved to be used in biblical Hebrew— there are isosyllabic passages among the quotations from certain lost books whose titles are referred to in the Bible—we should assume that this metre originated in Syria and came into the Hebrew language through the early *piyyutim*.[70]

Judaeo-Christianity held a strong position in Antioch: the *Didascalia* and part of the Pseudo-Clementines originated there; in the period from Barnabas to the great hymnodist Romanus and indeed until Bar-Hebraeus, we encounter a series of celebrated converts to Christianity. This was so even during Talmudic times: R. Tanchuma held a disputation there with a proselytizing Christian after 350. Soon after, the first Synod at Antioch (Canon I) declared that Easter must never be celebrated at the same time as the Jewish Passover.[71] From this and other laws one may conclude that the Christians often visited the Jewish synagogues and probably vice versa. Yet there arrived in Antioch one of these fiery homilists who saw his foremost aim as the destruction of this togetherness and finally in the annihilation of Jews and Judaism. This was, of course, St John Chrysostom. Here it is unnecessary to waste many words on this inveterate liar and rabble-rouser, and it may suffice to quote here Parkes' words concerning this pious man:

> In these discourses [the sermons of St John Chrysostom] there is no sneer too mean, no gibe too bitter for him to fling at the Jewish people. No text is too remote to be able to be twisted to their confusion, no argument is too casuistical, no blasphemy too startling for him to employ. . . .[72] It may well be that the Jews of Antioch were both powerful and aggressive. If they were so, they shared these characteristics with the Christians of that city. In such a situation it would have better become a priest to have tried to calm tempers rather than to inflame them with as complete an absence of interest in veracity as is shown by Chrysostom. . . .[73]

Indeed if the guilt of senseless hatred of Jews can be laid to one person in particular, it would be Chrysostom, the 'golden-mouthed'.

After the conquest by the Arabs the Christian patriarchate, which at times had rivalled that of Rome, faded away to a rather unimportant legalistic representation. From *c.* 100–600, Jews and Christians in Antioch were close neighbours, albeit enemies; and Parkes is certainly right in ascribing their mutual hatred to the 'too close fellowship of Jews and Christians in Antioch'.[74]

In an earlier chapter, we drew attention to a Syrian martyrology which included Jewish martyrs, also to the church in Antioch which once contained their relics.[75] We know, moreover, of the *Syriac Masora* which ran parallel to the first Palestinian group of Masoretes,[76] and the Syriac system of punctuation is so closely related to that of the Protopalestinian school that it is hardly possible to tell them apart.[77] In view of this common intellectual atmosphere embracing even poetry, grammar, chant and liturgy, we are inclined to view the Syrian Jewish converts of the first four centuries as the main bearers of Jewish tradition into the Church. This transference was not restricted to the Roman Church alone; it seems to have been active also in the Nestorian and later in the Jacobite (Monophysite) Churches.

To clinch the argument, there is both linguistic and liturgical evidence that some types of chants were common to Jews and Christians: (a) the Talmudic *'inyan* corresponding exactly with the Syriac *'enyana*; in the Jewish sources it stands for 'answer' or 'response' [to a benediction.] The connotation of chanted response is common to both terms. (b) Talmudic *sugia* = Syr. *soghita* = dialogue, study, lesson; (c) Hebr. and Syr. *Memra* = a saying, a proverb, a spoken or chanted aphorism; (d) *midrash* = Syr. *madrasha* which stands for a didactic or legendary, mainly narrative, piece of literature.[78]

The matter looks, however, quite differently if we ask ourselves how much of the once-common tradition survived. As far as can be established today, very little; nothing in musical notation. Yet we are confronted with a plethora of historical, theological, liturgical, and even personal elements in common, which once gave rise to West Semitic poetry and chant. Only by way of Byzantium did its remnants survive and sometimes find their way to the West.[79] As seen from the Syro-Judaic point of view the great and secure storehouse was Byzantium, also the juncture of the East-West road, the place of transshipment and relay, but not an original starting-point. A good deal of pristine material has survived in the original Syriac or Hebrew manuscripts. Yet the clergy, be it Christian or Jewish, saw to it that most of the common elements were veiled or at least weakened.

Different again was the situation in Rome during the first four or five centuries. From the period of apostolic Christianity there flourished in Rome a rather close social, economic, and even religious intercourse between Jews, Gentiles and Judaeo-Christians until the fourth or fifth century.[80] The eminent historian, Professor S. Baron, has repeatedly stressed the somewhat superstitious attraction as magicians or supernatural healers which the Jews held for the Gentile Romans. Many Christian women wore, as St Jerome laments, the Jewish phylacteries as talismans, sometimes with a cross or a pocket gospel.[81] Whether the third bishop of Rome, Clement, was of Jewish descent is not important: we know today of his being familiar with a good deal of rabbinical tradition, even with parts of the DSS, and of his being sympathetic to Judaism.[82] Shortly after his time a synagogue seems to have been built in Ostia—ruins of which were only recently discovered—whose history is still doubtful: was it a prayer-house of the Judaeo-Christians or was it a conventional synagogue?[83] Jews were buried in Christian cemeteries and vice versa, and the Rabbis supported the custom.[84] Even Christian saints were buried in Jewish cemeteries.

Although quite a number of Latinized Hebrew names have been found in the Christian catacombs, it is not always easy to reconstruct the interrelation as in the famous case of the deacons Deusdedit and Redemptus, who have been discussed in Vol. I.[85] At this occasion, I am happy to rectify an error of Vol. 1. There (pp. 54 f) I surmised that the term *levita*, the title of Deusdedit, hinted at his Levitical descent. As Prof. A. Stuiber, of Bochum, has kindly informed me, *levita* was the official title of a Roman deacon; thus the remark 'primus in ordine' indicates that Deusdedit was an archdeacon. At any rate, the famous legend of St Peter, protector of Roman Jewry, originated in Rome and indicates well the rather strange, but not hostile relationship in later centuries. According to the legend wherein Antioch is closely linked to Rome,[86] Peter, bearing his original Hebrew name Simon bar Kepha, was a sage feared by the

Christians. In vain they tried to proselytize him; it was only after a massacre of the Jews and upon their pleadings, that Simon sacrificed himself for his people. He appeared together with the Pope and the bishop (!) before the Christians and addressed them with the words: 'What do you want from me? Do what St Paul has commanded you in the name of Jesus: do not stone the Jews, admit them to your churches!' He did penitence for his baptism, living as an ascetic in a tower and protecting both the lives and the privileges of the Jews. According to that legend a famous Hebrew poem which is still sung every Sabbath was written by him. The oldest version of the legend originated in the fifth century, the two others in later centuries, but certainly before the year 1000.

The extraordinary interest of St Jerome in all things Jewish and Hebrew is well known and attested to, although one cannot call him a benevolent observer.[87] With his strong personality, his immense efforts to translate all of Scripture and his labours to reproduce the characteristic structure of Hebrew prose and poetry as accurately as possible in Latin, he added another pillar to the bridge between Synagogue and Church; moreover, he indoctrinated whole groups so that they became transmitters of Hebrew elements to the Church. His influence is most important in the fields of language, stylistics and literature. F. J. E. Raby has pointed out, and succeeding scholars have confirmed:

The language of the Vulgate gathers up the various influences which had been at work in creating the appropriate medium for the expression of Christian thought in the West. Jerome indeed owed much to his unknown predecessors who had based their versions on the Septuagint and had introduced along with Hellenic elements the flavour of the vulgar tongue. He combined with these elements others derived from the Hebrew; so a part of the Hebraic spirit passed into his version. New rhythms appeared, a new and more romantic imagery. The mystical fervour of the prophets, the melancholy of the penitential psalms or of the Lamentations could not be rendered in Latin without giving that severe and logical language a strange flexibility, an emotional and symbolical quality which had been foreign to its nature. The whole literary imagination of the West was to be fed on the sonorous sentences of the Latin Bible, and Christian poetry . . . could not escape the spell or fail to learn the new language. . . . Out of this music was to issue the poetry of the future, the poetry in which the Catholic emotion was to discover its final expression. It is the music of a new world. . . .[88]

Since the beginning of this century the existence and influence of so-called books of testimonies have become most probable. They contained, perhaps in midrashic, perhaps in aphoristic form, chunks of rabbinic literature and tradition, written in Greek. These 'testimony-books' seem to have been widely known and were in the hands of most early Christian theologians of the West.[89] Their importance was mainly of a theological nature. Yet when these ideas were expressed in poetical form, i.e., for the liturgy, another link is noticeable besides the biblical parallelism of verse structure. A kind of metre called homotony seems to have been brought from post-biblical Hebrew to Latin art prose—not to *poetry*—at least not while the classical system of quantitative metre was still alive and cultivated. Homotony keeps the number of accentuated words per line more or less constant. In the first volume one short example of this system was cited, a part of the *Te Deum*. To amplify the evidence, a few more illustrations may be adduced, chosen at random:

(1) Missale Romanum, Feria IV Cinerum, Oratio ante lect. Joelis Proph.:

Praesta, Domine, fidelibus tuis:
ut jejuniorum veneranda solemnia,
et congrua pietate suscipiant,
et secura devotione percurrant

(2) Miss. Rom.: Sabbato Sancto, Oratio ad bened. igneris:

Domine Deus,
pater omnipotens,
lumen indeficiens,
qui es conditor
omnium luminum:
benedic hoc lumen,
quod a te sanctificatum,
atque benedictum est. . . .

(3) Miss. Rom., Feria V in Coena:

Adesto. Domine, quaesumus,
officio servitutis nostrae:

200

et quia tu discipulis tuis pedes
lavare dignatus es,
ne despicias opera
manuum tuarum, quae
nobis retinenda mandasti. . . .[90]

The real reasons for the change from the classical verse to new, so-called rhythmic lines[91] lie deep. In our opinion they have intrinsically and organically grown out of the increasing interaction of the Graeco-Latin literature with the Hebrew-Aramaic through the translations of the Bible, the Greek, Syriac and Latin testimony books and the targumin and midrashim. This will be exemplified in a brief analysis of the first part of the *Te Deum* with regard to its choice of words and concepts.

The Te Deum

It is truly regrettable that the author of the most recent study on the *Te Deum*—it amounts to a most erudite essay—did not deem it necessary to say even one sentence about the art prose and the metre of the hymn. Neither did he deign to consult Judaistic literature on problems such as *Kabod, Doxa, Sanctus,* their variants and meanings.[92] Nonetheless, he reaches a tenable result in considering many of the concepts of the *Te Deum* as 'spät-jüdisch' (an expression invented by the German protestant Hebraists of the last century meaning the post-biblical or early Talmudic period).

(a) *te dominum confitemur.* Professor Kähler writes some pages on the word *confitemur* without an idea that the entire phrase is borrowed from the Hebrew *modim anachnu lach* written about three centuries before the *Te Deum.* Of course his conclusions are correct but rather cumbersome.[93]

(b) *incessabili voce proclamant.* Kähler subscribes to the notion of A. Jungmann that this expression originated in secular acclamations of emperors and the like and from there was brought into the angelic liturgy. A glimpse into the DSS (*Angelic Liturgy*) or into Ch. V of this volume will immediately correct these errors.[94]

(c) *te aeternum patrem. . . .* Kähler quotes here the Missale Gothicum which uses the *praefatio* (1) *dignum et justum est,* (2) *nos tibi gratias agere,* (3) *tibi debitas laudes pio honore deferre,* etc. These three phrases

201

are post-biblical Hebraisms and may be found in every traditional prayer book; all three originated in the first five centuries. The (1) occurs in the daily morning service of the Synagogue (translated 'true and firm, right and meet').[95] The (2) ibid., morning service (translated 'it is our duty to thank, praise and glorify thee').[96] The (3) ibid., morning service ('it is our duty to praise the lord of all things') (The famous 'Alenu prayer).[97]

The theological concept of the *rex gloriae,* alluding to Ps. 24 *melekh ha-kabod,* is obvious, and its transposition to Christ with the reference to the *Descensus ad inferos* shows clearly the continuous interaction of Judaeo-Christian concepts. The metrical form resembles, as observed in Vol. 1, that of Hebrew homotony which is found in numerous prayers of the third and fourth centuries, e.g., in 'May it be thy will',[98] or 'Blessed be He who spake',[99] and many other such compositions, where the number of accented words per line remains constant. The majority of the *Te Deum* lines can be grouped in lines of three or four accentuated words, whereby certain prepositions are not counted.[100] For the tune of the *Te Deum,* see page 124.

With all that interplay in literature and religion, the admonition of Firmicus Maternus addressed to Emperor Constantine after his victory at the Pons Milvius, has an ominous ring: 'It is better that you save [the Jews] against their own will than that you let them perish according to their will.'[101] Yet the very same writer and poet gave in his treatise against pagans and Jews a homiletic interpretation of Ps. 24:7, which apparently was introduced into the concepts of *Te Deum.*[102]

The Psalm Tones

The laws of Theodosius I and II treated the Jews severely and tried to hamper the exchange of ideas between Church and Synagogue. In spite of them, the mutual intercourse was still close and social relations between Jews and high clergymen were nothing extraordinary.[103] In spite of all the laws of Gregory the Great and the *Codex Theodosius,* the common celebrations of the Sabbath by Jews and Christians were continuing and even laws of Charlemagne and later councils thundered against such practices in vain.

If we now draw tentative conclusions from the evidence before us, we are forced to accept the theory that Antioch and Rome (perhaps also Jerusalem and later Byzantium) served as centres of transference of the liturgico-musical tradition, linking the two faiths. Having reached this important, yet tentative conclusion, we may ask what sort of chants were transmitted, and also whether they survived. The repertoire of the Synagogue was after all neither big nor variegated. It contained psalmodies, plain and ornate, responses and a few modest melismatic chants. The psalmodies were not rigidly organized with *tuba* and *flexa,* but contained usually two ténors, like the *tonus peregrinus.*[104] The punctuating melismata were, however, well developed and clearly performed as we learn from the grammarians of that age. We know next to nothing about the modes then in use; yet, if the continuity of oral tradition in the Mediterranean orbit means anything, we should expect modes with D, E and G as *finales* in tonal and subtonal ranges, which would correspond with the modes of the oldest chants, psalmodies, Graduals, and Tracts of the Roman Church. It may well be that one mode (not a scale!) much in use ended on E, whose ténor and *confinalis* was C;[105] such tunes belong also to the archaic structures of popular song in the Near East, and were not unkonwn in Byzantine chant. They appear quite regularly in the Lesser Doxology (Mode I, formula 12).[106]

In Gregorian chant, the ténor C for the third Psalm Tone has been admitted—albeit reluctantly. It is quite instructive to survey the various opinions of the scholars on this difficult stylistic question from about 1900 to the present day.

In his work, *Les Origines du chant romain* (1907), a book which advanced a radically new point of view, A. Gastoué bowed a little to the authority of A. Gevaert, who derived both tonality and the *octoechos* of the Psalm Tones from Greek theorists. Accordingly he speaks of the (Greek) *Echelles Doriennes,* where he means the third and fourth Tones; he mentions B as possible ténor but provides for 'certain formulas' the *Dorienne Modifiée* with ténor C.[107] And he had the courage to write, then and there: 'It is a bad error, and widely spread, to believe that this system [of the eight Psalm Tones] was originally applicable to *all* liturgical chants; it is true, though, that habit has sanctioned that practice. . . .'[108] P. Wagner, the grand master of this subject, explained as lucidly as possible the problems

203

of the ténor in the third and fourth Psalm Tones; he even permitted himself a little historical speculation about the forces that caused these 'irregularities';[109] he cautiously mentioned that the Psalm Tones and the modes refer to the same scalar model, never considering them as identical. Yet he is fully aware that the third Psalm Tone uses C instead of B.[110] P. Ferretti, O.S.B., on the other hand, evades the question of the 'irregular' ténor of the third and fourth Psalm Tones altogether; he considers the ténor C 'a corruption' of the original B without citing any reasons.[111] Eventually he recognizes these irregular ténors in the Tones of the canticles according to the *Commemoratio brevis*.[112] Yet he fails to give any reasoned elucidation of the structural differences between Psalm Tones and octave-species (or modes). G. Reese takes a major step forward in suggesting that 'the Psalm Tones are evidently not the least important of the formulas that helped to stamp the scalar modes with their ultimate characteristics'.[113] The latest serious and comprehensive book on Gregorian chant, by W. Apel, lists B and G as *tubae* of the third and fourth Psalm Tones respectively. But the author adds immediately the observation: 'This, however, is not entirely the actual state of affairs. In present-day practice as well as in the common usage of the Middle Ages the three ténors (B G B) are each a tone higher: for the third Psalm Tone the ténor is on C, for the fourth, on A, for the eighth, on C. . . .'[114] He goes on to prove that the original ténor of the third Tone was B, not C. If this conclusion were final, two results would spring forth from it: (a) one would have to set aside all those Oriental psalmodic structures altogether, or (b) one would have to conjecture that the change from B to C in the Occident happened due to continuous Byzantine or Near Eastern influence. We are as yet far from commanding sufficient evidence, written or oral, to warrant acceptance of either of the two alternatives.

Aside from the various psalmodic forms, only the liturgical recitation or cantillation and a few characteristic melismatic formulas might have crossed the bridge between Asia and the West during the first millennium. Some of the recurrent melismatic formulas were discussed in Vol. 1, and here only one observation needs discussion.[115] A certain melismatic formula, typical of Gregorian tracts, as quoted in Vol. 1 where also its Jewish counterpart was shown, appears also in older Alleluias; e.g., in the *Confitemini* on Holy Saturday, the *Confitemini* on Rogation Days (Greater and Lesser Litanies), *Haec dies* on Saturday in Easter Week, *Dominus in Sina* (on Ascension Day), etc. The two first mentioned *Confitemini* have the same text, namely the Egyptian *Hallel,* originally used only for the Jewish Passover; the *Haec dies* stems from Ps. 118, also *Hallel*; the *Dominus in Sina* (Ps. 68 : 17-18) sung on Ascension Day, is still part of the Oriental Jewish Pentecost liturgy. All this indicates old Judaeo-Christian traces in the customs of Eastertide; it does not prove them.[116]

There remains the liturgical recitation, also called cantillation. The Roman rite has stylized it much more rigidly than any other Catholic tradition; the Byzantine *ecphonesis* is considerably nearer to Oriental Jewish tradition. Unfortunately, the Syrian traditional cantillation has been lost since the tenth century.[117] A few enclaves of the Roman Church have maintained a fairly well preserved tradition of the old Latin cantillation, and in former chapters of this volume we referred to S. Corbin's excellent study on this subject. A comparison among these remnants of the Byzantine, Armenian, and perhaps the Nestorian traditions with the Oriental Jewish custom shows distinct similarity between the Byzantine and Armenian types on one hand, and Oriental Jewish cantillation on the other. Yet we must always bear in mind that the syntax, pronunciation and punctuation of a language have much more impact upon its musical rendition than all religious, ritual, local or racial characteristics may make upon it. Ethnic-linguistic identity has always begotten a folk music of its own, and inasmuch as all Synagogue chant, Moslem chant, Oriental Christian chant, *if sung in the vernacular,* is still extremely close to folk music, we realize that religious or even liturgical similarities do not necessarily condition musical ones. And yet in spite of the many divergencies—ethnic, linguistic, aesthetic—it will always be amazing to what extent the Roman *cursus* has preserved and stylized originally Jewish elements. P. Wagner's bold words, 'Only one answer is possible: the technique of migrating melismata functioning as punctuation is a heritage from the Synagogue',[118] are today as valid as when he wrote them more than fifty years ago; and every new comparison with groups of hitherto 'untouched' Oriental Jews confirms his words.

The Oldest Notated Source

It is well known that after the eighth century the Synagogue of the West began to adjust itself to the Church more and more. While the transmitters were not known, the evidence is clear: all Hebrew hymn forms are post-biblical and were at first imitations of Syriac or of Graeco-Latin models. Yet we never knew even one person who mustered enough authority to bring Christian notation and tunes into the supposedly ultra-conservative Jewish orbit. It was only within the last forty years that an extraordinary and interesting case of a musician's conversion to Judaism became known, together with some of his compositions or arrangements, written in neumes. Here is the story of the discovery.

E. N. Adler, a prominent barrister and collector of rare manuscripts in London, had in his library a Hebrew manuscript with neumes. After the end of World War I, he sent it to Abbé Mocquereau, the eminent musical paleographer of the Solesmes Monastery. Mocquereau and two assistants offered a transcription of the neumes, which they considered Lombardic, and dated in the late twelfth century. They admitted that they had not fully solved the problem of the clef, which was a Hebrew letter D crossing the third line. A number of scholars, including this author, have concerned themselves with the enigmatic manuscript. New light came into the matter, when two scholars, working independently, identified the scribe—a descendant of a Norman aristocratic family. Dr A. Scheiber of Budapest and Professor N. Golb of Chicago recognized the hand of a writer whose history had been known before from other sources. Obadiah the Norman proselyte, as he was called, was born Jean (Giovanni) baron de Drocos (or Dreux) in Oppido, a little town in Apulia, between 1050 and 1075. According to his own autobiography, Jean was 'a man who sought wisdom and understanding in books'. Hence, he engaged in a career leading to the priesthood or to a superior place in a monastic order, the usual position of a younger son of an aristocratic family. Through the discovery of his autobiography we obtained a most interesting document on the interrelationship between Jews and Christians just after 1100. The document opens with the dramatic statement:

Obadiah the Norman proselyte who entered the Covenant of the God of Israel in the month of Elul in the year 1403 of the Seleucides which is 4862 of the creation of the world [i.e. September 1102].

According to the prevailing laws, Obadiah-Jean would have been punished with death for apostasy into Judaism if he had remained in Europe. Thus he had to leave his home and land, and so went to the Near East, well provided with letters of introduction from eminent European rabbis to their Eastern counterparts. After many journeys in the Near and Middle East, about which he had himself reported, he settled in Cairo and died there, probably before 1150.

(a)

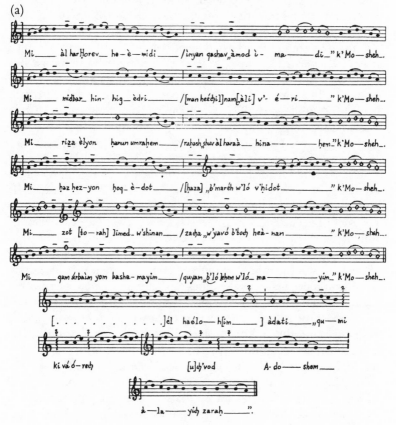

207

To date, three musical documents from his hand have come down to us: (a) a *piyyut* (liturgical poem) about Moses on Mt Horeb, (b) a fragment of another *piyyut,* and (c) a cento of biblical sentences culled from Jeremiah, the Proverbs, and Job.[119] Only the first piece exceeds the simple lines of biblical cantillation and shows a remarkable resemblance to Gregorian chant, but no identity! The many comparisons that have been undertaken since 1920 have only led this far: the resemblance with Gregorian chant is not accidental but organic. It may be caused by the monastic training of Obadiah, or by his wish to synthesize the songs of his youth with those of the Eastern Synagogue; perhaps the melody was Obadiah's arrangement and paraphrase of a tune which he heard in the Jewish communities of the Near and Middle East. He might have been but a scribe, recording tunes he had heard, or else a real composer—we may never know the true state of facts. Yet another question arises here: why did he write any music for the Synagogue in Italian neumes which none of his friends or acquaintances were able to read? If he did it to help his own memory, we must assume that he was an officiating cantor, yet his autobiography does not refer to it up to 1121, where it breaks off. We give H. Avenary's tentative transcription on page 209.[120]

The case of Obadiah the proselyte shows clearly the twofold direction in which tradition moved even after the Crusades. It reminds us that the road from the composer of art music to the recorder of stylized folk music was not very long. Nor can terms of folklore such as *aufsteigendes* or *absinkendes Kulturgut* be justly and wisely employed here as it would be hard to define the higher or lower status of the model and its imitation or paraphrase. Art-song or common popular tunes? It does not seem to matter at that time. Here I am unable to agree with a man of so profound an understanding of the subject as Professor E. Lowinsky who wrote: 'The beginning and the end of musicological studies lie in sympathetic and critical examination and of evaluation of the *individual work of art*' (italics mine). If this were indeed the alpha and omega of musicology, oral tradition, musical folklore, ethnomusicology, organology, etc., would not be parts of our discipline. But I am sure that Lowinsky's words must be understood in a wider context,

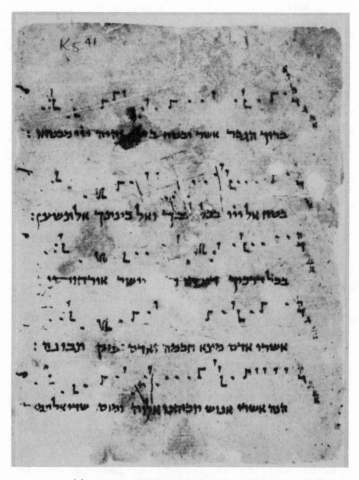

(c) Fragment Cambridge TS. K 5/41 verso

and he himself will be the first to clarify the questionable 'individual work of art'.

From here our way leads to specialization in the variegated aspects of our problem, to analysis, and again back to synthesis. Of the individual aspects the following seem to promise new findings:

209

(1) musico-calendaric comparisons of the ancient Near East and Early Christianity; (2) comparisons of lessons with their Graduals in the different liturgies; (3) special problems of a linguistic nature, connected with ancient musical structures. They are often neglected by musicologists. I shall quote here a lovely example, afforded us by Professor H. J. Moser.

The scholar writes apropos of an interesting question on 'the fate of the penultimate syllable': 'It is strange to realize now that years ago, during a conversation with the great Old Testament scholar H. Gunkel, I had learned that this phenomenon [the emphasis on the penultimate *in pausa*] occurs in the Hebrew psalms; I was privileged to gather some music examples to illustrate this for his commentary on the psalms'.[121]

Professor Moser refers here to a matter discussed at length in Ch. III, also in other publications of mine,[122] viz. the change of accent *in pausa* and the influence of the *pausa* on all psalmodic or even psalm-like tunes. The musical significance of the *pausa* common to all Semitic languages and cultures reaches farther than most scholars imagine, for it was carried at least in part to all the translations of the Bible. The comparative linguistic-musical treatment of the *pausa* remains a formidable task for a good musicologist who is also versed in Semitic languages.

All the problems and methods mentioned lead to 'by-paths' of orthodox musicology. But they can never lead anywhere without concomitant *musical* research. In a necessary stricture Professor Apel has warned against the establishment of:

> a chronology of musical evolution on the basis of liturgical or non-musical data. . . . Another notion of highly questionable validity is the idea that some of the most ornate chants such as Graduals or Tracts, possibly even Alleluias, may well be of an earlier date than many of the simpler syllabic or neumatic chants. . . .[123]

In full agreement with these critical observations, I have abstained from further investigation of any alleluiatic material; not because there might not be old traces to be found in them, but because they are hard to single out, harder to trace, hardest to date. And while I in general concur with P. Wagner's analysis and dating of the Tracts, some of the parallels of Tract motifs and synagogal melismata offered in Vol. I (pp. 518–19) are in all fairness not more than hypothetical. For the Jewish benedictions occur in their musical shape, as quoted in Vol. I, only in the Ashkenazic centres, and the specific melismata are not used at all among the Oriental Jews. This in itself, while not refuting my hypothesis, considerably weakens it. In emphasizing certain archetypes while rejecting others we shall by virtue of careful choice and elimination arrive at one of the goals of all musicology concerned with liturgical chant: an historically and ethnologically delineated *typology*. Into this realm fall all logogenic musical forms, all rhythmogenic and metrical melodies and their archetypes.

We shall, I hope, always return from minute and specific analysis and individual problems to survey and synthesis. Not even the fear of committing occasional blunders must keep us from striving ever and anew to synthetic, i.e., generalizing judgements. Professor F. Blume's words hit the mark: 'We lack the courage necessary for adventure, the courage to err—how rare are the exceptions! The danger is evident that we lose our aims in the thicket of research, concerned with minute problems, that we neglect the wider vistas, as yet unexplored, of musicology!'[124] The general self-limitation to highly specific problems without the redeeming synopsis and synthesis would reduce our discipline to the realm of a 'book-keeper of phenomena' (Lecomte de Nouy).

This danger is imminent whenever we are dealing with oral traditions. The insistence upon the most minute precision in the recording and transcribing of the original melodies, with the full knowledge that the same singer will after fifteen minutes deviate in text and intervals from his former performance, this obsession with *numerical* (not mathematical!) accuracy, with the letter, not the spirit, will, if it carries the day, annul all hope for any advance towards the establishment of general laws. *De minimis non curat lex* is a weighty principle of jurisprudence and so long as we do not treat folk music by methods suitable to the quantum theory, we would do well to heed the old dictum.

Even if we try to rival physics in the precision of our measurements, we should never forget that men like Coulomb and Faraday would never have discovered their celebrated laws if they had owned instruments of modern precision. Even Galileo might have

211

despaired of finding a general law of gravity since every experiment would have shown the influence of the variable conditions of weather, air-pressure, wind, etc. Yet he took the necessary risk of simplification and so must we. Without it, musicologists would relapse into a study of watermarks and inks, of medieval clausulae and rightly forgotten systems of notation, of echoing or correcting *obiter dicta* of former and greater generations.

The Sacred Bridge links continents and sanctuaries; many roads converge on each approach. If one has crossed the bridge, the roads seem to fan out in many distant directions. It is the intellectual as well as the moral obligation of the bridge's custodians to keep it accessible and serviceable at all times. Yet to be faithful to their duty they must be convinced of the bridge's value and even more that it is worth their effort to know the people *on the other side* and the cargo that is being carried over it in an endless stream. Let us remember, finally, that when the bridge is in peril, both sides must help to maintain it and to save it.

NOTES CHAPTER I

1. Josephus Flavius, *Antiquitates*, III, 7 : 6-7.

2. Philo, *Life of Moses*, 2 : 12; 3 : 10; Josephus, *De Bello Judaico*, V, 5 : 5; *Midrash Tadshe*, ed. Jellinek, *Beth Hamidrash*, III, 164 ff; ibid., V, 63 f; also in B. *Hag.* 12 b; for a brief, but reliable synopsis see R. Patai, *Man and Temple*, London, 1947, pp. 112 ff.

3. Josephus, *Contra Apionem*, 1, 7; a list of Josephus' ancestors is given in the first chapter of his autobiography.

4. F. J. Foakes Jackson, *Josephus and the Jews*, New York, 1930, pp. xii f, and 5-7.

5. The excavation of the Masada, the last fortress to hold out against the Romans during the Jewish War, has brought to light a scroll of hymns to accompany the Sabbath sacrifices. Their significance lies in the fact that they describe and praise a heavenly Temple, of which the Sanctuary in Jerusalem was the earthly counterpart. See Y. Yadin, *Masada*, Jerusalem, 1965, pp. 107 ff.

6. The best and most recent survey of the archaeological findings of musical *realia* is Bathyah Bayer's *The Material Relics of Music in Ancient Palestine and its Environs*, Tel-Aviv, 1963.

7. See the instructive article, 'Kinnor, Nebel-Cithara, Psalterium', by O. Kinkeldey in the *Joshua Bloch Memorial Vol.*, New York, 1960, pp. 40-54.

8. See H. Avenary in the article 'Jüdische Musik' in *MGG:* also C. Sachs, *The History of Musical Instruments*, New York, 1940, pp. 84-85; and S. Krauss, *Talmudische Archäologie*, III, Leipzig, 1912, pp. 81, 83; also Eric Werner in *Interpreter's Dictionary of the Bible*, New York, 1962, art., 'Musical Instruments'.

9. Horace, *Satirae*, 1, 2 : 1, where the *ambubaiae* are listed together with quacks, beggars, swindlers and parasites. See B. Bayer, op. cit., Nr. 184.

10. E. Werner, 'Musical Aspects of the Dead Sea Scrolls', in *Musical Quarterly*, 1957, Nr. 1; also E. Kolari, *Musikinstrumente und ihre Verwendung im Alten Testament*, Helsinki, 1947; note also Plutarch, *Quaest. conviv.*, IV, 6.

11. E. Werner, in *Interpreter's Dictionary* articles, 'Music' and 'Musical Instruments', where most of the literature is cited; also B. Bayer, op. cit., Nrs. 26-28, p. 8.

12. The συμφωνία—bagpipe equation seems to originate with the spurious epistle of St. Jerome, *ad Dardanum* (in Migne, *PL*, XXIII) to which the editor adds the cautioning NB: 'Erasmus ait, Hoc haud scio

213

cuius fragmentum, vix dignum est vel hoc ordine. Tantum abest ut Hieronymo sit tribuendum.' There the Hebrew *sumponya* is interpreted as '*chorus*', which was either a bagpipe or a kind of *kithara;* (cf. C. Sachs, *Real-Lexikon der Musikinstrumente,* 2nd ed., New York, 1964, q.v. *chorus*). See also E. Werner, 'Musical Instruments', in *Interpreter's Dictionary of the Bible,* New York, 1962. According to Sachs's plausible conjecture the *sumponya* was no instrument at all, but the designation of the musical ensemble.

13. According to N. Porteous, *Daniel,* Philadelphia, 1965, p. 58, the first instance of the word *symphonia* indicating a musical instrument occurs in the second century B.C.E. in connection with King Antiochus Epiphanes who, according to Polybius, seems to 'have shocked public opinion by dancing to its barbarous strains. . . .' The entire passage in Daniel 3 is a tough nut for the philologist. Here a few hints must suffice: *Sambykē:* see Athenaeus, IV, 175 e, with an etymology leading back to the Aramaic *Sabka* = net, lattice; cf. Strabo, *Geogr.,* X, 3 : 17 ('of barbaric origin along with *nablas*').

Mashroqita = *syrinx,* see Targum to Isa. 5 : 12.

Sumponya, symphonia: see Polybius, XXVI, 10; XXXI, 4. Long before C. Sachs, G. F. Moore opposed the translation 'bagpipe' (in *JBL,* 1905, pp. 166-75).

Psalterion = *psantrin:* see Augustine in *PL,* XXXVI, col. 474, 671, 900, 1964.

For the best recent commentary on the Book of Daniel, see J. A. Montgomery, *A Critical Commentary on the Book of Daniel,* 2nd ed., Edinburgh, 1950.

14. Some valuable material concerning the ancient translations and interpretations of the Daniel passage have been collected and critically edited by H. Avenary in his 'Hieronymus' Epistel über die Musikinstrumente und ihre altöstlichen Quellen', in *Anuario Musical,* XVI, Barcelona, 1961, pp. 56-80. From the organological and iconographic point of view the passage was treated by E. Kenton in a fine study on 'The Instruments in Jerome's Epistle to Dardanus', which is unfortunately not printed as yet.

15. Cf. C. Sachs, op. cit., pp. 84 ff, also his *Geist und Werden der Musikinstrumente,* Berlin, 1929, p. 196.

16. Cf. Polybius, XXVI, 10; XXXI, 4.

17. An excellent, though brief evaluation of Ben Sira is in V. Tcherikover's monumental work *Hellenistic Civilization and the Jews,* Philadelphia, 1959, pp. 142-51.

18. Cf. R. Patai, op. cit., ch. 11 (pp. 24-53); also L. Venetianer, 'Die Eleusinischen Mysterien im Tempel zu Jerusalem', in Bruell's *Monatsblätter,* Frankfurt-Berlin, XVII (1897), pp. 3 ff; D. Feuchtwang, 'Das Wasserop-

fer', in *MGWJ*, LIV-LV, Vienna, 1911, pp. 41 ff; R. Patai, 'The Control of Rain in Ancient Palestine', in *HUCA*, XIV, pp. 239 f; the rabbinic sources are M. *Succa* 4 : 2-7; B. *Succa* 48 b; 52-55.

19. M. *Succa* 5 : 2; B. *Succa* 52 a; Jer. *Succa* 55 b.

20. Th. Reinach, *Textes d'auteurs grecs et romains relatifs au Judaisme*, Paris, 1895, pp. 143, 139 ff (Plutarch): see also I. Heinemann (on Posidonius) in *MGWJ*, 1919, pp. 113 ff.

21. Th. Reinach, op. cit., pp. 130 f; 121 (Democritus).

22. It was generally believed that the water, poured out on the altar, would flow down to the fertile waters of the netherworld (*t'hom*), and would magically increase their fertilizing potential. See B. *Ta'an.* 25 b. A beautiful midrash is based upon this concept: King David sings, i.e., composes the fifteen psalms 'of ascent' (*cantus graduum*, Pss. 120-34) in order to bring up the waters of the *t'hom;* at the point where they had risen highest, the cornerstone of the Temple was erected. See R. Patai, op. cit., pp. 54-58, where many variants of the midrash are quoted.

23. Esp. M. *Arach.* 2 : 3-6; M. *Tamid* 7: 3-4; M. *Bikk.* 3 : 3-4.

24. The 'numerology', i.e., cosmologically meaningful measurements of the Temple, as suggested by Josephus, are well described in R. Patai, op. cit., p. 112.

25. On this difficult topic see the relatively unbiased and comprehensive study, *Sacrifice* by R. K. Yerkes, London, 1953; also *JE*, art., 'Atonement', where many rabbinic sources are given.

26. Although rabbinic Judaism was inclined to discourage martyrdom in times when senseless massacres abounded, when martyrdom was without discernible aim, or too much a display of heroism (cf. B. *Ber.* 61b; B. *Aboda Zarah* 18a), the virtues inherent in martyrdom were never denied. In our days a great German Jewish poet, Karl Wolfskehl, has memorialized the feelings of his unhappy generation on martyrdom in unforgettable words:

Who else holds dear so grim a pledge of grace?
Who else follows so live a pledge of conquest?
For the Law wills that shrieks of anguish,
Death-rattle and the moan of the maimed
Sound in your ears like prayer, oath and paean . . .

(in *1933, a Poem Sequence*, Schocken, New York, 1947, pp. 66-67).

27. Cf. Ecclesiasticus 50 : 16-19.

28. B. *Arach.* 11a.

29. B. *Rosh hashana* 31a.

30. B. *Ta'an.* 27a.

31. See Sir James G. Frazer's classic study on Golden Bells in his *Folklore*

in the Old Testament, III, London, 1918, where a plethora of sources is quoted, pp. 446 ff.

32. Josephus, being an 'enlightened' man, shies away from the common midrashic interpretation of the High Priest's bells; he replaces these 'legendary superstitions' with his general concept that everything in the Temple had a cosmological significance. Thus 'the vestments of the High Priest, made of linen, signified the earth; the blue denoted the sky, being as if lightning in its pomegranates of gold, and in the noise of the bells resembling thunder' (!). Yet in spite of such extravaganzas of interpretations, how much superior was his and Philo's thinking to the childish and gloomy superstitions about bells that persist to this very day all over the 'civilized world'! Cf. Josephus, *Antiquities,* III, 7 : 7, also Philo, *Vita Moysis,* III, 24 : 119; there is a parallel passage in Philo, *Wars,* V, 5 : 7.

33. 'Said R. Hanina: let an article of sound (the robe fringed with bells) come and atone for an offence of sound' (e.g., slander, name-calling, etc.).

34. According to some midrashim, the number of pomegranates-bells was 15, corresponding to the numerical value of the abbreviated Tetragrammaton. See also Philo, *Vita Moysis,* III, 29.

35. The connection with Gen. 22 was first stated by R. Abbahu in B. *Rosh hashana* 16a; for the biblical passages (Lev. 23 : 24; Num. 29) do not specify the instrument or its nature. The 'binding of Isaac', which today constitutes the most significant pericope of New Year's day, has not always remained uncontroversial among the theologians: the passages Jer. 19 : 5 and Micah 6 : 7 are understood by some Talmudic sages as critical of Isaac's sacrifice. Cf. B. *Ta'an.* 4a.

36. B. *Rosh hashana* 26a. For a good synopsis of the rabbinical material relating to the *shofar* see B. Finesinger, 'The Shofar' in *HUCA,* VIII, IX, 1931-2.

37. Cf. Vol. 1 of this work, p. 15, n. 37; also my study, 'The Common Ground', in *Atti del Congresso Internazionale di Musica Sacra,* Rome, 1952. The archaic significance of the *shofar* came to light again when it was sounded at the conquest of the 'Wailing Wall' of the Temple in Jerusalem in 1967.

38. Cf. R. Otto, *The Idea of the Holy,* 2nd ed., London-New York, 1957, pp. 73-75; the calls of the *shofar* are supposed to remind the listener that the New Year's day, on which they are sounded, is the 'birthday of the world'.

39. B. *Sota* 43a; B. *Sabb.* 36a.

40. C. Sachs, *Real-Lexikon der Musikinstrumente,* rev. ed., New York, 1964, art., *'Buccina'.*

41. The notation of the *shofar*-signals after A. Baer, *Der practische Vorbeter* (reprint), New York, Sacred Music Press, 1950; and E. Gerson-

Kiwi, 'Musique dans la Bible' (in *Dictionnaire de la Bible Supplem.*, Vol. V), Paris, 1956, col. 1419-20.

42. Josephus, *Antt.* VII, 12 : 3; also *Bell. Jud.*, 11, 9 : 15; XV, 8 : 1; III, 7 : 7; XI, 4 : 2; *Ecclus.* 1 : 18.

43. B. *Hull.* 29a.

44. M. *Arach.* 2 : 3-6.

45. M. *Tamid* 7 : 3-4.

46. M. *Bikk.* 3 : 3-4.

47. Recently a plausible explanation of that enigmatic instrument has been suggested by J. Yasser, In *JAMS*, 1960, *Kinkeldey-Festschrift*.

48. B. *Ta'an.* 27a; B. *Arach.* 11a-12a; also B. *Succa* 38b; B. *Sota* 20b; Jer. *Sabb.* XVI, 1 : 15 c.

49. B. *Rosh hashana* 31a.

50. Josephus, *Antt.*, XX, 9 : 6, ed. L. Feldmann in Loeb Classics, New York, 1965; see also the interesting study by H. Vogelstein, *Der Kampf zwischen Priestern und Leviten*, Stettin, 1889, esp. pp. 16 ff.

51. See my art., 'Music' in *Interpreter's Dictionary of the Bible*, New York, 1962, p. 460.

52. The literature on angelic liturgy and angelic concerts offers a sad spectacle: well-meaning, but totally unqualified scholars, whose field is really organology or history of art, have monopolized this subject, and the results are deplorable. Hardly one of them is aware of the importance, or, rather, of the *existence,* of the intertestamentary, especially of the apocalyptic literature, and none has bothered to study the Talmudic and midrashic sources, with one glorious exception: Prof. R. Hammerstein (*Die Musik der Engel*, Bern-Munich, 1965). These authors were so fascinated by the angels' concerts in medieval and renaissance sculpture and painting, that they took it for granted that the arrangement, the instruments, the conception, the symbols, in short, almost everything pertaining to angelic music is Christian in spirit, origin and character. How mistaken they are, may be demonstrated by a very brief listing of the sources neglected by them:

(1) Apocalypse of Abraham

(2) Apocalypse of Esdras

(3) Apocalypse of Moses

(4) Apocalypse of Sophonias

(5) Enoch I

(6) Enoch II

(7) Hebrew Daily Prayerbook (*Kedusha* of morning prayer)

(8) Cantic. *Rabba* 27a

(9) Leviticus R. 11e

(10) B. *Sota* 30b

(11) B. *Hagig.* 12b

(12) B. *Ta'an.* 31a

(13) Greater *Hechalot.*

The innumerable references in the corpus of Jewish mystic literature are best categorized in G. Scholem's standard work, *Major Trends in Jewish Mysticism,* sec. edition, New York, 1958-9, esp. Second Lecture. Yet how may we expect better results from serious scholars, if their own master frequently misguided them? A. Baumstark, who ought to have known better, wrote categorically (and falsely): 'The praise of God by angelic choirs is alien to the liturgy of the Synagogue' (in *Islam,* vol. 16: 'Jüdische und christliche Gebetstypen im Koran', p. 245). In the same study he claims that Judaism does not use doxologies in its liturgy, because, as Baumstark assumes, Christianity had monopolized them in its liturgy! As the book goes to press, K. E. Grözinger's study 'Gesang in der frühen jüdischen Literatur', Tübingen, fills the lacuna very well.

53. About dancing angels, see Leviticus R. 11e; B. *Hagig.* 12b; B. *Sanh.* 91b.

54. See J. Strugnell, 'New Fragments of the "Angelic Liturgy" ', in *Vetus Testamentum,* Suppl. VII, 1960, pp. 318 f; also in Y. Yadin, *Masada,* pp. 105, 107; and M. Baillot, 'Les paroles des luminaires', in *Revue Biblique,* vol. 68 (1961), pp. 195-250.

55. Philo, who usually views angels as allegories of 'natural powers', *(De cherubim,* 34; *De gigantibus,* 2, etc.) considers the concerts of the angels as purely spiritual events, as inaudible emissions of *logos,* and juxtaposes them with the Pythagorean harmony of the spheres.

56. G. F. Moore, *Judaism in the First Centuries of the Christian Era,* Cambridge, Mass., I, 66 f.; 253-4; also III, pp. 73-4.

57. Mark 7 : 1-13; Matt. 15 : 1-19; also G. F. Moore, op. cit., III, p. 81, n. 27.

58. This lacuna in the rabbinic sources against instrumental music is easily explained. While the Rabbis did everything to exclude instruments from the Synagogue, they could forbid only certain instruments, not all, for trumpets were fashioned and used according to divine command (Num. 10 : 2-6). They could not and would not set aside a divine command in plain language; all they could do was to put obstacles to the use of instruments.

59. Josephus, *Antt.,* XIV, 5 : 4.

60. The attitude of popular books, which more or less represent generally accepted ideas, shows that purely instrumental music was quite familiar to the people during the Hellenistic era; cf., e.g., Tobit 13 : 22; or the well-known passages of the apocryphal Thomas Acts.

61. Lam. 5 : 14-15.

62. B. *Sota* 48a.

63. Yet the same dignitary seems to have been very fond of music, for he is said to have gone to bed with songs and to have risen with songs. Cf. Jer. *Meg.* III, 7 : 74a; also B. *Gittin* 7a.

64. B. *Gittin* 7a.

65. This legalistic hodge-podge becomes outright chaotic, when the organ and its place in the Synagogue became the topic of discussion during the nineteenth century. A brief survey of the confusion can be found in *JE*, article, 'Organ'; a strict account of the problem was given by A. Berliner, 'Die Orgel', *Für und Wider*, Berlin, 1904. Also Maimonides, *Mishne Torah*, Shabbat 23 : 4.

66. See notes 62 and 60 above.

67. B. *Sota* 48 (end).

68. B. *Ber.* 24a.

69. The most recent interpretation of this old and controversial topic is found in Mr. McKinnon's study, *The Church Fathers and Musical Instruments*, New York, 1965. The author had limited himself to a few selected Fathers, mostly of the Western Church; also his knowledge is rather limited. The Syrian, Armenian, and most of the Byzantine Fathers have—luckily—escaped his attention, not to mention the rabbinic authorities. So has my study, 'If I Speak in the Voices of Angels . . .' escaped his attention, where St Paul's hostile attitude to all instruments is shown and explained, although this occurs in a document *before* the fall of the Temple. Nor has the author taken cognizance of my study, 'The Conflict between Hellenism and Judaism . . .' (*HUCA*, 1947) where a great many Hebrew, Greek and Syriac documents are adduced.

70. Cf. Werner and Sonne, 'The Theory and Philosophy of Music in Judeo-Arabic Literature', in *HUCA*, 1941, 1943, esp. vol. XVI, pp. 255-9.

71. This attitude of the Rabbis, hostile to any and every art music, began fairly early. Yehuda Halevi's *Kuzari* (II, n. 70-74) contains already a doctrine of music that is 'theologically acceptable' for worship. Needless to add that this kind of music is little more than a sort of primitive improvisation designed to correspond to the 'outpouring of the soul'. A collection of similar decisions by authoritative rabbis during the Middle Ages was published by Prof. Boaz Cohen under the title, *The Responsum of Maimonides concerning Music*, New York, 1935.

NOTES CHAPTER II

1. The recently published *Temple Scroll* will emphasize, as Prof. Y. Yadin has kindly informed me, even more strongly the proper calendar of

the feasts and their celebration, confirming the calendaric origin of the *octoechos*.

2. Cf. the Dead Sea Scrolls, Vol. I, *The Isaiah Manuscript and the Habakkuk Commentary*, ed. M. Burrows, New Haven, 1950, p. xvi.

3. Millar Burrows, *The Dead Sea Scrolls*, New York, 1955, p. 99.

4. Quoted from the source mentioned in note 2.

5. Published as *Monumenta Musicae Byzantinae Subsidia*, Vol. III, Copenhagen and Boston, 1953.

6. Destroyed in 1944 during the bombardment of Chartres.

7. Cf. E. Werner, 'Hebrew and Oriental Christian Metrical Hymns', in *Hebrew Union College Annual*, Vol. XXIII, Pt. II, pp. 415-25.

8. Cf. P. Verdeil, op. cit., p. 113 (see n. 5).

9. Cf. M. Burrows, *The Dead Sea Scrolls*, p. 298.

10. Cf. A. Dupont-Sommer, *The Jewish Sect of Qumran and the Essenes*, London, 1954, pp. 74 ff.

11. P. Kahle, 'The Karaites and the Manuscripts from the Cave', in *Vetus Testamentum*, Leyden, 1953, pp. 82-4.

12. Dupont-Sommer, op. cit., p. 139.

13. My emendation of Burrows's translation is based upon the text in *Megillot Midbar Yehuda*, p. 69, Jerusalem, 1959.

14. Philo reports the very same fact about the Therapeutae in Egypt, who celebrated the *Pannychis* (the pentecontade), of which the system of *octoechos* is the lasting musical symbol. Cf. E. Werner, 'The Origin of the Eight Modes of Music', in *Hebrew Union College Annual*, 1948.

15. I Cor. 14:15.

16. Clement of Rome, *I. Ep. to the Corinthians*, 40.

17. Philo, *Quod Deus sit*, ed. Cohn-Wendland, II, 61.

18. Philo, *De fuga et inventione*, ibid., III, 115.

19. Philo, *De posteritate Caini*, XXXI, 104 f.

20. I Cor. 13:1.

21. I Cor. 14:7.

22. I Cor. 14:15.

23. Literally, 'measuring cords'.

24. Cf. F. C. Conybeare, *Philo about the Contemplative Life*, Oxford, 1895, p. 247.

25. Quoted from M. Wallenstein's excellent translation, in *Bulletin of the John Ryland Library*, Manchester, Vol. 38, No. 1, p. 254.

26. The instrument, a cittern with ten strings, a close relative of the *psalterion*, is referred to in Pss. 92:4; 33:2; 144:9.

27. Cf. E. Werner, 'The Origin of the Eight Modes of Music', *HUCA*, 1948.

28. Prof. T. H. Gaster, *The Dead Sea Scriptures*, New York, 1956, p. 291.

29. The *War-Scroll* actually quotes the passage Num. 10 : 9.

30. Burrows, *The Dead Sea Scrolls,* 2nd ed., New York, 1958, p. 397.

31. Yigael Yadin, *Megillat Milhemet,* etc., Jerusalem, 1955.

32. All these passages occur in the *War-Scroll,* VIII: 3-10. In attempting to give a translation of my own I was most ably assisted by Dr. A. Giat, to whom I am indebted.

33. II Chron. 5 : 13.

34. Cf. Curt Sachs, *Geist und Werden der Musikinstrumente,* Berlin, 1929, p. 52.

35. My translation. Cf. Philo, *De vita contemplativa,* M. 484 (Loeb Classical Library, Philo, Vol. IX, p. 162). Some of the terms are somewhat ambiguous. A very similar description is offered in Clement of Alexandria, *Paedagogus,* II, 4.

36. Conybeare, *Philo about the Contemplative Life,* pp. 101 ff, seems to understand this as a reference to Pentecost; actually, however, there is no valid reason for this assumption, since the ancient pentecontade-calendar appears to have been used by the Therapeutes. Cf. Eric Werner, 'The Origin of the Eight Modes of Music', where all sources are given.

37. Cf. Dupont-Sommer, op. cit., pp. 99-100.

38. Ibid., p. 103.

39. Cf. Yochanan Rufos de Mayuma in *Patrologia Orientalis,* VII, 180 ff. Also E. Werner, 'The Origin of the Eight Modes of Music', pp. 232-3.

40. Cf. M. Burrows, op. cit., 2d ed. pp. 385-7. Dr Sukenik's hypothesis that the 'Teacher of Righteousness', the central figure of the Scrolls, was the author of these hymns, is very plausible.

41. This rough simplification does justice only to the antiphons of the First Millennium and their usual method of performance.

42. Translation and annotation after M. Wallenstein, *Hymns from the Judean Scrolls,* Manchester, 1950, pp. 9-13.

43. Cf. Lou H. Silberman, 'Language and Structure in the *Hodayot*', in *Journal of Biblical Literature,* Vol. 75, June, 1956.

44. For examples of such statements, cf. G. F. Moore, *Judaism,* Vol. II, pp. 85 ff; also Hillel's dictum: 'Be of the disciples of Aaron, loving and pursuing peace, loving all creatures and drawing them near to the Law' (*Abot* I : 12).

45. The term 'Pharisee' is used here in the sense in which Paul and the modern comparative history of religion have understood it, not in the derogatory meaning frequently found in the Gospels. The protagonists of this unorthodox interpretation were George F. Moore (*Judaism,* II, pp. 159 f; 192 ff) and R. Travers Herford (*Pharisaism: Its Aim and Its Method,* London, 1912; and *The Truth about the Pharisees,* New York, 1925).

46. For a cogent and most eloquent comparison between Pharisees and

New England Puritans, see L. Finkelstein's monumental work *The Phari-sees*, 2nd ed., New York, 1952; also J. Klausner, *From Jesus to Paul*, New York, 1943.

47. Cf. my 'Conflict between Hellenism and Judaism in the Music of the Early Christian Church' in *HUCA*, Vol. XX (1947), pp. 407 ff.

NOTES CHAPTER III

1. J. Huizinga, *Homo Ludens*, New York, 1950, pp. 158 ff.

2. Cf. E. Werner, 'The Attitude of the Church Fathers to Psalmody' (in *Review of Religion*, Chicago, 1943).

3. John Chrysostom, *De compunctione cordis*, II, 1. It is noteworthy that this postulate of Chrysostom exactly corresponds with the Talmudic position which demands from the worshipper the 'attitude of repentance and supplication' (B. *Ber.* 29b).

4. Andreas of Caesarea in *PG*, 106, 1072.

5. Eusebius, *Comment. in Psalmos*, beginning.

6. Augustine, *De civitate dei*, VII, 14.

7. Ambrose, in *PL*, 14, 178.

8. Ibid., *PL*, 14, 924.

9. John Chrysostom, *In Psalm 100*.

10. *La Paléographie musicale*, III, pp. 10, 11.

11. Cf. *The Sacred Bridge*, Vol. 1, pp. 106, 129.

12. About the connection between psalmody, the Levites and prophetic singers, see A. Arens, *Die Psalmen*, pp. 51 f (Trier, 1961) and W. Rothstein, *Kommentar zum I Chronikbuch*, pp. 446 f; cf. III Macc. 6 : 32; 7 : 13, 16; most recently H. H. Rowley, *From Moses to Qumran*, London, 1963; also in *Journal of Jewish Studies*, London, 1956, pp. 1 ff; also *Worship in Ancient Israel*, London, 1967.

13. Cf. N. Wieder, *The Judean Scrolls and Karaism*, London, 1962, pp. 96 f, 254-5; also Arens op. cit., pp. 201-2. The last psalm of each book carries a doxology which clearly harks back to early post-exilic times.

14. Cf. *The Sacred Bridge*, Vol. I, pp. 138 f. On Christian collections see A. Baumstark, *Nocturna Laus*, ed. O. Heiming, Münster, 1957, pp. 164 ff.

15. Ibid. pp. 144-58.

16. The etymology of *Marmitha* is not quite clear: H. W. Codrington (*Studies of the Syrian Liturgies*, London, 1953, pp. 35 f) derives it from the root *'armi*, 'to throw, to hurl'; while Payne-Smith's *Syriac Lexicon* links it to the Hebrew *ram*, 'to make high, to exalt'. Perhaps the 'missile'-etymology was an all too literal translation of the Greek, *anapémpein* (scil. *tàs euchás*)—in the last analysis both explanations may be correct. On the

system of division see A. Baumstark, *Nocturna Laus,* Münster, 1957, pp. 162 ff.

17. Etymology not sure; either from *Shur~Incipium* (of the day), call of the rooster; or from the Hebrew *Shir*=song, poem.

18. Codrington, op. cit., p. 41.

19. R. H. Connolly, O.S.B., *Expositio Officiorum Ecclesiae Georgio Arbeleusi vulgo adscripta,* Rome, 1913-14; this is a most erudite edition of a Nestorian text of the tenth century.

20. Ibid., pp. 94-95, 'Per primum hullalam, qui 10 psalmos habet, significantur 10 generationes ab Adam usque ad diluvium'.

21. Ibid., p. 165, cf. Brockelmann, *Syrisches Lexikon,* who suggests that the word *Krh* means 'at the end' (*punctus*). For a brief discussion of the Syriac terms and their history, see J. Mateos, S. J., *Lelya-Sapra,* Rome, 1959, pp. 410 ff.

22. R. H. Connolly, op. cit. pp. 167 ff.

23. To the enormous liturgico-midrashic literature, L. Zunz's standard work *Die gottesdienstlichen Vorträge der Juden,* 2nd ed., Frankfurt, 1892, gives a solid introduction, esp. see pp. 346-423.

24. *Manual of Discipline,* VI : 6-7 (in M. Burrows, op. cit.).

25. N. Wieder, *The Judean Scrolls and Karaism,* London, 1962, pp. 98-99. About the division of the night and its watches see A. Baumstark, op. cit., pp. 21 ff, 26 ff, 152 ff.

26. G. Diettrich, 'Bericht über eine neuentdeckte handschriftliche Urkunde zur Geschichte des Gottesdienstes in der Nestorianischen Kirche' (in *Nachrichten der Ges, der Wissensch, Phil.-Hist. Klasse,* Göttingen, 1902, Heft 2).

27. R. H. Connolly, op. cit., pp. 179 ff.

28. R. Lach, 'Das Wiederholungsprinzip' in *Öster. Akademie der Wissenschaften Wien, Phil.-Hist. Klasse,* 1923-4, also in the same author's *Beiträge zur Entwicklungsgeschichte der ornamentalen Melopoie,* Vienna-Leipzig, 1913, pp. 391, 593, 613 ff.

29. Psalms 114 : 3; 121 : 1. For an exceedingly useful discussion of biblical parallelism see Theodore H. Robinson, *The Poets of the Old Testament,* London, 1947, pp. 21-46.

30. Apparently most scholars have failed to notice that the Oxyrhynchus Hymn is actually a paraphrase of Psalm 93.

31. W. F. Albright on Psalm 68 in *HUCA,* Vol. 23, Part One, p. 2.

32. Winfred Douglas, *Church Music in History and Practice,* New York, 1937, pp. 18 ff. The book is of great value in many respects.

33. C. Sachs, *The Rise of Music in the Ancient World, East and West,* New York, 1943, p. 101.

34. C. Sachs, *The Wellsprings of Music,* The Hague, 1962, p. 70.

35. Cf. Payne-Smith, *Syriac Lexicon*, q.v.

36. C. Sachs, *The Wellsprings of Music*, pp. 168-71. the term *periheletic* (erroneously derived by C. Sachs), denoting a musical ornament circling a central tone, was coined by R. Lach, in his standard work on musical ornaments, Vienna-Leipzig, 1913 (see n. 28). Not unjustly did E. Bloch ridicule the naïveté of those who believe in the 'Indian file march' (*Gänsemarsch historicher Epochen*) of human evolution.

37. B. *Sota* 30b and the parallel passages in B. *Succa*.

38. The passage of St Augustine, 'Ut pronuntianti vicinior esset quam canenti,' in *PL*, 32, 200; about Cassian's remark see A. Baumstark, *Nocturna Laus*, ed. O. Heiming, O.S.B., 1957, p. 107.

39. H. Avenary, *Studies in the Hebrew, Syrian and Greek Liturgical Recitative*, Jerusalem, 1963, p. 3.

40. Psalmody cannot reasonably be termed 'art music', as Avenary does, although it is the result of intellectual effort, for it admits several variants of the same tune, a criterion of oral tradition of folk music. A cogent proof of this criterion is the newly discovered 'Sabbath-psalm', excavated at Masada; see Y. Yadin, *Masada*, 1965, p. 106 ff.

41. In the theory of plainchant these three are called *positurae*, after Isidore of Sevilla, *Etymologiae*, 1 : 20, see WGM, II, pp. 83 f, III, pp. 37 f.

42. See J. Chailley, 'Essay analytique sur la formation de l'Octoechos Latin' (in *Essays Presented to Egon Wellesz*, Oxford, 1966, p. 85) from which we quote: 'Les usages universels de la cantillation nous enseignent que la tendance la plus courante de celle-ci conduit d'un part à des broderies autour de la teneur, d'autre part á une chute mélodique finale grave de celle-ci, chute qui va parfois ailleurs jusqu' à devenir un veritable parlando. . . .'

43. S. Corbin, 'La Cantillation des rituels Chrétiens', in *Revue de musicologie*, XLVII, July 1961, Paris. About modal (pitched) recitation see Dom Gajard, 'Les récitations modales', in *Etudes Grégoriennes*, I, Solesmes, 1954, pp. 9 ff.

44. CF. Avenary, op. cit., pp. 26, 29. While the author adduces an abundance of literary and musical sources to his essays, he endeavours to 'cover his tracks', so to speak; that the Syriac form of '*Enyana* developed out of the antiphon, as he claims, is tantamount to saying that a battle developed out of a war. What does he mean by stating that 'the tonic accent *sometimes* occurs in Roman and Jewish chant'? (p. 33).

45. As e.g., S. Finkelstein, *Composer and Nation*, New York, 1960, pp. 29 ff, who approximates such a formulation. Much more profound, due to its phylogenetic foundation, is R. Lach's fine essay 'Das Wiederholungsprinzip in der Musik' (in *Proceedings of the Vienna Akademie der Wissenschaften, Phil-Hist. Kl.*, Nr. 201-2, 1924).

46. B. Bartók, *Hungarian Folk Music,* London, 1931.

47. Yehuda Halevi, *Kuzari,* ed. D. Cassel, 1920. The counterpart to the metrical *Anshadiya* was called *Tartil;* the non-metrical improvisation on a modal pattern (*Lahan*) as the spontaneous outburst of the God-seeking soul, it is preferred by Halevi for theological reason (*Kuzari,* 11, 72-73; pp. 171 ff).

48. Not even such an apparently obvious representation of Eastern and Western conceptions of musical (or literary) form will remain undisputed; see the interesting study by P. Lucas Kunz, O.S.B., 'Untersuchungen zur Textstruktur solistischer Psalmen', in *Kirchenmusikal Jahrbuch,* XLV, 1961, pp. 1-37, where mathematical concepts play a considerable—however hypothetical—role.

49. Cf. C. Sachs, *The Rise of Music in the Ancient World,* p. 101: 'Its style before 1000 B.C.E. as a whole was logogenic, basically syllabic, and only moderately spiced with . . . melismas'.

50. Socrates, *Hist. Eccles.,* 11, 8; also Jerome, *Comm. in Ep. ad Ephes.,* 284 : 2, in *PL.*

51. Basilius, *Homilia I in Psalmos.*

52. Methodius, *De libero arbitrio,* in *PG,* 18 : 240 ff.

53. That psalmodic chant was well organized seems indicated by the Talmudic adage, 'If it be a tradition, learn it by heart, word for word, as a song'! (B. *Sabbath* 106b).

54. For this and similar information regarding Iranian and Sanskrit, I am indebted to the late Prof. Bernard Geiger of Columbia University.

55. W. Bacher, *Die Anfänge der hebräischen Grammatik,* 1895, pp. 57, 101; also *Kuzari,* 11, 80, supra n. 47.

56. Bauer and Leander, *Historische Grammatik der Hebr. Sprache,* p. 186, and note on the subject.

57. I am indebted for this piece of information to Prof. Bernard Geiger. Cf. also O. Fleischer, *Neumen-Studien,* I, Ch. 1 and 2, where, however, no chronological synopsis of the accentual systems is provided.

58. It is of interest to note that Jerome was well aware of these difficulties; witness his three separate attempts at translating the Psalter. Cf. J. M. Harden, *Psalterium juxta Hebraeos Hieronymi,* London, 1922, especially pp. xxv f.

59. Ibid. p. xxvi.

60. P. Wagner, *Gregorianische Melodien,* III, p. 368. See also my article, 'The Common Ground', in *Atti del Congresso Internazionale di Musica Sacra,* Rome, 1952.

61. R. Lach, *Ornamentale Melopoie,* Vienna-Leipzig, 1913, pp. 241 f.

62. Ibid., pp. 245-6.

63. Ibid. It is worth mentioning that A. Machabey considers the punctuating melismata as primary facts and the *syllabes excédentaires* as their consequences—just the opposite view. Machabey gives no proof at all for his wild hypothesis. See A. Machabey, 'La Cantillation Manichéenne', in *La Revue musicale,* Paris, 1955, p. 227.

64. Dom Gajard, 'Quelques reflexions sur les premières formes de la musique sacrée', in *Etudes Grégoriennes,* II, Solesmes, 1957, p. 9. The learned author is quite familiar with the medieval sources and writers on his subject; but he carefully avoids any reference to contemporary scholars, their opinions or achievements.

65. H. Anglès, 'Die Sequenz und die Verbete im mittelalterlichen Spanien' (in *Festschrift for C-A. Moberg,* in *Svensk Tidskrift For Musikforskning*), Stockholm, 1961. The study deals only with Mediterranean and Western music.

66. Ibid., p. 47.

67. As early an authority as Tertullian testifies to it in his *De oratione,* 27 (in *PL,* Vol. 1); for other cases, see *The Sacred Bridge,* Vol. 1, pp. 198-9 and 205, notes 105-7.

68. Cf. Jerome, *Comment. in Psalmos,* ed. Morin, in *Anecdota Maredsol.,* III, 76.

69. E. Gerson-Kiwi, 'Hallelujah and Jubilus in Hebrew-Oriental Chant', (in *Festschrift for H. Besseler,* Leipzig, 1962, p. 45).

70. The Talmud permits isolated Hallelujahs as salutations at the end of the service (B. *Yoma* 53b); the apocryphal and apocalyptic literature, however, is full of isolated Hallelujahs, e.g., the Apocalypse of Moses. A good collection of the pertinent rabbinic passages is in H. Avenary, 'Formal Structure of Psalms and Canticles', in *Musica Disciplina,* VII, Amsterdam, 1953, pp. 10 ff.

71. Cf. E. Werner, *The Sacred Bridge,* Vol. 1, pp. 169, 202 (n. 9); also 'The Doxology in Synagogue and Church' (in *HUCA,* XIX, 1945), pp. 324-5.

72. Gerson-Kiwi, op. cit., p. 48; and B. Stäblein, *MGG,* 'Gradual', col. 644. See also B. Stäblein on 'Modes of Underlaying a Text', in *Report of I.M.S. Congress,* 1961, New York, Vol. 1, pp. 14-15, Vol. 2, pp. 49-50, containing some of my observations.

NOTES CHAPTER IV

1. L. Duchesne, *Christian Worship,* New York, 1903, pp. 114, 167 ff; P. Wagner, *Gregorianische Melodien,* Vol. I, pp. 81 f; J. A. Jungmann, *Missarum Sollemnia,* I, pp. 520 ff, does not commit himself to the Jewish origin of the

Gradual; Lechner and Eisenhofer, *Liturgik des römischen Ritus,* 6th ed., Freiburg, 1953, pp. 218 f, deny it categorically without giving reasons; A. Baumstark, *Liturgie comparée,* ed. Botte, Chevetonge, 3rd ed., 1953, pp. 26-27, 51, emphatically confirms it; so does Th. Klauser in his excellent *Kleine abendländische Liturgiegeschichte,* Bonn, 1965, p. 1; G. Dix in his *The Shape of the Liturgy,* 1945, cites the pros and cons, as we shall see.

2. G. Morin, "Une nouvelle théorie sur les origines du Canon', in *Revue bénédictine,* XXI (1904), p. 378.

3. Gennadius, *De viris illustribus,* 79, in *PL,* 56, col. 1103-4. It can hardly be assumed that Musaeus compiled such a lectionary and gradual completely *de novo,* as will be shown below. Cf. O. Bardenhewer, *Geschichte der altkirchlichen Litteratur,* IV, pp. 578 f.

4. Apollinaris Sidonius, *Epist.,* IV, 11; V, 14 f (ed. Luetjohann, p. 63), Berlin, 1887. See also Th. Mommsen, *Reden und Aufsätze,* Berlin, 1905, pp. 132-43.

5. It is rare, and should be appreciated, for a serious scholar such as A. Fortescue (*The Mass,* New York, 1912) to have the courage to ask boldly: 'Why and when did our Mass begin to be affected so profoundly by the calendar?' and, 'Who chose the special Introits and Graduals, etc., for the various days, and why was such a Gradual chosen for such a day?'

6. *Liber Pontificalis,* I, ed. Duchesne, Paris, 1886, p. 230

7. *Peregrinatio Aetheriae Silviae,* ed. W. Heraeus, Heidelberg, 1939. (Most recently called *Egeria.*)

8. *Constitutiones Apostolorum,* ed. F. X. Funk, Paderborn, 1905.

9. G. G. Willis, *St. Augustine's Lectionary,* London, 1962; also the musicologically most instructive article, 'Graduale' by B. Stäblein, in *MGG,* Vol. V.

10. The tabulation follows G. G. Willis's book, pp. 14 ff, in part, and in the other part epitomizes the author's examinations of more recent lectionaries.

11. It is unfortunate that we have hardly any opportunity of comparing the practice of the two great doctors with each other. In general it can be maintained that during the fourth and fifth centuries only the NT lesson, in some cases also the OT lesson, was determined by the feasts to which the Gospels or the Early Church refer, including anniversaries of martyrs. The rest was left to the discretion of the bishops. But again, there are some regional exceptions, esp. the Syriac lectionary which F. Burkitt edited (esp. in *Proceedings of the British Academy,* XI, London, 1923). See also G. Dix, op. cit., with our excerpts below.

12. Cf. *The Sacred Bridge,* Vol. 1, pp. 58-101.

13. Ed. Mecheln, 1874.

14. Cf. Missale Sarum, ed. F. H. Dickinson, Oxford and London, 1861-83, pp. 218-19.

15. The numeration of verses, the order of clauses, indeed, the very meaning of the entire verses used in the texts of the Missal deviate considerably from the TM (Textus Masoreticus), the Vulgate and the LXX; nor is there a recognizable system or method for the deviations of the *Vetus Itala*.

16. Cf., eg., the Offertory for the 21st Sunday after Pentecost (Job 1 : 1 plus free paraphrase mentioning both Satan and Job's boils). If an allusion to the Epistle (Eph. 16 : 10-17) is intended, the Alleluia-verse Ps. 114 : 1 makes no sense, nor the Gospel lesson of the 15th Sunday after Pentecost, which is identical with the 5th day after the 4th Sunday in Lent, but whose Gradual simply quotes the Sabbath psalm (Ps. 92).

17. Cf. J. A. Jungmann, S. J., *Missarum Sollemnia,* 2nd ed., Vienna, 1949, I, p. 536.

18. See, e.g., the difference in the Gospel lessons for the first Sunday in Advent between the Sarum and the Roman Missal; in Sarum we find Matt. 21 : 1-9; in Rom., Luke 21 : 25-33; yet the Graduals and responses are more consistent: Ps. 25: 3, 4, plus Ps. 85 : 8.

19. The DSS only hint at the practice of martyrs' veneration; in early rabbinic literature it became quite popular. See also Th. Klauser, *Kleine abendländische Liturgiegeschichte,* Bonn, 1965, p. 88.

20. From the beginning, the martyr's day (either birthday or day of his death) was reckoned according to the civil (secular) calendar, not according to the ecclesiastical year. We read: 'Festa igitur Sanctorum agebantur *semper die fixa in mense* [Ital. in original] independenter ab hebdomada, vel a festis et temporibus anni liturgici.' (C. Callewaert, J. C. D., *De Breviarii Romani Liturgia,* Bruges, 1939, p. 28.) in this way, the feasts of the martyrs and saints contributed to the establishment of the secular calendar. See my recent study 'Traces of Jewish Hagiolatry', in *HUCA,* LI, 1980.

21. The rather intricate distinction between saint, confessor and martyr is irrelevant for the purpose of this discussion. The statement quoted above is found in *Martyrium Polycarpi,* 18, in Lightfoot's edition of the *Apostolic Fathers,* London, 1891. A brief introduction to the *Martyrium* is given in J. Quasten, *Patrology,* Westminster, Md., 1950, I, pp. 77 ff.

22. Yet the martyrdoms of Pope Telesphorus and St Justin Martyr in Rome, which were nearly contemporaneous with that of St Polycarp, were not inscribed in the ecclesiastical calendars at the time of Emperor Constantine. It has been stressed that even an epitaph of a pope, that of Cornelius, while bearing the inscription 'Cornelius martyr ep. (251-253)', does not state the day or month of his martyrdom, or his birth either. See J. A. Jungmann, S. J., op. cit., II, p. 212.

23. The best modern critical edition is by H. Lichtenstein, in *HUCA*, VIII–IX (1931-32). The editor treats the *scholion* a little too concisely and hardly comments on it.

24. Following D. Kaufmann in his *Gesammelte Schriften*, III, Frankfurt, 1915, p. 517 ff, where the various sources are quoted. Kaufmann paid no attention to the fact that the litany has fifteen stanzas, the number which in Hebrew characters represents the abbreviation of the Divine Name. See also ELB.

25. BLEW, p. 32.

26. Ibid., p. 129.

27. Ibid., pp. 169-70.

28. The first critical study of this martyrology was given by L. Zunz in *Die Synagogale Poesie des Mittelalters*, 2nd ed., Frankfurt, 1920, pp. 139-41; also *JE*, art., 'Martyrs, the Ten' (*'asarah haruge malkut*).

29. For a brief description of the customs on that occasion, see *JE*, art., 'Lag be-'Omer'.

30. Cf. B. *Meg.* 13b; B. *Kidd.* 38a. Before the banquet the members of the *Hebra kadishah* usually fast.

31. For this instance, we rely on the exhaustive list of sources given by L. Zunz in his *Synag. Poesie, Beilage 20*.

32. Cf. ELB, pp. 202 f. Other forms of such (rhymed) martyrologies were the so-called *pizmonim* (on the word, see my *The Sacred Bridge*, Vol. 1, pp. 137, 143), or *taidi*, or *Taydye*. This term has not been convincingly explained. I venture to derive it from the Greek *a(i)do* (to sing), or *t'aidoia* (sacred chants).

33. Cf. B. *Sanh.* 44b; Jer. *Kidd.* I (end); also Zunz, op. cit., pp. 148 f. In this connection we might mention a curious, possibly anti-Christian allusion in B. *Sanh.* 92b, referring to angels who punish Nebuchadnezzar for praising God (Dan. 3 : 25; 4 : 3) and ask him (answering his observation, 'and the form of the fourth is like the son of God'), 'Has God a son?'

34. Text according to R. Saadya Gaon, *Siddur*, ed. J. Davidson, J. Assaf, B. J. Joel, Jerusalem, 1941, pp. 327-329. For the translation of this difficult text I am deeply indebted to my late friend Professor J. Schirmann, Jerusalem.

35. See L. Zunz, *Zur Geschichte und Literatur*, Berlin, 1845, I, pp. 324-30. The LXX already uses the term martyr in connection with the suffering servant (Isa. 55 : 4 ff). For later martyrdom see P. Browne's extensive study, 'Die Judenbekämpfung der Kirche im Mittelalter', in *Zeitschrift für kath. Theologie*, LXII, 1938, pp. 349 ff, which in view of the time of its publication must be considered a courageous work.

36. B. *Yoma* 23a, referring to Judges 5 : 31.

37. R. H. Charles, *The Ascension of Isaiah*. For a more critical interpreta-

tion see H. W. Surkau, *Martyrien in jüdischer und frühchristlicher Zeit,* Göttingen, 1938, pp. 30 ff. The Talmud has only part of the legend in B. *Yeb.* 49a and B. *Sanh.* 40b–41a.

38. Jer. *Hag.* II, 2, 16a.

39. See Gregory Dix, *The Shape of the Liturgy,* Westminster, 1945, pp. 153, 344.

40. Ibid., p. 369.

41. Si eos sequi non valemus actu, sequamur affectu; si non gloria, certa laetitia; si non meritis, votis; si non passione, compassione; si non excellentia, connexione (*Sermo* 280, in *PL,* 38, col. 1283).

42. Cf. B. *Sanh.* 74a; Jer. *Sanh.* III, 6; also B. *Baba Kamma* 17a.

43. See G. Scholem, *Major Trends in Jewish Mysticism,* New York, 1941, pp. 146, 356, n. 3.

44. *Authorized Daily Prayer Book,* ed. Hertz, Funeral Service; also ELB, p. 203.

45. H. Cohen, *Die Religion der Vernunft ans den Quellen des Judentums,* Leipzig, 1919, pp. 262, 356. His point of view is fully supported by the *Mekhilta,* ed. Horovitz (*Mishpatim*) XVIII, 313.

46. H. Cohen, op. cit., p. 377, also pp. 383, 512, 517.

47. *Constitutiones Apostolorum,* VI, 30: 'Ne igitur observetis huiusmodi legalia et naturalia. . . .'

48. Injuria est enim pro martyre orare, cuius nos debemus orationibus commendari. (*Sermo* 159, I, in *PL,* 38, col. 868).

49. H. Cohen, op. cit. Neither the kabbalists nor the miracle-hungry masses of oppressed Jewry were prepared to endorse this brave, austere, sober and intensely philosophical derogation of martyrdom. In his homily in honour of the Maccabean martyrs St Augustine breaks out in the contemptuous words quoted above: 'What of this kind [of martyrdom] have the Jews ever understood to celebrate?' (in *Acta Sanctorum*).

50. J. Jeremias, *Heiligengräber in Jesu Umwelt,* Göttingen, 1958.

51. Jeremias used as his main source and guide-book the *Vitae prophetarum* in the edition of Th. Schermann, Leipzig, 1907 and its modern American edition, *The Lives of the Prophets,* ed. C. C. Torrey, Philadelphia, 1946. This is an apocryphal, frequently redacted and interpolated work, whose origin harks back to the times of primitive Christianity, but whose substance is certainly older, almost certainly of Jewish nature and authorship. On this question see H. A. Fischel in *JQR,* XXXVII (1946-7), p. 375; also Luncz, *Luah Eretz Yisrael,* Jerusalem, 1895, with important material for the calendar of martyrs.

52. On the question of the ritual purity of a house of worship above a grave, see p. 96, and Jeremias, op. cit., pp. 122 ff.

53. Jeremias, op. cit., pp. 144–46, and cf. LXX, Jos. 24 : 33.

54. I Macc. 13 : 25; also Josephus, *Antiquitates,* XIII, 211, and Eusebius, *Onomasticon,* ed. Klostermann, 132, 17.

55. The historicity of the 'ten martyrs' has been seriously questioned ever since L. Zunz's penetrating scrutiny of the story of his *Geschichte der synagogalen Poesie,* pp. 139 ff, see *infra* n. 65.

56. In *Revue de l'art chrétien,* Vol. XLII, 1899; see also *DACH,* 1, 2, col. 2357 ff.

57. Wilhelm Bacher, 'Jüdische Märtyrer im christlichen Kalender', in *Jahrbuch für jüdische Geschichte und Literatur,* IV, 1901.

58. For a list of midrashic passages referring to such intercessions, see Jeremias, op. cit., pp. 135-38. It seems that Jeremias was unaware of Bacher's older and in some respects more profound study.

59. B. *Ta'anit* 16a. A list of some pilgrimages, together with the persons celebrated, is given in *JE,* art, 'Pilgrimage', section, 'Customs'.

60. Josephus, *Bellum Judaicum,* IV, 532. See also A. Schlatter, *Zur Topographie Palästinas,* Stuttgart, 1893, pp. 223 ff.

61. As e.g., the 'Pilgrim of Bordeaux' (*c.* 333) and Antonius Placentinus, both edited by P. Geyer, in his *Itinera Hierosolymitana saec. IV-VIII,* in *CSEL,* Vienna, 1898.

62. For this and other festivities in honour of OT personages, especially in Christian lectionaries, see my *The Sacred Bridge,* Vol. 1, pp. 64 f, and p. 98, n. 60, where some recent bibliography is listed. It is not clear why David and James were celebrated together. Possibly some confusion of James with Jacob had taken place, and the festival (after Christmas) was a remnant of ancestor worship.

63. According to R. Petachya's *Itinerary,* I, 19 : 3 f; II, 26 : 6 f (ed. Grünhut), the Babylonian Jews of his time knew of 550 graves of prophets, heroes, and rabbinic sages.

64. From Karl Wolfskehl, *Die Stimme spricht,* Berlin, 1933-4. In German: 'Ein Krumenkorn vom Grab der Ahnen/Bewahrt als Letztes, was euch bleibt. . . .'

65. On the 'ten martyrs' see L. Finkelstein, 'The Ten Martyrs', in *Essays and Studies in memory of L. R. Miller,* New York, 1938, pp. 29 ff; also G. Scholem, op. cit., p. 360, n. 39. Lately Professor S. Lieberman has cast serious doubt on the authenticity of the whole episode; cf. his study, 'The Martyrs of Caesarea', in *Annuaire de l'institut de philologie et d'histoire orientales et slaves,* Vol. VII, New York, 1939-44, p. 430, n. 115. Also S. Krauss, *Talmudische Archäologie,* II, pp. 78-81, Leipzig, 1911.

66. On pilgrimages to Hebron, see J. Jeremias, op. cit., pp. 139 f.

67. For a list of these midrashim, see L. Zunz, *Die Gottesdienstlichen Vorträge der Juden,* 2nd ed., Frankfurt, 1892, pp. 130 ff.

68. The first patristic references, aside from St Jerome and St Augustine,

are found in St Gregory of Nazianzus (see *Acta Sanctorum Augusti*, I, 19); cf. Rampolla, op. cit., pp. 301-3.

69. The conjecture that Hebr. 11 : 35 refers to the seven brothers is not convincing.

70. J. Oberman, 'The Sepulchre of the Maccabean Martyrs', in *JBL*, Vol. 50, 1931, pp. 250-65, where the name of their mother Shmonit or Smuni is correctly identified as 'Hasmonaean'. This was first proved by W. Bacher, see n. 57.

71. Ed. M. Gaster in *The Chronicles of Jerahmeel*, London, 1899, pp. 263-67.

72. Cf. Baer, *Seder Abodath Israel*, pp. 624 f, where the text is given.

73. Cf. Rampolla, op. cit., p 381.

74. See W. Bacher, op. cit., also Rampolla, op. cit., p. 458.

75. Cf. Rampolla, op. cit., p. 301.

76. Cherateia or Cherataion was the old Jewish part of Antioch. According to the chronicler Malalas, Demetrius I Soter (162-150 B.C.E.), or, according to M. Maas, Antiochus Eupator, left the remains of the martyrs to the Jews of Antioch. See E. Bickerman, 'Les Maccabées de Malalas', in *Byzantion*, XXI, 1951, pp. 63 ff.

77. This text is according to the most recent edition of the document, translated into Latin, under the title, *Breviarium Syriacum, seu martyrologium Syr. juxta Cod. SM. Mus. Brit. Add. 12150*, ed. Bonaventura Mariani, O.F.M., Rome 1956. The document of which it forms a part seems to be the basis of the martyrology mentioned above; if the historical text was really written by Eusebius of Caesarea, which is not fully established, the solemnization of the Maccabean martyrs in the Church might have originated at or before the time of Constantine the Great.

78. *Passio SS Machabaeorum*, ed. H. Doerrie, in *Abhandlungen der Gesellschaft der Wissenschaft zu Göttingen, phil.-hist. Klasse*, 3. Folge, Nr. 22, Göttingen, 1938.

79. H. Delehaye, *Les Origines du culte des martyrs*, Paris, 1933.

80. St John Chrysostom, *Panegyric on the Maccabees*, in *PG*, 50; also Rampolla, op. cit., p. 303.

81. James Parkes, *The Conflict of the Church and the Synagogue*, London, 1934, pp. 163 ff.

82. J. Oberman, op. cit., p. 262; also E. Bickerman, in *Louis Ginzberg Jubilee Volume*, New York, 1945.

83. A Greek apocryphal book on the Maccabees, falsely attributed to Josephus Flavius, deserves some attention, as it was quite popular in the fourth century.

84. *Tosefta*, III, 2: 'The ministering angels, say the rabbis (B. *Meg.* 10b)

desired to sing a song of triumph to God when the Egyptians were overwhelmed at the Red Sea. But God refused permission, saying: "Shall ye sing praises unto me while my children are sinking in the sea. . . ?" ' See also I. Abrahams, *Companion to the Authorized Prayer-book,* London, 1919-20, p. clxxxv. On the fasting of the firstborn, see *Sofrim* XXI, and *Machzor Vitry,* p. 222.

85. Cf. S. Lieberman, op. cit., p. 445. A quite different picture appears in St Ambrose's story of the exhumation of the Christian martyrs Vitalis and Agricola, who had originally been interred in a Jewish cemetery. At their second burial in a Christian cemetery, under Ambrose's supervision, the Jews participated and sang verses from the Song of Songs, the Psalms, etc., in the Latin version, whereupon the Christians responded (*PL,* 16, col. 350). The entire story is highly dubious and does not enhance Ambrose's credibility.

86. See *JE,* art., ' 'Omer, Lag be-'. The averted martyrdom of the Three Children, recorded in Daniel, falls outside the scope of this examination. For a new interpretation of the *Lag be-'Omer* festival, see J. Morgenstern, 'Lag be-'Omer—its Origin', in *HUCA,* XXXIX, 1968, pp. 81 ff.

87. This idea of a transcendental union achieved by martyrdom is also found in Christianity; see P. Louis Bouyer, F.O., *Liturgical Piety,* Notre Dame, Ind., 1955, pp. 218 ff.

88. See n. 66 *supra.* See also W. Bacher, *Die Aggada der Tannaiten,* Strassburg, 1890-1903, 11, p. 124.

89. Ibid.

90. After E. Gerson-Kiwi, in *International Folk Music Journal,* 1966.

91. ELB, 3rd ed., pp. 203, 335 ff, and Zunz, op. cit. (see n. 35), pp. 136 ff. Long lists of *piyutim* and elegies for these days are given in ELB pp. 336 f. It is hardly surprising that the existence of these martyrologies was familiar to many Christians and kept alive in medieval mystery-plays. The St Nicolas play of MS Orleans 201 contains the so-called *Planctus Judei,* the caricature of a Jewish musical lament, in which we find elements of the *'Alenu* tune, which the Jews in Blois intoned when they were at the stake in 1171. It was adapted in Gregorian chant as *Sanctus* IX. See H. Wagenaar Nolthenius, 'Der *Planctus Judei*', in *Mélanges offerts à René Crozet,* Poitiers, 1966, pp. 881 ff. Further documents on that event are in my *A Voice Still Heard. . . ,* State College, Pa., 1976-7, Ch. III.

92. Cf. ELB, p. 203; also S. Freehof, '*Hazkarath Neshamoth*', in *HUCA,* XXXVI, 1965, pp. 179 ff. See also S. Freehof's edition of MAHARIL's responsum on the holiness of martyrs, (in *A Treasury of Responsa,* Philadelphia, 1963, pp. 56 ff).

93. Ibid.

94. Ibid., pp. 184 ff; also S. Salfeld, *Martyrologium*, Berlin, 1898, pp. 81 f.

95. Cf. *JE*, art., 'Jahrzeit'; also Freehof, op. cit., and L. Zunz, *Die Monatstage des Kalenderjahres*, Berlin, 1872.

96. Applying a well-founded hypothesis of S. Freud to this strange phenomenon, we might consider it a 'disavowal of death' in Freud's terminology.

97. Jerome, *Epistle*, 107 : 9.

98. Tertullian, *De corona*, 111; see also *DACH*, art., 'Martyr'.

99. *Constitutiones Apostolorum*, ed. Funk, VIII, 42 : 1-3. According to St Ambrose the third, thirtieth (or fortieth) day after burial and the anniversary are the special days of mourning (*PL*, 16, col. 1386, and *De obitu Theodosii*, 3).

100. See Freehof, op. cit., pp. 179 ff.

101. S. Lieberman, op. cit., pp. 395-445, and H. Cohen, op. cit. (see nn. 45, 46).

102. For a full description see P. Batiffol, *History of the Roman Breviary*, London-New York, 1912, pp. 99-106; also G. de Rossi, *Roma sotterranea*, III, p. 495, where important archaeological evidence is presented.

103. A Baumstark, *Nocturna Laus*, ed. O. Heiming, O.S.B., Münster, 1957, p. 141. The fixed number of three for the nocturns and their psalms may now be explained by the model of Jewish monks of Qumran with their three shifts of readings per night. The same practice was observed in the Sinai monastery.

104. See Juan Mateos, S.J., *Lelya-Sapra, Essay d'interpretation des matines Chaldéennes*, Rome, 1959, pp. 98 ff.

105. Batiffol, op. cit., pp. 111 f.

106. Plentiful examples and documents are cited by Delehaye, *Les origines du culte des martyrs*, 2nd ed., Brussels, 1933, pp. 100-40; also Duchesne, op. cit., pp. 283 ff.

107. The crux of the problem lies in two hitherto unanswered questions: (1) What was read and chanted at the martyrs' graves before the Roman Sacramentaries, esp. the Gelasian, standardized the customs? And (2) To what extent were the vigils secular and socializing functions, perhaps even pseudomorphoses of ancient pagan festivals, as, e.g., the Kermesse?

108. G. Dix, *The Shape of the Liturgy*, 2nd ed., 1945, Westminster, pp. 39 f.

109. A. Baumstark, op. cit., p. 51. The psalms between the lessons are not called *zmirot* but *tehillim*. As *zmirot* the synagogal liturgy knows metrical, frequently Cabbalistic poems of the High Middle Ages. These are usually chanted on the Sabbath Eve, Sabbath afternoon or Sabbath Close,

both in the synagogue and at home, usually after the three traditional meals. Baumstark, in his *Liturgie comparée,* p. 142, reaches more or less the same conclusion as this author in *The Sacred Bridge,* Vol. 1, p. 205.

110. A. Fortescue, *The Mass,* London, 1912, pp. 265 f.

111. G. Kunze, *Die gottesdienstliche Schriftlesung,* Göttingen, 1947, p. 142.

112. *Musik in Geschichte und Gegenwart,* Kassel, 1956, art., 'Graduale' by B. Stäblein.

113. Duchesne, op. cit., p. 167.

114. Cf. Jacob Mann, *The Bible as Read and Preached in the Old Synagogue,* Cincinnati, 1940, Vol. 1. The posthumous second volume of this monumental work, edited by my late colleague and friend, I. Sonne, appeared in 1966, also in Cincinnati. It is extremely difficult to peruse, even for a scholar, because Sonne died before he could put the enormous material into orderly shape.

115. All these books were published after 1960, yet neither Ehrlich nor Willis took cognizance of Mann's *magnum opus.* In the first case the reference was not indispensable, since the institution of the scriptural lesson is treated rather perfunctorily. Willis, however, might have profited by comparing synagogal OT lessons with those of St Augustine.

116. E. G. King, 'The Influence of the Triennial Cycle upon the Psalter', in *Journal of Theol. Studies,* V (1905), pp. 203 ff; I. Abrahams and E. Kiug, 'The Influence of the Triennial Cycle upon the Psalter', in *JQR,* XVI (1904), pp. 579 f; H. St. J. Thackeray, 'The Song of Hanna and other Lessons for the Jewish New Year's Day', in *Journal of Theol. Studies,* XVI (1916), pp. 177 f.

117. N. H. Snaith, *Hymns of the Temple,* London, 1951; also 'The Triennial Cycle and the Psalter', in *Zeitschrift für die alttest. Wissenschaft,* NF X (1933), pp. 302 f. Nowhere in these studies has the problem of the numbering of the Psalms been touched. It certainly antedates the LXX, but by how many years? As there was no *lectio continua* of the Pentateuch in the Temple, the co-ordination of the Triennial Cycle with the performance of the Psalter can make sense only in the Synagogue, yet from what time on may one assume a regular Sabbath liturgy in the Synagogue? The elements of the *'amida* hardly reach further back than the end of the second century B.C.E., if as far. Where and when was that early co-ordination of Torah and Psalter practised?

118. L. Rabinowitz, 'Does Midrash *Tehillim* Reflect the Triennial Cycle of Psalms?', in *JQR,* n.s. XXVI, 1935-6, pp. 349 ff; J. Mann, op. cit. (Cincinnati, 1940); W. Braude, *The Midrash on Psalms,* New Haven, 1959, Introduction.

119. 'The Psalms in Jewish Liturgy', in *Historia Judaica*, VI (1944), esp. pp. 121 f. Yet it must be added that Mann gives some conclusive proof for the existence of the Triennial Cycle of lessons in the pre-Christian era. This in turn seems to demonstrate the well-established function of a number of synagogues in Palestine at least a century before Christ. If certain scholars have more recently overlooked these facts in order to be 'newsworthy', and claim that there is no evidence of a synagogue before the fall of the Temple (in 70 C.E.), they are either ignorant, or less than honest, or both.

120. Z. D. Levy, 'The Question of Cyclic Readings of the Hagiographa in the Synagogue, and its Relation to Christian Liturgy' (unpublished thesis), Hebrew Union College—Jewish Institute of Religion, New York, 1962.

121. A. Arens, *Die Psalmen*, pp. 170 f.

122. To this practice Leviticus *Rabba* P. 29 : 3 already refers unmistakably; also B. *Rosh hashana* 30b. For a fine check-list of the older Hebrew literature on the subject of the Triennial Cycle and its pericopes, see ELB, pp. 539-42 (in the Notes).

123. The complexities of the various theories are critically analysed by L. Morris, *The New Testament and the Jewish Lectionaries*, London, 1964, esp. p. 15: 'The evidence is so confused that different experts can come to mutually exclusive conclusions. Moreover the position of most of them means that the Synagogue's lectionary was established somewhere near the beginning of our era. . . .'

124. L. Rabinowitz, 'Does Midrash *Tehillim* Reflect the Triennial Cycle of Psalms?', in *JQR*, n.s. XXVI, 1935-6, pp. 349-68, and art. cit. in *Historia Judaica*. As a matter of fact, the Chief Rabbi of Rome edits a psalm lectionary for every Sabbath of the Jewish year.

125. See also the philological study of the late C. Høeg: 'Les rapports de la musique chrétienne et de la musique de l'Antiquité classique', in *Byzantion, Mélanges E. Dyggve, 1955-7*, Brussels, 1958, p. 398.

126. Dom Gregory Dix, *The Shape of the Liturgy*, 2nd ed., Westminster, 1945, pp. 39-40.

127. During the last twenty-five years the views represented by Dix, formerly held by most Christian theologians except the more cautious, such as Msgr Batiffol, E. Bishop and Th. Klauser, have been somewhat modified by the younger generation like von Unnik, Peterson, J. Krauss, O. Michel, et al. The appearance of the DSS and the literature connected with them has shattered many rigidly-held convictions and made the theologians somewhat more cautious. Certain prejudices—or shall we call them axioms?—of a scholastic nature are, however, still evident, *in spite of contrary evidence*.

128. Tertullian, *De oratione*, in *PL*, I, col. 1194, where he speaks of

'Diligentiores [Christiani] in orando subjungere in orationibus Alleluia solent, et hoc genus psalmos, quorum clausulis respondeant qui simul sunt.'

129. Pseudo-Athanasius, *De virginitate*, 20, in *PG*, 28, col. 276. Here he stands in surprising contradiction to his Egyptian brethren, who so often follow his example and instruction.

130. Cf. Cassian, *Institutiones*, 2, 11, in *CSEL*, 17 : 27. On a possible modification of the practice as described by Cassian see A. Baumstark, *Nocturna Laus*, ed. O. Heiming, Münster, 1957, pp. 128 f. We shall not engage in controversy about the use of the terms *psalmi, antiphona* and *hymuus*, in the *Peregrinatio* of Aetheria Sylvia.

131. R. H. Connolly, *The So-called Egyptian Church-Order*, Cambridge, 1916, p. 189.

132. Completely separated from OT context is the Alleluia of the celebrated Fayum papyrus. It is added to the Lesser Doxology (in Greek). About the Alleluia in the Doxology see *Reg. S Benedicti*, c. 15, also my study, 'The Doxology in Church and Synagogue', in *HUCA*, XIX (1945). About psalmody in the statutes of St Benedict see esp. S. Hilpisch, *Der Psalmenvortrag nach der Regula S Benedicti*, 1941-2, pp. 105-15.

133. In the Vol. of *Decretalia* of *PL*, 130, col. 659.

134. In his fine article about Alleluia in *MGG*, B. Stäblein lists this letter, strangely enough, as authentic. See also P. Blanchard, 'La correspondence apocryphe du Pape St Damase', in *Ephemerides Liturg.*, Vol. 63, p. 376, and P. Batiffol, *History of the Roman Breviary*, London, 1912, pp. 35, 45, and notes thereto. See also BLEW, Appendix J, pp. 506 f.

135. The many references by Jerome to Alleluia allude almost exclusively to the first category, i.e., the Alleluia as end of a psalm which contains it as part of its text. Still, passages like the following make even this assumption questionable: 'In septimo vero, quia et ipse sub Alleluia cantatus est, quia in illa alia dominica die lectus est sextus psalmus, et nos pro aegrotatione interpretari non possumus: nunc autem lectus est septimus psalmus,' or in *De psalmo 148:* '. . . sed ille psalmus, qui in principio habet Alleluia ipse ut in fine habet Alleluia. Hoc totum quare dixi? Ut sciatis quare in isto psalmo duo Alleluia proposita sint . . .' (in Jerome, *Tract. in Psalmos*, ed. Morin, in *Anecdota Maredsol.*, 1897, Maredsous, p. 7, 171). Yet neither Ps. 6 nor Ps. 7 have an Alleluia in their texts, whether LXX or TM. To what recension does Jerome refer here?

136. Cf. Victor Vitensis, *De persecutione Vandalica*, 13, in *PL*, 58, col. 197 ff: [during Easter-time] the [Arian] presbyter Anduit or Adduit 'ad expugnandum turbam accendit innocentium. . . . Et tunc forte audiente et canente populo Dei lector unus in pulpito sistens alleluiaticum melos

canebat. Quo tempore sagitta in gutture jacalatus [sic], cadente de manibus codice, mortuus post cecidit ipse. . . .' This was written in or about 481 and reports an incident which happened after 427.

137. J. M. Hanssens, *Institutiones liturgicae de ritibus orientalibus,* Rome, 1930.

138. Ibid., no. 990 f (pp. 187 f).

139. Ibid., no. 989: '. . . nimirum antiphona in papyro quadam Faiumensi scripta et mysterium nativitatis memorans'. See also 'Papyr. collect. archiducis Rainer', ed. Bickell and C. Wessely, in *Les plus anciens monuments du Christianisme,* II, Paris, 1901.

140. E. Wellesz, 'Gregory the Great's letter on the Alleluia', in *Annales Musicologiques,* II, Paris, 1954, pp. 18, 22, 24, which, in our opinion, settles the matter once and for all.

141. For a tabulation of the usage of this verse, see *DACH,* art., 'Communion', III, col. 2428-33. Also *La Paléographie musicale,* V, pp. 22-23.

142. M. Andrieu, *Les Ordines Romani,* III, pp. 223 f, where some old sources are collated, Louvain, 1931.

143. ELB, pp. 495 f; Jer. *Shabb.* XVI, 1 : 15; B. *Succa* 38b; also B. *Pes.* 117a, b, which argues against a 'free' Hallelujah. But see also above Ch. III, p. 79, and note 70.

144. Cf. E. Werner, 'Musical Aspects of the Dead Sea Scrolls', in *MQ,* 1957, January; also by the same author: 'Musikalische Bedeutung der Toten-Meer-Rollen', in *Sitzungsberichte der Ungarischen Akademie der Wissenschaften, phil.-hist. Klasse,* 1962. The best English version of the DSS is Th. H. Gaster, *The Dead Sea Scrolls,* 3d ed., New York, 1976.

145. N. Wieder, *The Judean Scrolls and Karaism,* London, 1962, pp. 103 f.

146. Not all translators of the Bible left the Hallelujah untranslated: thus Theodotion uses instead *'ainete ton hon'.* Cf. M. A. Habermann, *Dictionary of the DSS,* Jerusalem, 1959, where the Hallelujah is not listed. Most recently the Hallelujah was discovered as epithet in the superscription of the apocryphal Psalm 151, found in Qumran. See Ch. VI below.

147. The critical edition of the Odes by Rendel Harris, Cambridge, makes no reference to the Hallelujah refrain.

148. The literature on the Temple cult is immense, and only the most significant contributions are listed here: A. Büchler, *Die Priester und der Cultus im letzten Jahrzehnt des Jerusalemischen Temples,* Vienna, 1895; H. J. Kraus, *Gottesdienst in Israel,* 1959; G. B. Gray, *Sacrifice in the Old Testament,* Oxford, 1925; Holm-Nielsen, 'The importance of late Jewish Psalmody', in *Studia Theologica,* Lund, 1960; R. de Vaux, *Ancient Israel,* 2nd ed., London, 1965, and the monumental *Worship in Ancient Israel,* by H. H. Rowley, London, 1967.

149. Cf. Dom Paolo Ferretti, *Esthétique Grégorienne*, Paris, 1938, pp. 164-5.

150. E. Gerson-Kiwi, in the *Besseler-Festschrift*, cf. Ch. III, pp. 43–49. Considering the ubiquity of ecstatic *jubili*, e.g., the Bedouin's 'trill li-li' (E. Littman) and similar expressions as *elelizo, ululare,* etc., we should pay serious attention to R. Lachmann's observation that the alleluiatic songs by Djerba women are always chanted in Arabic. This demonstrates the adaptability of *jubili* and similar ecstatic acclamations to many languages, either as a process of organic acculturation, or as atavistic usage of the syllables *'l'l* for expressions of ecstasy. See. R. Lachmann, *Jewish Cantillation and Song in the Isle of Djerba,* Jerusalem, 1940, pp. 67 f. See also above, pp. 79 f.

151. The function of 'meaningless' expletives, cries, calls, or interjections in liturgical chant is not new. The subject was treated *de novo,* extensively and with special emphasis upon Oriental usage, by E. Gerson-Kiwi, 'Der Sinn des Sinnlosen in der Interpolation sakraler Gesänge', in *Festschrift für W. Wiora,* Kassel-Basel, 1967.

NOTES CHAPTER V

1. These deviations are treated in A. Baumstark, 'Trishagion und Qeduscha', in *Jahrbuch für Liturgiewissenschaft,* III, 1923, pp. 18 ff; also Vol. I of this book, pp. 282 ff, also in my 'The Doxology in Synagogue and Church' (*HUCA,* 1945).

2. Cf. G. Kretschmar, *Studien zur frühchristlichen Trinitätstheologie* (Tübingen, 1956).

3. The word *ophan* (wheel) has undergone a remarkable change of meaning, so that in later mystical literature it stands for 'musical mode'.

4. Cf. G. Kretschmar, op. cit.

5. It almost appears as if in this instance the LXX was based upon a better text, because among the DSS we encounter the passage 'according to the number of the sons of God'. On this point, see G. F. Moore, *Judaism,* 1, pp. 227 f; M. Burrows, *The Dead Sea Scrolls,* 1956, p. 319; E. Werner, 'Midrashic Elements in The Prima Clementis' (in *Harry Wolfson Jubilee Vol.,* New York, 1965); and D. S. Russell, *The Method and Message of Jewish Apocalyptic,* London-Philadelphia, 1964, pp. 248 ff.

6. J. Strugnell, 'Angelic Liturgy at Qumran', in *Congress Volume,* Oxford, 1959, pp. 318-45.

7. Translation after R. H. Charles's edition of the Ethiopic text, Oxford, 1893, p. 117. According to A. Baumstark, 'The praise by angelic choirs is alien to synagogal liturgy' (in *Islam,* Vol. XVI, 'Jüdische and christliche Gebetstypen im Koran', p. 245). Quantum rapitur in errorem!

8. The etymology of 'Metatron' is a most controversial subject among scholars. Cf. H. Odeberg, *III Enoch*, Cambridge, 1928, pp. 125-46 containing a full analysis of the question; also G. Scholem, op. cit., pp. 67 ff and 366.

9. Cf. Acts 23 : 8.

10. The arguments listed above were for the most part collected and cogently put forth in L. Finkelstein's study, 'La Kédouscha et bénedictions du Schma' (in *Revue des Études Juives*, Paris, 1932), pp. 3 ff.

11. Cf. *Sifre*, in *Corpus Tannaiticum, zu Deuteronom*, II, ed. L. Finkelstein, Breslau, 1935, pp. 348 ff, (no. 306).

12. K. Kohler, 'Ursprünge und Grundformen der synag. Liturgie' (in *Monatschrift für Geschichte und Wissenschaft des Judentums*) Breslau, 1893, pp. 447 ff. Kohler shows there quite clearly the parallelism between Hebrew prayers of the earliest Christian times and the liturgies of Books VII and VIII of the *Apostolic Constitutions*, the so-called Clementine Liturgy. Much later the gist of this pioneering study was 'written out', not to say copied, by W. Bousset in his 'Eine jüdische Gebetssammlung in der Clement. Liturgie' (in *Silzungsber. der Göttinger Akademie der Wissenschaften, phil. hist. Kl.*, 1925-6).

13. A Baumstark, op. cit., and *Liturgie comparée*, 3rd ed., 1953. Baumstark makes an error by confusing R. Yehuda with the rabbi of the same name, called the Prince (fl. 190 C.E.). Actually the rabbi mentioned was R. Yehuda ben ll'ai, who lived at least one and a half generations before the Prince. (Cf. H. L. Strack, *Introduction to the Talmud and Midrash*, Philadelphia, 1931, p. 115.)

14. London, 1944. The author confuses the third benediction of the eighteen benedictions with the K itself and argues from that erroneous position. Cf. my *Sacred Bridge*, Vol. I, p. 308, notes 64 and 66.

15. Joseph A. Jungmann, *Missarum Sollemnia*, Vienna 1949-50; esp. II, pp. 157 ff.

16. Kenneth Levy, 'The Byzantine Sanctus and its modal tradition in East and West', in *Annales de Musicologie*, Paris, 1964, pp. 7-67.

17. Mr. Levy apparently knows the Books VII and VIII of the *Apostolic Constitutions*; is he unaware of the attention drawn to them in modern research which asserts that the Clementine Liturgy exerted a distinct influence on the Byzantine Anaphora?

18. Cf. B. F. Westcott, *A General Survey of the History of the Canon of the New Testament*, 5th ed., Cambridge, 1881, pp. 69, 77 and 121 ff.

19. David Flusser, 'Sanktus und Gloria', in *Festschrift für Otto Michel*, Leiden-Köln 1963, pp. 129 ff.

20. On this similarity Flusser writes: 'The resemblance of the Gloria and the Targum of Isa. 6 : 3 is neither accidental nor indirect; it flows from the

direct dependence of the Gloria on the K, where words from prophetic books are introduced.'

21. Best critical edition by J. B. Lightfoot, *The Apostolic Fathers*, rev. ed., London, 1890; also A. von Harnack, *Das Schreiben der Römischen Kirche an die Corinthier*, Leipzig, 1929; and W. C. van Unnik, 'I Clement 34 and the Sanctus', in *Vigiliae Christianae*, V, Amsterdam, 1951, pp. 214 ff; most recently E. Werner, 'Midrashic Elements in the Prima Clementis' (in the *Harry Wolfson Jubilee Volume*, New York, 1965).

22. The redactor of Revelation has managed to combine the two visions of Isaiah and Ezekiel in one verse. The S goes back to Isaiah; the 'four living creatures', and the conception of them as holy beasts covered with eyes stems from Ezekiel 1 : 3-19. The appositive clause 'The one who was and is', etc., is an attempt to christologize the Hebrew *tetragrammaton* YHWH.

23. *Stromata*, VII, 12, ed. O. Stählin, in *CGES*, 12, 2nd ed., Leipzig, 1939. Clement speaks of beasts, not of angels; although he mentions Isaiah by name, he avoids the expression 'seraphim'. Is again a mixture of the two visions the reason for this strange phraseology? A quotation of the Apocalypse of Zephaniah by Clement is known (*Stromata*, V, 11 : 77), which seems to indicate his familiarity with Jewish angelology and alludes to the K; see also Clement of Alexandria, *Excerpta ex Theodoto*, ed. Casey (1934), No. 78, where the Alexandrian refers to the *Merkaba* vision as *plērōma*.

24. St Ignatius, *Ad Eph.*, in Lightfoot, op. cit., I, pp. 30, and II, p. 40 ff. The term ὁμονοία is a favourite expression of Clement of Rome. The old legend that Ignatius introduced the custom of antiphonal singing in the Church (Socrates, *Hist. Eccl*,, VI, 8) was often repeated and can even today be found in some books. Lightfoot adds to this (more than seventy years ago!): 'A tradition which appears so late does not deserve consideration. . . . Antiphonal singing indeed did not need to be suggested by a heavenly vision . . . It was practised with much elaboration of detail in the psalmody of the Jews, as appears from the account given of the Egyptian Therapeutes by Philo. . . .'

25. Tertullian, *De oratione*, 3 (*CSEL*, VII, 70)—Tr. 'and to Him the surrounding host of angels ceased not to exclaim: "Holy, holy, holy is God . . ." hence we, also potential candidates for angels, if we have so deserved, can already here on earth learn that heavenly word and service of future splendour. . . .'

26. *Passio SS Perpetuae et Felicitatis*, ed., I. M. Beck, in *Florilegium Patristicum*, Bonn, 1938, pp. 4-42: 'and we entered and heard one word spoken in unison: "Agios, agios, agios", incessantly exclaimed and to the right and to the left four presbyters. . . .'

27. Here 'scale' or 'hue' of God; see also Aristides Quintilianus, *De*

THE SACRED BRIDGE II

musica: λευκοῦ καὶ μέλαινος χρῶμα, and Clement of Alexandria, *Stromata*, VII, 14.

28. Cf. Origen, *Hom., in Isa. 1-6* (*GCS*, VIII, 244 ff); also *De principiis*, IV, 3 : 14; and Victor Vitensis, *Hist. Persec. Afr. Prov.*, II, 100 (*CSEL*, VII, p. 70); see also Jerome, *Epist.*, 18 : 6 (in *CSEL*, 54, p. 73). Origen's *De principiis* (ed. G. W. Butterworth, London, 1936, p. 32) contains the significant words: 'And my Hebrew master used to say that the two six-winged seraphim in Isa. 6 : 3, who cry one to another and say "holy, holy, holy . . ." are the only-begotten Son of God and the Holy Spirit. And we ourselves think that the expression in the song of Habakkuk, "In the midst of two living creatures Thou shalt be known" is spoken of Christ and the Holy Spirit.'

29. Cf. Gregory Dix, *The Shape of the Liturgy*, Westminster, 1945, pp. 158 ff; for an opposite view see H. Engberding, 'Das angebliche Dokument römischer Liturgie aus dem Beginn des 3. Jahrhunderts', in *Miscellanea Liturgica in honorem C. Mohlberg* I, pp. 47-71.

30. The remarks of the great patrologist Bardenhewer on Hippolytus are still true: 'Hippolytus is, in his exegesis, much more down-to-earth than Origen. He loves the allegorical method . . .' (in his *Patrologie*, Freiburg, 1894).

31. Between the version of Hippolytus and that of Cyril lie about a hundred years. On the lacunae in Cyril's description see F. E. Brightman, *Liturgies Eastern and Western*, Oxford, 1896, p. 469, n. 9. One may not assume that Cyril was familiar with the Clementine Liturgy, although there appear to stand out some identical phrases; the *Apostolic Constitutions* and their liturgy are known as a remnant of the Judaeo-Christian Church, yet Cyril was, next to St John Chrysostom, the most fanatical Jew-baiter and -hater in the garden of patrology.

32. Hippolytus knew this tradition well himself. In his *Apostolic Tradition*, IV he admonishes all faithful Christians to worship at midnight, for at that moment 'stars and trees and waters stand still with one accord, and all the angelic host does service to God by praising Him, together with the souls of the righteous. . . .' This is, of course, pure Jewish doctrine, and Hippolytus refers to it as 'the tradition taught to us by the elders', i.e., of Apostolic origin. The recent editor, B. S. Easton (New York, 1934), pp. 67-70; 76 ff; 95; 99; 101-3, adds: 'The ancient Law is still fully binding'; 'many prayers have a distinct Jewish background . . .' The editor proves conclusively that the entire section on presbyters and their prayers is completely dependent upon the Hebrew Mishnaic tradition.

33. Cf. *Didache*, ed. K. Lake (in *The Apostolic Fathers*, London-New York, 1930, end of chap. 9).

242

34. E. Werner, 'The Hosanna in the Gospels' (in *Journal of Biblical Literature*, New Haven, July 1946).

35. This term for the S and its additions seems to occur first in Gregory of Nyssa's *De baptismo* (*PG*, 46, col. 421) and in *Christi resurr.* (*PG*, 46, col. 654). See *infra* n. 39.

36. Cf. Sophocles, *Dictionary of the Later Greek Language*, q.v. ἐπινίκιος.

37. Cf. Pauly-Wissowa, *Real-Encyclopaedie des classischen Altertumswissenschaft*, q.v. ἐπινίκιος.

38. Cf. Gregory of Nyssa, *Oratio de occursu Domini* (in *PG*, 44, col. 1140 f) where reference is made to 'quocumque carmine, quo Deus celebratur' ("*tà epiníkia*").

39. See Brightman, op. cit., pp. 479, n. 20; 536, line 15, where the verse is called *hagiastikè doxología* = K.

40. Cf. J. Jungmann, op. cit., II, p. 164. Yet the expression 'militia exercitus coelestis' has a somewhat militaristic connotation, just as the Hebrew *Saba'oth*. See J. M. Hanssens, S.J., *Institutiones Liturgicae*, III, pp. 402 ff.

41. In fairness to the memory of Prof. Baumstark it must be said that he modified his original conception expressed in the article quoted above (see note 1). His *Liturgie comparée* (3rd ed., by Bernard Botte, O.S.B.) stresses anew the importance of the *K-Yotzer* and links it with the *Apostolic Constitutions* and their Judaeo-Christian worship. Had he, who eagerly expected new findings in early Christian liturgies, lived to examine the DSS, we might have benefited greatly by his views on the Qumran literature and its impact on the early Church.

42. My own translation after Pseudo-Dionysius, *De caelesti hierarchia*, ed. P. Hendrix, Leiden, 1959, p. 17. About the Hebraisms of that text, see J. Stiglmayr, S.J., 'Dionysius and Severus' (in *Scholastik*, III, 1928, and VII, 1932). Also the German edition of Dionysius' work on the heavenly hierarchy edited, translated, and annotated by Hugo Ball, Munich, 1955. As these authors have demonstrated, the Areopagite was quite familiar with Hebrew expressions, also with Gnostic and Jewish mysticism. He was probably the one Church Father, who was, without rancour, fully aware of the synthesis of Judaism and Hellenism in Christianity. Hence his Neo-Platonic interpretation of Jewish angelology comes close to later Hebrew philosophy. Cf. Leo Baeck on the 'Book of Creation' in *Monatschrift für Geschichte und Wissenschaft des Judentums*, 70 (1926), pp. 371-6, and 78 (1934), pp. 448 ff.

43. Oslo, 1956, pp. 233 f; see also M. Richard, on the same topic, in *Symbolae Osloenses*, 1952, pp. 24-33; 93-98.

44. Cf. E. Hammerschmidt, in *Texte und Untersuchungen*, Vol. 80 (*Studia*

patristica, V. ed. F. L. Cross), Berlin, 1962, pp. 59-61, where all sources and references are given. See also the same author's *Die koptische Grego-riosanaphora*, Berlin, 1957, pp. 112-28. He is fully aware of the great impact of the Synagogue's *Yotzer* prayer upon the early liturgies: 'In the West Syrian anaphoras of Gregory of Nazianzus, of Jaqub of Sarug, and of Gregory Bar-Hebraya we find still the *ophanim* (wheels) and the divine chariot (*Merkaba*), of the Jewish morning service.' As to Hammerschmidt's lengthy discussion of the attributes of God—indescribable, invisible, without origin, etc., which he ascribes to Hellenistic influence: these negative epithets occur in almost identical order in the Apocalypse of Abraham 17 : 8, where we read: 'Eternal, powerful, . . . Self-created, impeccable, unblemished, immortal', etc. Hellenistic influence is here certainly possible in such passages, for the original *scriptural* attributes are mainly positive.

45. Cf. Brightman, op. cit., p. 531, n. 2, where the first sources are quoted.

46. Apocalypse of Abraham (ed. G. H. Box, London-Cambridge, 1919) 17 : 7, 8; 20 : 6; 22 : 1; 26 : 1. In apocalyptic literature the expressions 'holy' and 'unique' (*monos*) are often interchangeable. E. Bishop, the great historian of Christian liturgy, discusses the origin of the T according to some information by Dom Connolly; they differ considerably from Brightman's sources and indicate a possibly Nestorian origin of the T. See Edmund Bishop, *Liturgica Historica*, Oxford, 1918, p. 132, note 3.

47. It is well known that the passage, Matt. 21 : 9, (εὐλογημένος ὁ ἐρχόμενος κτλ) which follows the LXX, Ps. 117 : 26, is an erroneous translation from the Hebrew; the intent of the verse is: 'Blessed by the Name of YHWH be he, who cometh'. See E. Werner, 'The Hosanna in the Gospels', in *Journal of Bibl. Literature*, July 1946.

48. I Enoch 39 : 12; 12, 13, *et passim*.

49. K. Levy's study on the Byzantine *Sanctus*, quoted above (note 16) contains not only a vast list of palaeographic sources, but also most of the pertinent *musicological* literature on the subject.

50. The Rabbis objected to melismatic chant, which they called 'hymns without words'; they feared, not without good reason, heretical influence. The appearance of the S in the *Te Deum* is amply discussed in the *Jahrbuch für Liturgik und Hymnologie* Vol. 25 (Kassel, 1981), pp. 69–82.

51. Cf. E. Werner, 'The Oldest Sources of Synagogue Chant' (in *Proceedings of the American Academy for Jewish Research*, XVI, 1947, pp. 228 f), and the subsequent rectification of my previous views, as described by Dr. D. Plamenac in his admirable 'Reconstruction of the French Chansonnier in the Biblioteca Colombina, Seville', in *Musical Quarterly*, XXXVII (1951-2), p. 524, note 59.

52. Clement of Alexandria, *Stromata*, VII, 7 : 40, ed. Stählin (in *GCS*, 12); translation by Oulton and Chadwick, *Alexandrian Christianity*, London

and Philadelphia, 1954, p. 117. See also R. B. Tollington, *Clement of Alexandria*, London, 1914, II, p. 150: 'Standing was the usual attitude in worship, with head erect and hands raised and the heels lifted from the ground, and the face turned to the East.'

53. This response seems to date from a time after Clement, as he nowhere alludes to it. See on this point the interesting note in Brightman, op. cit., p. 509, notes 25, 26, where St Cyril of Alexandria is quoted as saying that the closing phrase of the Anaphora (and Mass) was the τὰ ἅγία τοῖς ἁγίοις pronounced by the liturgists, i.e., the priests. The formula Εἷς ἅγιος is mentioned by St Didymus, but nowhere in connection with the liturgy.

54. Cf. Philo, *De vita contempl.*, II, 63 (VI, 68 ed. Cohn-Reiter); also my study on 'The Musical Aspects of the Dead Sea Scrolls' in *Musical Quarterly*, XLIII, 1957, pp. 21 ff.

55. Clement of Alexandria, *Paedagogus*, I, 4. For a full discussion of that interesting passage, see the bibliography in the next note.

56. E. Werner: 'Notes on the Attitude of the Early Church Fathers towards Hebrew Psalmody', in *Review of Religion*, New York-Chicago, May 1943; 'The Conflict between Hellenism and Judaism in the Music of the Early Church', in *Hebrew Union College Annual*, XX, 1947, Cincinnati, pp. 427-9; 'The Common Ground in the Chant of Church and Synagogue', in *Atti del Congresso Internazionali di Musica Sacra*, Rome, 1952, pp. 1-15; *The Sacred Bridge*, Vol. 1, New York-London, 1959, pp. 441-5; 366; 369, note 51, *et passim*.

57. Cf. Dionysius of Halicarnassus, *De compositione verborum*, 17; H. Abert, *Die Lehre vom Ethos in der griechischen Musik*, Leipzig, 1899, pp. 133 ff; Plutarch, *De musica*, XI (ed. R. Volkmann, Leipzig, 1856, pp. 14-15 and 94 f); also H. Riemann, *Handbuch der Musikgeschichte*, 3rd ed., Leipzig, 1923, Vol. I, I, pp. 49 ff; and R. P. Winnington-Ingram, *Mode in Ancient Greek Music*, Cambridge, 1936, pp. 22 ff.

58. It is astounding that Kenneth Levy reaches exactly the same group-ings of melodies as I did, with the exception of the Jewish examples, which he does not mention, and the *Tropos Spondeiakos*, of which he does not seem to be aware. Mr Levy arrived at these conclusions by *original* and careful comparisons and collations of manuscripts; yet the fact that he reached them without ever noticing my studies in the same field, as well as the identity of our results can only be termed a *remarkable coincidence*, the more so, as he quotes from the very same volume (*Atti del Congresso*), where I published my analysis of the *Tropos Spondeiakos* and its parallels in Grego-rian, Byzantine, and synagogal chant.

59. P. Wagner, *Gregorianische Melodien*, III, Leipzig, 1921, p. 456; also K. Levy, op. cit., p. 27.

60. Cf. my *The Sacred Bridge*, Vol. 1, pp. 455, 459, 477.
61. P. Wagner, op. cit., III, p. 59, note.
62. Ibid., p. 366; also *The Sacred Bridge*, Vol. 1, p. 356.
63. K. Levy, op. cit., p. 56. I have, in similar fashion, listed a number of examples of this type of recitation, also of 'pre-octoechic' character on the E-mode, in my *The Sacred Bridge*, Vol. 1, p. 498, Table VI.
64. Cf. my *The Sacred Bridge*, Vol. 1, p. 443, ex. 7.

NOTES CHAPTER VI

As this book goes to press, the author gladly recognizes and gratefully acknowledges the action of the Episcopal Church of America eliminating the *Improperia* from its Holy Week ritual.

1. L. Finkelstein, 'Pre-Maccabean Documents in the Passover-Haggada' (*Harvard Theological Review*, XXXVI, 1943), pp. 1-3; 35; also E. D. Goldschmidt, *Seder haggada schel Pessach* (Tel-Aviv, 1947), pp. 44-47, where the rabbinic sources are quoted.

2. Another explanation of the number 15 is given in *Encyclopédie Chrétienne Hier, Aujourd'hui, Demain* (Paris, 1963), Vol. V, art., 'Impropères'. There the number 15 is constituted by the fifteen antiphons which alternate with the lessons on Good Friday. This is only a shift away from the true reason; why just fifteen antiphons?

3. Durandus, *Rationale divinorum officiorum*, etc., 2nd ed., Venice, Bernardus de Vitalibus (1519), fol. C v verso. (lib. VI, cap. 77).

4. On the *Acta Pilati*, see W. Michaelis, *Die apokryphen Schriften des Neuen Testament* (Bremen 1956), p. 156. The Latin and Greek texts with crit. apparatus are here quoted after C. Tischendorf, *Evangelia Apocrypha*, 2nd ed., Leipzig, 1876, pp. 242, 299 f, 358 ff; also M. R. James, *The Apocryphal New Testament* (Oxford, 1953); and K. L. Schmidt, *Kanonische und apokryphe Evangelien und Apostelgeschichten* (Basel, 1944), pp. 51-63.

5. On the Gospel of Nicodemus and its constituent parts, see also J. Quasten, *Patrology*, I (Westminster, Md. and Brussels, 1953), pp. 115-18, where most modern critics are listed.

6. Cf. A. Baumstark's hypothesis of a possible first tradition of the *Improperia* at the time of Theodosius, in his *Liturgie comparée*, 3rd ed., ed. B. Botte, O.S.B. (Chevetonge, 1953), pp. 105-6. See also the instructive remarks by E. Wellesz on the Byzantine tradition in his *Eastern Elements in Western Chant* (Oxford, 1947), pp. 22-24.

7. *DACH*, art., 'Impropères'. A letter of Gregory VII to the Archbishop of Synnada (Armenia) alludes to that 'scandalum' connected with the event. On a parallel remark in the apocryphal Gospel of Bartholomew, see A. Baumstark, 'Der Orient und die adoratio crucis', in *Jahrbuch für Liturgiewissenschaft*, II (1922), pp. 16-17, no. 2.

8. Dom Martène, *De antiquis Ecclesiae ritibus* (Bassani, 1788), Vol. III, cap. 23. Martène dates the MS of the Colbertina 'ante 400' (!) Baumstark, on the other hand, recommends 'strictest reserve' vis-à-vis Dom Martène's material (*Jahrbuch für Liturgiewissenschaft*, II, p. 2.)

9. Cf. Dom Férotin, *Le Liber ordimun* Paris, 1904, p. 200.

10. The text of Melito's homily which is used here, follows exactly Campbell Bonner's edition, *The Homily on the Passion by Melito of Sardes* (London, 1940); see also: E. Wellesz, 'Melito's Homily on the Passion', in *Journal of Theological Studies,* 44 (1943), pp. 42 ff; and P. Kahle, 'Was Melito's Homily originally written in Syriac', in *Journal of Theol. Studies,* 44 (1943), pp. 52 ff; also E. Peterson, *Frühkirche, Judentum und Gnosis* (Freiburg-Vienna-Rome, 1959), pp. 137 f; and J. Blank, *Meliton von Sardes, 'Vom Passa'* (Freiburg, 1963).

11. Cf. Philo, *De mut. nom.,* 81 (ed. Cohn-Wendland); also in Hippolytus, *Commentarii in Genesim,* 16. Justin (*Dialogue,* 125 : 3) follows here the correct interpretation of Gen. 32 : 30-31.

12. Cf. J. Blank, op. cit. (note 10). Blank, pp. 34 f, refers to the relationship between the *Improperia* and Melito, but is unaware of the Hebrew prototypes of the 'benefit-litany'. He also overlooked the fact that the quartodeciman fasting on the day of the 14th *Nissan* was not only a 'Sühnefasten für das Heil und die Bekehrung der Juden' (p. 36), but the exact continuation of the ancient Jewish fasting of the first-born on that very day, in memory of the day of the slaying of Egypt's first-born.

13. The form ἀφικάμενος does not occur in the LXX, while other forms of the verb ἀφικνέομαι were used. They appear as the equivalents of seven Hebrew verbs (acc. to the concordance to the LXX by Hatch and Redpath). The passages closest to Melito's usage are to be found in Judith 1 : 14; Ecclesiasticus 43 : 17, and 47 : 16; e.g., καὶ ἀφίκετο ἕως 'Εκβατάνων, κτλ (Judith 1 : 14).

14. Justin, *Dialogue (Contra Tryphonem),* 40, and III : 3.

15. Cf. II Baruch (Apocalypse), Syriac text, ed. Wright, Chaps. 6-8; see also Dr Rist's fine discussion of that motif in *Harvard Theological Review,* XXXI, pp. 249 f.

16. The quotation from Isho'dad is given in C. Bonner, op. cit., p. 44.

17. As for the Judaeo-Christian apocryphal literature, and IV Esdras in particular, George F. Moore's statement is still valid: 'The entire tradition of the Jewish apocalyptic literature . . . is Christian, and the many versions of IV Esdras show how wide and lasting its influence was.' In *Judaism,* I, p. 127 (Cambridge, Mass., 1950). See also J. Quasten, *Patrology* (Westminster-Brussels), I, p. 109, and B. Altaner, *Patrologie,* 4th ed., Freiburg, 1955, p. 48; also W. Michaelis, *Die apokryphen Schriften des Neuen Testament* (Bremen, 1956), pp. 464 ff.

18. A. Marmorstein, 'Judaism and Christianity in the Middle of the Third Century', in *HUCA*, X (1935), p. 230.

19. A. von Harnack, *Marcion*, 2nd ed., Leipzig, 1924, p. 341; see also H. J. Schoeps, *Theologie und Geschichte des Judenchristentums* (Tübingen, 1949), pp. 62, 182.

NOTES CHAPTER VII

1. R. K. Yerkes, *Sacrifice in Greek and Roman Religion and in Early Judaism*, London, 1953, p. 124. A good and trustworthy bibliography on the subject of sacrifice and sacrificial cults may be found in H. H. Rowley, *Worship in Ancient Israel*, London, 1967, pp. 111 f. See also 'Ritual and the Hebrew Prophets' in S. H. Hooke, ed., *Myth, Ritual and Kingship*, Oxford, 1958.

2. Susanne Langer, *Philosophy in a New Key*, Cambridge, Mass., 1942; L. Meyer, *Emotion and Meaning in Music*, Chicago, 1956.

3. We may here well ask if categories such as art music *v.* folk music are at all applicable to the cultures of the old Near East. To state a few opposing opinions, separated by centuries: J. G. Herder thought of certain biblical books as a kind of 'elevated folklore', esp. of the Song of Songs, Psalms, etc., and attributed their creation to a collective *Geist der Ebräischen Poesie;* in sharp contrast stand, paradoxically enough, certain Arabic theorists, of whom Saffi-Yu-D-Din Abdul-L-Mumin (fl. 1375) traces every tune, however 'folkish', to its composer, every text to a poet. We might consider some of his sources as legendary or mythical, but the concept of folklore is totally alien to him, except in its most vulgar and contemptible examples. (In D'Erlanger, *La Musique Arabe*, III, *Kitab al Adwar*, pp. 539-51, Paris, 1938). R. Lachmann (*Jewish Cantillation and Song in the Isle of Djerba*, Jerusalem, 1940, p. 38) takes quite a different view: 'Since the *Gestalt* in [folklore]—melody is not, or not capable of being determined by ratio, we have . . . to resort to analogies and paraphrases.' In general Lachmann shows nowhere that he would recognize such a distinction between art and folklore in music. B. Nettl (*Theory and Method in Ethnomusicology*, New York, 1964) generally evades questions like these and contents himself (and his readers must be content with him) with a limited bibliography on recent authors on folk music. Yet the very existence of a dividing line between two postulated categories of music in antiquity is problematical, to say the least.

4. Ch. Seeger, art., 'Tradition', in Funk and Wagnalls, *Encyclopedia*, New York, 1960.

5. E. B. Tylor, *Primitive Culture*, London, 1871; W. R. Smith, *The Religion of the Semites*, 2nd ed., 1889; W. K. C. Guthrie, *The Greeks and their*

Gods, London, 1950; H. C. Trumbull, *The Blood Covenant,* 2nd ed., London, 1896.

6. M. Jastrow, *The Civilization of Babylonia and Assyria,* Philadelphia, 1915.

7. J. E. Harrison, *Prolegomena to the Study of Greek Religion,* 3rd ed., Cambridge, 1922.

8. Cf. Boisacq, *Dictionnaire etymologique de la langue Grecque,* 5th ed., Paris, 1962, q.v. *theos;* also Yerkes, op. cit., p. 25.

9. Sir James Frazer, *Folklore in the Old Testament,* London, 1918; also R. de Vaux, *Ancient Israel,* 2nd ed., London, 1965, pp. 442, 465.

10. J. M. Robertson, *Pagan Christs,* London, 1903, pp. 203, 345, 356; also Yerkes, op. cit., p. 43; J. Klausner, *From Jesus to Paul,* New York, 1943, p. 115. Also F. Cumont, *Les Religions orientales dans le paganisme romain,* 4th ed., Paris, 1929; A. Loisy, *Les Mystères païens,* 2nd ed., Paris, 1930.

11. How deeply the loss was felt is shown in one of numerous anecdotes: R. Yohanan b. Zakkai was walking in Jerusalem, accompanied by his disciple, R. Joshua b. Hananya. At the sight of the Temple's ruins, Joshua broke out in bitter laments, 'Woe to us, for the place where Israel's iniquities were atoned for is destroyed'. R. Yohanan replied: 'Do not grieve, my son, for we have an atonement which is just as good, namely deeds of mercy, as Scripture says: "For I desire mercy and not sacrifice" ' (Hos. 6:6). On the significance of the cessation of sacrifices, see the penetrating observations by G. F. Moore in his *Judaism,* Cambridge, Mass., 1950, I, pp. 503-6; II, pp. 14 ff. Recent modifications of this view were offered by A. Guttmann's article, 'The End of the Jewish Sacrificial Cult', in *HUCA,* XXXVIII (1967), pp. 138-9. For a modern bibliography on the Passa sacrifice, see H. Rowley, op. cit., pp. 48 ff, and notes thereto.

12. Pindar and Pausanias use the word *prophētēs* as expression of the ecstatic ravings of the seeress in Delphi, intoxicated by the vapours of Apollo's cave. Literally it means 'to speak in front of' (probably the cave). When the Hebrew Bible was translated into Greek by the Rabbis (the LXX), the term *nabi'* was rendered by *prophētēs.* Yet *nabi'* signifies a person that proclaims, calls, speaks in inspired words. It has little to do with 'predicting things to come', as latinized Christianity understood it in its Christology, often introduced by the phrase 'sicut scriptum est apud prophetas'.

13. G. F. Moore, loc. cit., (note 11); also R. de Vaux, op. cit., pp. 454 ff.

14. G. Dix, *The Shape of the Liturgy,* Westminster, 1945, pp. 36 f. Dix's point that in the ancient Synagogue prayers came before the reading of Scripture, while in the early Church the procedure was reversed, is problematic in view of the DSS, especially the *Manual of Discipline* that

resembles the *Didache.* See E. Peterson, 'Probleme der Didache-Über-lieferung' (in *Rivista Archeologica Cristiana,* Rome, 1952, pp. 37 f). Also H. Rowley, op. cit., pp. 51, 115, 131, 147 ff.

15. On this and similar problems, see *Theologisches Wörterbuch zum Neuen Testament,* q.v. *Agape,* and *Eucharist;* also *The Interpreter's Dictionary of the Bible (IDB),* New York, 1962.

16. We should, however, caution ourselves against the assumption that such heterogeneous positions as worship by deed *v.* worship by word, were clearly understood in the ancient world. One may conjecture that this antinomy sprang into existence only with the emergence of monotheism. Before that time, many kinds of 'mixed practices', employing pantomime, sacrifice, dance, pageant, sacred marriage and other fertility rites or apotropaic priestcraft, as well as solemn dirges and laments, were in regular use without any generally discernible preference.

17. Our knowledge of Hittite music has not been enriched by a pre-sumptuous little book on that subject by A. Machabey (*La Musique des Héthites,* Paris, 1950), which indulges in all sorts of ludicrous and phantas-tic speculations without any literary or factual intelligence.

18. H. Hartmann, *Die Musik der sumerischen Kultur,* Frankfurt a/M, 1960, by far the best and most reliable work on that thorny and remote subject. Thereafter, W. Stauder's fine and comprehensive study, 'Die Musik der Sumerer, Babylonier und Assyrer', has appeared, in *Handbuch der Orientalistik,* Ergänzungsband IV, Leiden-Köln, 1970, where the latest findings and a solid bibliography are given.

19. Hartmann, op. cit. pp. 165 ff, 253.

20. E. D. van Buren, 'The Sacred Marriage in Early Times in Mesopota-mia' (in *Orientalia,* XIII, 1944, pp. 1 ff). Also Thureau-Dangin, *Rituels accadiens,* Paris, 1921.

21. W. Stauder, art., 'Sumerisch-babylonische Musik', in *MGG,* XII. The author examines cautiously and carefully the earliest traces of a 7-tone scale and the division of the octave. By contrast, H. G. Farmer in *NOHM,* I, pp. 254 ff, indulges in all sorts of abstruse conjectures, yet does not hesitate to draw on my *octoechos* theory, when it suits his purpose, without citing any of his sources.

22. At the sacrifice of propitiation of Apollo, Chryses prays, and the Greek youths 'sang a fair paean with music' (*Iliad,* 472-4).

23. The name Phemios, from Gr. defective *phaō-phēmi* signifies 'the sayer', 'the proclaimer', Germ. *Künder.* As such the word comes near to the meaning of the Hebrew *nabi'* = prophet, which etymologically derives from a root 'to say, to utter, to proclaim'.

24. Cf. Herodotus, VII, 6; also Aristotle, *Politics,* VIII, 5, 1339b, where a verse is attributed to Mousaios. In Alexandria he was sometimes equated

with Moses; see E. Bickermann, in *Havard Theol. Review*, 1965 (LVIII, pp. 136-41).

25. W. K. C. Guthrie, op. cit., pp. 221-2. The peripheral role played by music in Greek sacrificial ritual is hardly worth mentioning; it was no more than a necessary ingredient for the festive mood.

26. *Antt.*, XX, 9 : 6. For many more examples, see art., 'Soziologie der Musik', in *MGG*, also E. Werner, art., 'Music', in *IDB*. For a good bibliography on this subject see H. H. Rowley, op. cit., pp. 149-75, who also provides a critical survey.

27. For the modern interpretation of this and other terms, see E. Werner, in *IDB*, art., 'Music'.

28. From the enormous literature on this subject, only K. Bücher's classic *Arbeit und Rhythmns* (4th ed., Leipzig, 1909), F. Leitner's *Der gottesdienstliche Volksgesang im jüdischen und christlichen Altertum* (Freiburg, 1906), and Herder's still inspiring *Vom Geist der Ebräischen Poesie* should be named here, as they are of historical importance.

29. A. C. Welch, *Prophet and Priest in Old Israel*, London, 1936, p. 111.

30. S. Mowinckel, *The Psalms in Israel's Worship*, Oslo, 1941, p. 57.

31. Ibid., p. 60.

32. A few scholars have identified these cultic prophets with the biblical 'false prophets', in this writer's opinion with unconvincing arguments. See J. Jocz, *The Spiritual History of Israel*, London, 1961, p. 69; also H. Rowley, op. cit., pp. 165-8; and A. R. Johnson, *The Cultic Prophet in Ancient Israel*, 2nd ed., Cardiff, 1962, pp. 69 f.

33. S. Mowinckel in *HUCA*, Jubilee Vol. XXIII, pt. I, p. 205, Cincinnati, 1950-1; also H. Gordon May, '*Al* . . . in the Superscriptions of the Psalms,' in *American Journal of Semitic Languages and Literatures*, LVIII, 1941, Nr. 1, pp. 72 ff.

34. S. Mowinckel, op. cit. (*HUCA*, XXIII), p. 226.

35. At the end of *Man.*, IX; 4-5 we read: 'atonement will be made . . . more effectively than by any flesh of burnt-offerings or fat of sacrifices. The "obligation of the lip" will be in all justice like the erstwhile "pleasant savour" on the altar; righteousness and integrity like that free-will offering which God deigns to accept . . .' (Th. Gaster's translation).

36. B. Gärtner, *The Temple and the Community in Qumran and the New Testament*, Cambridge, 1965, p. 21.

37. Ibid., p. 44.

38. The text quoted here is according to J. A. Sanders, *The Dead Sea Psalms Scroll*, Cornell Univ. Press, 1967.

39. Cf. M. Jastrow, *Dictionary of Talmudic and Rabbinic Hebrew*, q.v. *pethi*; cf. also Prov. 19 : 25, where the Vulg. simply translates 'stultus sapientior erit'; LXX, ibid., *aphron* = silly, foolish.

40. The poetic personification of wisdom, which already occurs in Prov. 8 : 4 f, and Ecclus. 1 : 15 f, is carried to an erotic extreme in the Qumranite version of Ecclus. 51 : 11-17. Cf. J. A. Sanders, op. cit., pp. 115 f, and the commentary thereto.

41. S. Holm-Nielsen, 'Ich in den Hodayot' (in H. Bardtke, *Qumran-Probleme,* Berlin, 1963, pp. 217 ff), believes that many of the *Hymns of Thanksgiving* served for community singing. In his opinion their style was fashioned for the worship at the 'Erneuerungsfest der Bundesgemeinde' (Feast of consecration and rededication).

42. This *Temple Scroll,* which has just been published seems to contain new and incontrovertible evidence for the link between the festal calendar and the system of musical modes.

43. J. A. Sanders, op. cit., pp. 97 f. The psalm is ascribed to David, who was considered a prophet in Qumran—exactly as in the Church. According to the *Psalm-Scroll* (p. 137), 'All these [psalms] he [David] composed through prophecy which was given him from before the Most High'. Prof. Th. Gaster has directed my attention to certain resemblances with poems by Theocritus.

44. Perhaps the editor overlooked here the many rhymes and assonances that permeate the entire poem—a sure sign of its popularizing style. Verses 3-6 especially are replete with such pure and impure rhymes. The instruments associated with David are exactly those of Jubal, the 'father of all those that play the lyre and pipe' (Gen. 4 : 21). This is probably more than a chance allusion. It is, all other things considered, not very amusing to read about David as a '*Musikant*' as he is consistently called by M. Delcor, '*Zum Psalter von Qumran*' (in *Biblische Zeitschrift,* NF 1966, pp. 15 f).

45. For a list of the Syriac MSS, see *Publications of Peshitta Institute,* Leiden University, Leiden, 1961, p. 113.

46. With many apologies to Prof. J. A. Sanders, whose translation I have altered in a few details in order to preserve certain characteristics of style.

47. '. . . et incipit canite dissimili voce et melodia ut a circumstantibus altare tantum audiatur. . . .' M. Andrieu, *Les Ordines Romani du haut moyen age,* I-III, Louvain, 1931, 1948, p. 103; and II, p. 221: '. . . pontifex tacito intrat in canonem'; also WGM, I, pp. 34 and 84, where P. Wagner sets the time for the decline of congregational participation at about 450. The reader will here, and in the subsequent pages, have to forgive the author for not joining the chorus of the writers, who in these matters invariably use hymnic language enthusiastically preferred by J. A. Jungmann, S. J., and his school. 'Severus sit clericorum sermo', said St Augustine, and in this instance we shall follow his advice.

48. As to the common chant *Sanctus* and Doxology, see my 'The

252

Doxology in Synagogue and Church', in *HUCA,* XIX (1945) and Ch. V of this book, as well as the recently discovered *Angelic Liturgy* of the DSS, referred to in Ch. V. It is regrettable that musicologists refuse to take cognizance of nonmusical discoveries, regardless of their importance to our knowledge of Jewish or Christian liturgies. Thus P. J. Thannabaur (in his art. on *Sanctus* in *MGG*) ignores all new liturgical evidence and is satisfied with the repetition of the main ideas of the nineteenth century.

49. Cf. the remarks by the Church Fathers as quoted above in Ch. IV, p. 88; also Augustine, *Enarr. in Psalmos,* II, on Ps. 32 : 5, *PL,* 36, 279; and Jerome, *Epist.,* 107, 9 : 2, in *CSEL,* LV, p. 300.

50. See the extensive discourse on that period in F. Blume's outstanding work, *Geschichte der evangelischen Kirchenmusik,* 2nd ed., Kassel, 1965. For a shorter discussion of the problem, see *MGG,* art., 'Gemeindegesang', by B. Stäblein and W. Blankenburg, where also an extensive bibliography may be found.

51. On the influence of the counter-reformation on music, see *MGG,* art., 'Gemeindegesang'; also O. Ursprung, 'Katholische Kirchenmusik', in *Handbuch der Musikwissenschaft,* 1931, pp. 223-5.

52. J. S. Bach, a music director of a collegiate church, took a professional choir for granted; and this institution saved the polyphonic art music in his day, which, for theological reasons, has recently fallen into discredit. The nucleus of the Protestant music remained, however, at all times the congregational chorale. Leipzig's main churches were, before the Reformation, under the jurisdiction of a chapter of Augustinian Canons. See Ph. Spitta, *J. S. Bach,* 4th ed., Leipzig, 1930, vol. II, p. 6 ff.

53. I. Henderson in *NOHM,* I, p. 376.

54. G. Murray, *The Rise of the Greek Epic,* 4th ed., London, 1934, p. 66.

55. Herodotus, II, 79; Linos was not a historical person, and while the Ailinos-wail was quite common in the Near East, it was not taken very seriously, for Euripides (quoted by Athenaeus, *Deip.,* XIV, 619) claimed that Linos and Ailinos are suited for joyous occasions as well. See W. Christ, *Geschichte der griechischen Litteratur,* 4th ed., Munich, 1905, p. 21; also H. Gordon May, op. cit., and H. G. Farmer, in *NOHM,* I, pp. 251 f, who, as usual, goes far beyond established facts. Not as uncritical is E. Reiner, in *Die rituelle Totenklage der Griechen,* Berlin, 1938, pp. 109 f.

56. Perhaps the most notorious of these songs was: 'Gallias Caesar subegit, Nicomedes Caesarem; ecce Caesar nunc triumphat qui subegit Gallias, Nicomedes non triumphat qui subegit Caesarem' (Caesar laid Gaul, Nicomedes laid Caesar, now Caesar triumphs because he laid Gaul, but Nicomedes, who had laid Caesar, does not triumph) (in Suetonius, *Divus Julius,* 49).

57. See M. P. Nilsson, *Geschichte der griechischen Religion*, II, Munich, 1950, p. 614 ff.

58. Cf. H. Brown, 'The Chanson Rustique: Popular Elements in 15th and 16th cent. Chanson' (in *JAMS*, XII, 1959), pp. 17 f: 'As opposed to what is badly termed "art music", folk song, whatever its original sources, may be defined as music which is transmitted orally and which circulates primarily among rural populations. Therefore(!), specimens of genuine folk music from before the nineteenth century are unlikely ever to be found'. I wonder what the author thinks of the famous collections of folk music and popular songs established before the nineteenth century, especially the Hussite, Taborite, or German songs of the sixteenth-eighteenth centuries?

59. B. Nettl, 'Unifying Factors in Folk and Primitive Music', in *JAMS*, IX, 1956, pp. 196-7.

60. C. Sachs, *Rhythm and Tempo*, New York, 1953, pp. 180-1.

61. That the nationalistic schools cultivated such structures is undeniable, either to parade their close links with the 'grass roots' of their nations, or because it was a most convenient technique of continuation ('*Fortspinnungstechnik*'). We may find similar repetitious rhythms in the music of the Vienna classics, especially in dance forms, also in note for note accompanied harmonisations of chorales.

62. E. Ferand, 'What is Res Facta?' (in *JAMS*, X, pp. 141-50).

63. Ibid., pp. 146 ff.

64. S. Langer, op. cit., p. 195.

65. J. Kuckertz, *Gestaltvariation in den von Bartók gesammelten rumänischen Colinden*, Regensburg, 1963.

66. R. Lachmann, *Musik des Orients*, Breslau, 1929, p. 59.

67. A discernible coherence is by definition also demonstrable; the statement is, however, not reversible. The virtual abandonment of the postulate of discernible coherence coincides with the weakening of tonality in the works of Reger, Debussy, Schoenberg, Stravinsky, and others; it is not by mere accident that in folk music the postulate of coherence by tonality has retained much of its force and validity. (Since this was written, Zofia Lissa's excellent essay, 'Prolegomena to the theory of musical tradition', has appeared in *International Revue of Music Aesthetics*, I. Zagreb, 1970. While it goes far beyond my brief discussion, it contains some similar ideas.)

68. Cf. A. Z. Idelsohn, 'Songs and Singers of the Synagogue in the 18th century', in *HUCA*, 1925, Jubilee Volume.

69. The two extreme positions, viz. that each ethnic tradition of music is strictly autonomous and only understandable by its own terms and

principles, and the opposite one, which looks for interdependence and interrelations without too much regard for specific historical, geographic and cultural elements of either of the two traditions to be compared, are no longer dominant in the scholarly world, yet the more so in the sphere of nationalistic political propaganda. The smaller the nation, the greater its claims, the fiercer its pride.

70. C. C. Gillispie, *The Edge of Objectivity*, Princeton, 1960, which describes and defines precisely the dilemma of natural science between preciseness and generalization; esp. pp. 15-21; 45-59, and *passim*. Every natural scientist is perfectly familiar with these ideas, but they are, up to this day, rarely at home in the halls of the humanities. And vice versa!

71. The choice of the best suited parameters varies from tune to tune, but it must be emphasized that a bad choice of parameters cannot distort the curve of distribution of the resulting values; it may, however, make it less clear and less precise. The parameters suggested above tend in the limit (diatonic melodies with no omissions or singularities, where the final note is also the lowest, and where the text is treated strictly syllabically) to 1, except the first parameter NT, which gives the number of discrete tones. It is easy to see that, e.g., in a strict recitation upon one tone the resulting number will equal the number of syllables recited, as all other parameters reduce to 1.

72. The literature on this and related subjects in mathematics and statistics is enormous; here we recommend for beginners without any background of calculus the wittily written *Facts from Figurers* by M. J. Moroney (a Pelican book), London, 1958; for advanced students W. M. Smart, *Combination of Observations*, Cambridge, 1958.

73. For concrete examples, see my study 'Numerical Representation of Orally Transmitted Tunes' (in *A. Z. Idelsohn Memorial Vol.*, Hebrew University, Jerusalem, 1984).

NOTES CHAPTER VIII

1. The ambivalence is most clearly felt in the writings of St Paul. See J. Klausner, *From Jesus to Paul*, New York, 1943, esp. Bk. VII, Ch. 2 and 5. Reading between the lines of Eusebius's *History of the Church*, one seems to sense traces of guilt feelings in those Judaeo-Christians, who, in the year 66, fled to Pella, thus evading the siege of Jerusalem. See Eusebius, *Eccl. Hist.*, X, 4 : 23, where Constantine is called 'the New Aaron'!

2. *Didascalia Apostolorum*, ed. Gibson, in *Horae Semiticae*, II, 21, p. 96, London, 1903.

3. For a more extensive discussion, see W. Wiora, *Europäische Volksmusik*

und abendländische Tonkunst, Kassel, 1957; for the Anglo-American orbit, see D. K. Wilgus, *Anglo-American Folksong Scholarship since 1898,* New Brunswick, 1959.

4. Cf. W. Danckert, *Das europäische Volkslied,* Bonn, 1970, where most of these theories are discussed.

5. Cf. *The Sacred Bridge,* Vol. 1, Pt. 2, Ch. II, pp. 373 ff. The author of the art., 'Octoechos', in *MGG,* Maria Stoehr, failed to clarify the significance of the term as a collective name for the eight Psalm Tones, also to mention its calendaric meaning, which it has retained to the present day. L. Richter, in his 'Antike Überlieferungen in der byzantinischen Musiktheorie' (in *Jahrbuch Peters,* VI, Leipzig, 1962, pp. 75 ff), utilizes some of my findings anonymously. Of the Semitic origin of the syllables *Neannoe* in the *octoechos* neither he, nor Miss Stoehr, nor Prof. O. Strunk is aware, although no other etymology has been offered. Cf. E. Werner, 'The Psalmodic Formula *Neannoe* and its Origin', in *MQ,* XXVIII (1942), pp. 93 ff.

6. Prof. J. Handschin, being an exception, preferred to state that I, in tracing the *octoechos,* have 'followed uncritically' Prof. Quasten; he does not explain where and when, nor quote any sources, he just says so (*NOHM,* 11, 160). For the reader's information my source is quoted in *The Sacred Bridge,* Vol. 1, p. 408, nn. 66, 67.

7. See, e.g., *The Hymns of Thanksgiving* of the Dead Sea Scrolls, Also H. Rowley, op. cit., p. 269, and S. Mowinckel, *The Psalms in Israel's Worship,* II, p. 211.

8. E. Werner, 'The Eight Modes of Music (Octoechos)', in *HUCA,* XXI (1948), p. 217.

9. Ibid., p. 220; see also *The Sacred Bridge,* Vol. 1, pp. 379 and 407 n. 37.

10. Text in *The Sacred Bridge,* Vol. 1, p. 307.

11. E. Werner, 'The Eight Modes of Music', (see n. 8) p. 238.

12. Hippolytus, *Refutatio omnium haeresium* (in *Antenicean Fathers,* V), VI, 26, 27.

13. Tertullian, in *Antenicean Fathers,* III, p. 514.

14. E. Werner, *The Sacred Bridge,* Vol. 1, pp. 396 ff.

15. M. Gaster, *Studies and Texts in Folklore, Magic, . . .,* London, 1925-8. Excellent examples are Nos. 11, 12, 16, 17, of Vol. I, and 34 of Vol. II. The author's ingenious sense of combination and detection came close to discovering the DSS by sheer historical and philological reasoning.

16. In order to avoid a dull chronological description, we shall group the answers according to the respective reasoning and motivation that underlie them.

17. *The Sacred Bridge,* Vol. 1, pp. 355 f.

18. As the equation $Y_x = [r!/x!(r-x)!]q^{(r-x)}p^x$ seems to be valid for the diatonic octave, where r approaches infinity, the result cannot differ too much from $(1/x!)q^{(r-x)}p^x$, whereby p represents the positive, q the negative probability of the event. How complicated the problem is in reality, can be seen in R. von Mises's extensive discussion of the similar problem posed by K. Marbe, in von Mises, *Wahrscheinlichkeitsrechnung*, Vienna, 1938—New York, 1945, p. 101.

19. J. N. Forkel, *Allgemeine Geschichte der Musik*, Leipzig, 1788, 1801, I, No. 90, n. 134, where the author quotes as his expert Millot's *Elements d'Histoire générale*.

20. R. G. Kiesewetter, *Geschichte der europäisch-abendländischen oder unserer heutigen Musik*, 2nd ed., translated into English by R. Müller, London, 1848, p. 3.

21. K. C. F. Krause, *Darstellungen aus der Geschichte der Musik*, Göttingen, 1827, pp. 96, 100.

22. G. A. Bontempi, *Historia musica . . . secondo la dottrina de' Greci, i quali inventata prima da Jubal avanti il Diluvio . . .*, Perugia, 1695, p. 173: '. . . estimandosi superfluo pe'l canto de Salmi, delle Antifoni, degli Hinni, e dell' altere cose da cantarsi nel Coro l'uso ai tanti Modi antichi, da Noi nella Seconda Parte . . . ne furono da' Musici Greci Ecclesiastici elletti solamente quattro . . .' etc.

23. J. Handschin, 'Geschichte der Musik', in *Musica Aeterna*, Zurich, 1948, pp. 41 f. In his interpretation the hymns of Paul's exhortation are 'newly composed songs'. It is well known among NT scholars that the hymns mentioned by Paul are OT canticles.

24. And yet Gevaert wrote: 'We shall have to observe the influence of the Syrian—half Greek, half Semitic—Church upon Roman plainchant even in later epochs.' (*Der Ursprung des römischen Kirchengesanges*, trans. H. Riemann, Leipzig, 1891, p. 13.).

25. Michael Praetorius, *Syntagma Musicum*, I, Epistola dedicatoria, Wittenberg, 1615.

26. W. C. Printz, *Historische Beschreibung der Edelen Sing- und Kling-Kunst*, Dresden, 1690, pp. 86 f. He found this (correct) interpretation probably in Pseudo-Dionysius Areopagita.

27. G. B. Martini, *Storia della Musica*, Bologna, 1757-81, I, pp. 354, ff.

28. M. Gerbert, *De cantu et musica sacra*, St. Blasien, 1774, I, cap. 8: 'Nec dubito . . . quin et hoc canendi genus, vel praecipue commendat Paulus (Ephes. 5 : 19) mansit diu is mos Ecclesiae veteris' (H. Grotius).

29. Arthur Bedford, *The Temple Musick: or an essay concerning the Method of Singing the Psalms of David in the Temple, before the Babylonish captivity. Wherein the musick of our cathedrals is vindicated as conformable not only to that of*

primitive Christianity, but also to the practice of the Church in all preceding, London, 1706. Bedford was a strict Puritan and he does not hesitate to quote John Calvin (*Comm. in I Cor. 14*), 'I doubt not but from the beginning they followed the Jewish Usage in singing of Psalms'. See also the sharply worded essay by P. Scholes, *The Puritans and Music in England and New England,* London, 1934, where this fine historian convincingly disproves the legend of the Puritan antimusical attitude. Bedford, by the way, was quite a learned author having published treatises on astronomy, mathematics and Semitic languages besides books on music. See *Dictionary of National Biography*.

30. This conflict, so interesting for the musical sociologist, still demands detailed examination. W. Douglas's serious book *Church Music in History and Practice,* New York, 1937, has been superseded by the various encyclopedic articles in *Grove* 5th ed., London-New York, 1954; see also E. Routley, *Hymns and Human Life,* New York, 1953, also John Westrup, art., 'England III', in *MGG*.

31. Charles Burney, *A General History of Music,* 1776-89, I, p. 212, II, p. 41. On the conception of history in Burney and Hawkins see E. Hegar, *Die Anfänge der neueren Musikgeschichtsschreibung,* Leipzig-Strasbourg, 1932.

32. Ch. Burney, op. cit., I, p. 413.

33. Although a fine musician and a well-read man of the world, it is doubtful if Burney knew genuine Greek Temple hymns.

34. Voltaire and Montesquieu would have expressed similar opinions: the enlightened rationalists were not too self-critical when it came to their own knowledge of ancient cultures, unless they were Latin or Greek.

35. Sir John Hawkins, *A General History of the Science and Practice of Music,* 2nd ed., London, 1853, Preface.

36. Ibid., III, Ch. 22.

37. F. J. Fétis, *Histoire générale de la Musique,* Vol. IV, pp. 8-12, Paris, 1874.

38. Ibid., pp. 10-11.

39. A. W. Ambros, *Geschichte der Musik,* Breslau, 1864, Vol. II, pp. 7, 8.

40. Sir H. Parry, *Evolution of the Art of Music,* London, 1893, pp. 53 f.

41. S. Naumbourg, *Recueil de Chants Religieux; Étude Historique,* Paris, 1874.

42. J. Singer, *Die Tonarten des traditionellen Synagogengesanges,* Vienna, 1886.

43. A. Ackermann, *Der synagogale Gesang in seiner historischen Entwicklung* (in Winter and Wünsche, *Die jüdische Litteratur seit Abschluss des Kanons*), Vol. III, Trier-Berlin, 1896.

44. A bibliography of this eminent scholar is found in my article,

'Manuscripts of Jewish Music in the Eduard Birnbaum Collection', in *HUCA*, XVIII (1944), pp. 397-428.

45. Prof. C. Palisca, of Yale University, has omitted the name of A. Z. Idelsohn in his 'authoritative' survey in Frank H. Harrison, Mantle Hood, and Claude V. Palisca, eds., *Musicology,* Princeton Studies of Humanistic Scholarship in America, Englewood Cliffs, N. J., 1963. Idelsohn was an American citizen, had lived in this country for thirteen or fourteen years, and created new concepts in modern musicology. In this instance Heine's bitter words are surely applicable: 'Blamier mich nicht, mein schönes kind, und grüss mich nicht Unter den Linden'.

46. Idelsohn's *Jewish Music in its Historical Development,* New York, 1929, was a very popular book, but contains quite a few inaccuracies.

47. H. Riemann, *Handbuch der Musikgeschichte,* 3rd ed., Leipzig, 1923, I, 2; pp. 33, 56, 82.

48. In his contribution to Adler's *Handbuch,* P. Wagner again offered his conjecture of Jewish proselytes as the bearers of Jewish tradition into the Church. He had done so first in his *Gregorianische Melodien,* Vol. I, p. 17, published in 1911; meanwhile C. M. Kaufmann had drawn attention to some early Judaeo-Christian cantors, in his *Handbuch der Christlichen Archäologie,* Paderborn, 1922. See also *The Sacred Bridge,* Vol. I, pp. 54 ff.

49. *OHM,* ed. P. C. Buck and Sir W. H. Hadow, Introductory Vol. (VII), pp. 88 f.

50. A. Einstein, in 3rd ed. of H. Riemann's *Musiklexikon,* Berlin, 1929, art., 'Jüdische Musik'.

51. C. Sachs, *Our Musical Heritage,* N.Y., 1948; 'Musik der Antike' (in Bücken's *Handbuch der Musikwissenschaft,* Potsdam, 1932); *The Rise of Music in the Ancient World,* New York, 1943.

52. H. Besseler, 'Musik des Mittelalters und der Renaissance' (in Bücken's *Handbuch,* see n. 51). Although racist principles were taken for granted in the book, the author still took some pains to shed new light on the problem under consideration.

53. G. Wille, *Musica Romana,* Amsterdam, 1967, p. 400. The author of this massive book attempts to save the musical reputation of the Romans, yet did not escape some serious mistakes; was he not aware of the complex etymology (Hebrew-Latin) of *jubilaeum?* Why does he cite St Arnobius as a prototype of allegoristic exegesis: had he never heard of Philo of Alexandria and his school?

54. A fair bibliography on the subject may be found in *MGG,* arts., 'Jüdische Musik', and 'Psalm'. Also, see R. Lachmann, whose excellent study on the chants of the Jews of Djerba (Jerusalem, 1941) touches the basic problem.

55. H. Anglès *La Musica de las Cantigas de Santa Maria del Rey Alfonso el Sabio*, I-III, Barcelona, 1957-64 (with complete bibliography); E. Wellesz, 'Early Christian Music,' in *NOHM*, II, Oxford, 1954; *Eastern Elements in Western Chant*, Oxford-New York, 1947; *A History of Byzantine Music and Hymnography*, 2nd ed., Oxford, 1961; bibliographies of K. G. Fellerer and of B. Stäblein in their respective *Festschriften*, 1962 and 1967.

56. P. H. Lang, *Music in Western Civilization*, New York, 1941, pp. 42 ff.

57. D. Grout, *A History of Western Music*, New York, 1960, esp. pp. 20-21.

58. A few rectifications are better than a list of *errata: Tersanctus* and *Trisagion* are not identical and should not be confused with each other; the songs of the Temple in Jerusalem were not the common ground between the Jewish and Christian chant; the Oxrhynchus Hymn was not discovered in 1896, but in 1922, etc.

59. Professor O. Strunk is the author of *Source Readings in Music History*, New York, 1950, among which the Bible is conspicuously absent. Does he not consider the Bible to be a source, or to be relevant to music history? Apparently to him the collection of erudite after-dinner gossip—the *Deipnosophists*—has more historical value than, say, the Book of Chronicles.

60. Eusebius, *Eccl. Hist.*, and *Martyrs of Palestine*, ed. Lawlor and Oulton, London, 1927 (the end of the Passage paraphrased by me); our quotation is from the *Martyrs*, pp. 384-5. Also Eusebius, op. cit., III, 27 : 1-6; IV, 22 : 5-9; VI, 16 : 3 Eusebius quotes Origen as claiming to have found an ancient text of psalms in a jar near Jericho(!).

61. Ibid., IV, 6.

62. *JE*, art., 'Jerusalem', p. 128.

63. J. Parkes, op. cit., p. 173.

64. Epiphanius, in *PG*, Vol. 45, col. 411 f; also *JE*, arts., 'Hillel II', 'Gamaliel V' and 'Joseph the Apostate'.

65. *The Sacred Bridge*, Vol, 1, pp. 235 f.

66. J. Parkes, op. cit., pp. 259-62. We hear of a mass conversion of Jews in Jerusalem before 932, but the facts are not clear. See S. Baron, op. cit., III, p. 182 ff.

67. *JE*, art., 'Jerusalem', p. 130. The story goes back to Bar-Hebraeus, *Chronicum Syricum,* and can hardly be proved or disproved today. If the story is true, Omar broke his word, for he permitted the Jewish community in Jerusalem to grow and prosper.

68. Josephus, *Bellum Jud.*, VII, 3 : 3; also *Antiqu.*, XII, 3 : 1.

69. G. Dix. op. cit., pp. 173 ff.

70. E. Werner, 'Oriental Christian Metrical Hymns', in *HUCA* Jubilee Volume, 1950-1, Vol. II, pp. 399-400, 427 ff.

71. G. D. Mansi, *SS Concil. Coll. (Synopsis)*, I. 51.

72. J. Parkes, op. cit., pp. 163 f, 245 f.

73. In the recently published *Patrology*, Vol. III, p. 452, the editor, Father J. Quasten, makes the following observations about Chrysostom's *Homilies against the Jews:* 'The 8 homilies against the Jews delivered at Antioch from 386 to 387 were intended chiefly for Chrysostom's Christian listeners and only incidentally for Jews. We gather from them that Christians were frequenting synagogues, attracted by the charms and amulets in which Jews of the lower class dealt freely. . . . All of these sermons try to show that the Jews have rejected the Messias, as the prophets foretold, and that they have been rightly and permanently punished for their treatment of Christ. They reveal, however, that the Jews at that time were still a great social, and even a religious power in Antioch.' The work appeared in 1960 (i.e., after Vatican II). Elsewhere, the editor remarks of Chrysostom: 'He remains the most charming of the Greek Fathers and one of the most congenial personalities of Christian antiquity. His remarkable purity of speech reflects his noble and natural thought and reminds one of classical times' (p. 429). To this writer it seems an ominous sign that two Christian theologians of the very same generation can so widely differ in their assessments of a notorious hate-monger. Apparently, S. Kierkegaard's categorical separation between the Morally Good and the Aesthetically Beautiful has made inroads into theology, which sheds new light on the effectiveness of the *Vaticanum* II.

74. J. Parkes, op. cit., p. 300.

75. See *supra* p. 90 f.

76. *The Sacred Bridge,* Vol. 1, pp. 117 f.

77. On Syrian ecphonetic accents, see C. Høeg, *La Notation ekphonèti-que,* Copenhagen, 1935, pp. 142 ff; also E. Werner, 'Preliminary Notes for a comparative study of Jewish and Catholic musical punctuation', in *HUCA,* XV (1940), pp. 335 ff; also E. Wellesz, *A History of Byzantine Music,* 2nd ed., Oxford, 1961, pp. 121 ff. On the closeness of Syriac and Hebrew, see *Syrische und hebräische Inschriften,* ed. B. Moritz and J. Euting, Leipzig-Baltimore, 1913, p. 163.

78. *The Sacred Bridge,* Vol. 1, pp. 212 ff.

79. E. Wellesz, *Byzantine Music and Hymnography,* 2nd ed., London, 1961, pp. 43 ff; also E. Werner, 'Oriental Christian Metrical Hymns', in *HUCA,* XXIII, pt. 2 (Jubilee Vol.), 1950-1.

80. S. Baron, op. cit., II, pp. 163 ff; also H. Vogelstein, *Geschichte der Juden in Rom,* I, Berlin, 1896, pp. 113-70.

81. S. Baron, op. cit., II, pp. 188 ff. Cf. Jerome, *Comment. in Matt. 35 : 6,* in *PL,* XXVI, 175.

82. E. Werner, 'Post-Biblical Elements in the Prima Clementis', in H.

A. Wolfson Jubilee Volume III, p. 793 ff, Jerusalem-New York, 1965.

83. R. Wischnitzer, *The Architecture of the European Synagogue,* Philadelphia, 1964, p. 8; see here also the church (former synagogue) of Elche (Spain).

84. S. Baron, op. cit., II, pp. 188 f. Recently the strange case of SS Vitale and Agricola, who were originally buried in a Jewish cemetery and later exhumed under the auspices of St Ambrose, has aroused my curiosity, for it is full of contradictions which make me doubt the veracity of St Ambrose's report (in *De exhortatione virginitatis,* in *PL,* XVI, 350 f); see also G. Vecchi, *Medioevo Musicale a Bologna,* Bologna, 1970; also L. Ruggini, 'Ebrei e Orientali nell'Italia Settentrionale', in *Studia et Documenta Historiae,* XXV, Rome, 1959, pp. 197-217.

85. *The Sacred Bridge,* Vol. I, pp. 54 f.

86. H. Vogelstein, op. cit., I, pp. 166 f. According to another variant the prophet Elijah founded a monastery in Antioch and gave to the Christians sage and benevolent advice for their dealings with Jews. He opposed a Christian Nestore (scil. Nestorius), who recommended circumcision, etc., to the Christians.

87. For instance, *Epistle CXXI,* in *PL,* XXII, 1006: 'I could not tell you how many Pharisaic traditions there are today, told by the Talmudists, and I do not care for their old wives' tales. Many of them are so atrocious that I blush to mention them'.

88. F. J. E. Raby, *A History of Christian-Latin Poetry,* Oxford, 2nd ed., 1953, pp. 10-11.

89. E. Peterson, *Frühkirche, Judentum und Gnosis,* Rome-Vienna, 1959. Also R. Harris, *Testimonies,* Cambridge, 1917; see, for a different approach, W. L. Knox, 'Pharisaism and Hellenism', in *Judaism and Christianity,* II, ed. H. Loewe, London, 1937.

90. It would be extremely difficult to distinguish in these texts what is cursus, habitus, eloquentia, style, formula, and sheer chance. These elements are perhaps intrinsically and organically interlaced with each other.

91. F. J. E. Raby, op. cit.

92. E. Kähler, *Studien zum Te Deum,* Göttingen, 1958. His approach does not, fortunately, hark back to Wellhausen's, Lagarde's, or Baumstark's wilful and one-sided neglect of the contemporary Judaistic scholarship. For a more recent approach, see my study 'The Hebrew Background of the Te Deum', in *Eretz-Israel,* XVI (H. Orlinsky volume), New York-Jerusalem 1982.

93. Cf. *Prayer of the 19 Benedictions:* benediction no. 18 (*Hoda'a*).

94. A. Jungmann, S. J., op. cit., II, p. 161. It would not harm these learned Thebans to familiarize themselves with the old epithets of the angels—but it would spoil their hypotheses.

95. *The Authorized Daily Prayer Book,* rev. ed., Dr. J. H. Hertz, Chief Rabbi of England, London-New York, 1948, p. 127.

96. Ibid., p. 29.

97. Ibid., p. 209.

98. Ibid., p. 26.

99. Ibid., p. 50.

100. A good parallel is the Greek *Sanctus* text, quoted by A. Baumstark, in *Oriens Christianus,* Vol. 34, 1937, pp. 1-26. Here it happens that Baumstark failed to recognize the isosyllabism of his text, with eleven syllables per line plus assonance—a clear sign of Syrian influence!

101. Firmicus Maternus, *De errore profanarum religionum,* 6 : 5, in *PL,* XII.

102. E. Kahler, op. cit., pp. 69 f. For a full discussion of the *Te Deum,* see my study on it (in *Jahrbuch fur Liturgik und Hymnologie,* Vol. 23, Kassel, 1982). The verse Ps. 27 : 7 was mistranslated in the LXX and in the *Te Deum.*

103. H. Vogelstein, op. cit., p. 159.

104. E. Werner, 'Preliminary Notes', etc., in *HUCA,* XV, 1940 (*supra* n. 77).

105. The expression *tuba* may be a translation of the name of the Hebrew accent *shofar munach* (resting *shofar*) or vice versa. It corresponds to the Byzantine accent *Ison.* Note the opposite direction of the script!

106. Cf. E. Wellesz, op. cit. (n. 79), pp. 328-9; also p. 347, *Domesticus.*

107. A. Gastoué, *Les Origines du chant romain,* Paris, 1907, p. 137.

108. Ibid., p. 146.

109. WGM, III, pp. 110-12.

110. See in this connection the Pseudo-Guidonic treatise *De modorum formulis,* in Coussemaker, *Scriptores,* II, p. 90b.

111. D. Paolo Ferretti, O.S.B., *Esthétique Gregoriénne,* I, Paris, 1938, pp. 282 f.

112. Ibid., pp. 302-3.

113. G. Reese, *Music in the Middle Ages,* New York, 1940, p. 174.

114. W. Apel, *Gregorian Chant,* Bloomington, Ind., 1958, p. 211.

115. *The Sacred Bridge,* Vol. 1, pp. 531 ff (examples of Tone VIII).

116. These indications, plus the identity of the musical phrases and their structure, seem to be fairly convincing; not to Mr H. Hucke, however, who refuses all such hypotheses for reasons not stated (see art., 'Tractus' in *MGG*).

117. E. Werner, 'Preliminary Notes', etc., in *HUCA,* XV, 1940, p. 338; also Bar-Hebraeus, *Buch der Strahlen,* ed. A. Moberg, II, pp. 108 ff, Lund and Leipzig, 1907-10; also *The Sacred Bridge,* Vol. 1, p. 126, n. 58.

118. Here quoted from W. Apel's translation in his *Gregorian Chant,* p.

362; the clear and lucid representation of so complex a matter is most refreshing to read in Apel's work; yet he is mistaken in his belief that the earliest MSS of Jewish accents (*Ta'amim*) date form the ninth century. Today MSS of the late seventh and early eighth century are not too rare.

119. A fairly comprehensive if unsystematic bibliography on this enigmatic subject is to be found in the notes to I. Adler, 'Les Chants Synagogaux par Abdias le Proselyte Normand' (in *Revue de Musicologie*, Vol. LI, 1965, No. I, Paris, pp. 19-51). Also H. Avenary, 'Genizah Fragments of Hebrew Hymns' (in *Journal of Jewish Studies*, Vol. XVI, Nos. 3-4, 1966, London, pp. 87-104), and L. Levi, *Le due piu antiche trascrizioni musicali di melodie ebraico-italiane* (in *Memorial Vol. for G. Bedarisda*, Florence, 1966, pp. 106-36).

120. I. Adler, loc. cit., (n. 119).

121. H. J. Moser, *Musik in Zeit und Raum*, Berlin, 1960, p. 289. Any scholar familiar with the structure of Hebrew language and poetry will smile when reading Moser's remarks—but is it not one of the signs of our age (of so-called specialisation) that cautious and prudent scholars rush to judgements about subjects of which they possess a mere smattering of notions, hardly any tenable ideas!

122. E. Werner, 'Preliminary Notes', etc. . . . and especially see Ch. III of this book!

123. W. Apel, op. cit., p. 507.

124. Fr. Blume, 'Historische Musikforschung in der Gegenwart' (in *Acta Musicologica*, Vol. XL, 1968, fasc. I, pp. 8-21, Basel-Kassel).

General Index

(R. after a proper name indicates the title of Rabbi.)

A

Aaronides, play trumpets, 12, 35 ff
Abrahams, I., 98
Abub, 2
Accents, Masoretic, 28 ff, 62 f, 268 n. 77
Ackermann, A., 88, 258 n. 43
Acts of Pilate, traces of 'benefit litany' in, 132, 136
Adler, E. N., 206
Adler, G., 189 f, 266
Adler, I., 191 ff
Aetherea Silvia, 76
Agrippa II, King, 20
Ahab, King, 93
Ailinos-wail, 167
Akiba, R., 83, 85, 93
Albright, W. F., 59
Alleluia, 41 f; in the liturgy, 101–107; 'free' A, 103 ff
Al-Qirqisani, 30
Ambros, A. W., 187 f
Ambrose, St, 52, 61, 90 f, 76; lectionary of, 77
Amram, R., *Siddur* of, 146
Angelic Liturgy (DSS), 109, 111 f
Angelology: Jewish, 17–18; controversy about, 108–112; in Christian liturgy, 134–141
Anglès, H., 69, 191
Antioch, 87, 91 f, 194–196
Antiochus Epiphanes, King, 4
Antoninus Pius, addressed by Melito, 146
Apel, W., 204 ff, 210 f
Apion, 7
Apollinaris Sidonius, Bishop, 75 f
Arens, A., 98, 100
Ars Nova, 169
Art music, 150 f, 157 f, 167 f
Asaph, Heman, Jeduthun (Temple singers), 158
Asterius the Sophist, 119 f
Athanasius, 65, 102
'Atnah, see Accents, Masoretic
Augustine, St, 4, 52, 61, 76, 85, 90 f, 128; lectionary of, 76 f
Auschwitz, 25
Avenary, H., 191, 208
Ayrus (bronze gong), 44 f

B

Bacchus, 7
Bach, J. S., 181
Bacher, W., 87
Ball, H., 120
Bar-Hebraeus, 196 f, 244, 260, 263
Bar Kokhba, 2, 113, 195
Baron, S., 198 f
Barthélémy, Paul, 33
Bartók, B., 63
Basilius, 65
Bauer-Leander, 67
Baumstark, A., 61, 74, 96 f, 113–119, 179 f
Bedford, Arthur, 184 f
Bells, on High Priest's robe, 9 f
Ben Arza, 12, 44
Ben Sira, 5, 13, 44, 47 ff
Berenice, 20
Besseler, H., 190
Birnbaum, E., 189 ff
Blank, J., 142
Blume, F., 211
Bonner, Campbell, 137, 140, 142, 145
Bontempi, G. A., 182, 257 n. 22
Braude, W., 98
Brightman, F. E., 120
Buccina, 10 f; see also *Shofar*
Bultmann, R., 45
Burney, Charles, 185 f

C

Caesarius of Arles, 165
Cage, John, 170
Calendar, 96 f (ch. IV)
Calvin, John, 166, 169
Cassian, St, 61
Celestine I, Pope, 76
Chalcedon, Council of, 193
Chryses, priest of Apollo, 156
Chrysippus, 147
Chrysostom, John, see John Chrysostom, St
Clement of Alexandria, 51, 122 f; see also *Tropos Spondeiakos*
Clement of Rome, Pope, 32, 115, 120 f, 198
Cohen, Hermann, 85 f
Combarieu, F., 190
Common of Martyrs, 94 f

269

GENERAL INDEX

T

Tabernacles (*Succot*), ritual of, 6–7
Tanchuma, R., 196
Taurobolium, 153
Tchaikovsky, P. I., 169
Te Deum: parallelism in, 58–59; chant belongs to *Tropos Spondeiakos,* 125; metre (homotony), 203 f; Hebraisms in, 201 ff
Temple (Jerusalem Sanctuary): as symbol of the universe, 1 f, 7–8, 213, 215, 216; music described by St Paul, 43–50; orchestra, 3, 13–15
Temple Scroll (DSS), 163, 179, 219 n. 1, 252 n. 42
'Ten martyrs,' 82 f
Tersanctus, see *Sanctus*
Tertullian, 95, 101, 116 f, 136, 180
'Testimony-books,' 192, 200, 201, 262 n. 89
Thackeray, H. St. J., 98
Theodosius I, 132, 193 f
Theodosius II, 202 f
Theory of errors, 172 ff
Therapeutes, see Essene sect
Tonus peregrinus, 66, 203
Tradition's intermediaries between Synagogue and Church, 180 ff
Trisagion, see *Kedusha,* also *Sanctus*
Tropos Spondeiakos, 123–126
Trumpets: used by priests, 3; in Temple, 35 f, 38 ff; in *War-Scroll,* 39–43

U

'Ugab, 2
Unison, in trumpet-signals, 37–38

V

Vaux, R. de, 152 f
Verdeil, Mme Paralikova, 28 ff

Victor Vitensis (of Vita), 117, 242
Vigil: in sacred banquet of the Therapeutes, 39–40, 44; in worship of Qumran sect, 39–40

W

Wagner, Peter, 68, 125, 126, 189, 190, 191, 203, 205, 210, 225, 226, 245, 246, 252, 259, 263
Wagner, R., 178
War of the Children of Light against the Children of Darkness (DSS), 3, 35–38
Welch, A. C., 157
Wellesz, E. 122 f, 191 f, 263 n. 106
Wieder, N., 98
Wille, G., 190
Willis, G. G., 76, 98, 227, 235
Wiora, W., 69
Wolfskehl, Karl, 88, 235 n. 64

Y

Yadin, Y., 36–37, 213, 218, 219, 221, 224
Yannai, 139
Yehuda Halevi, R., 63–64, 219, 225
Yerkes, R. K., 149–150, 215, 248, 249

Z

Zadokite (Damascus) Document (DSS), 162; priests and Levites in, 160
Zeitlin, S., 30
Zera, R., 9, 15
Zunz, L., 223, 229, 231, 233, 234

271